Basic Psychopathology: A Programmed Text
2nd Edition

Basic Psychopathology: A Programmed Text 2nd Edition

Edited by **C. W. Johnson, J. R. Snibbe,** *and* **L. A. Evans,**
all of The University of Southern California School of Medicine,
Los Angeles, California.

PMA PUBLISHING CORP.
New York

NOTICE: The editors, contributors, and publisher of this work have made every effort to ensure that the drug dosage schedules and/or procedures are accurate and in accord with the standards accepted at the time of publications. Readers are cautioned, however, to check the product information sheet included in the package of each drug they plan to administer. This is particularly important in regard to new or infrequently used drugs. The publisher is not responsible for any errors of fact or omissions in this book.

Library of Congress Cataloging in Publication Data

Basic Psychopathology: A Programmed Text, 2nd Edition
    1. Psychology, Pathological – Programmed instruction
I. Johnson, C. Warner (Clayton Warner), 1930-
II. Snibbe, John R.   III. Evans, Leonard A. [DNLM:
1. Psychopathology – Programmed texts. WM 18 B311]
RC336.B37   1981   616.89   81-8571

ISBN 0-89335-155-5 (pbk)

Printed in the United States of America

Contributors

William G. Crary, Ph.D., Associate Professor in Psychiatry
(Psychology), Director of Adult Psychology Service,
Clinical Psychology Division

David B. Friedman, M. D., Professor of Pediatrics

Brian P. Jacks, M. D., Associate Clinical Professor of
Psychiatry

C. Warner Johnson, M. D., Associate Professor of Psychiatry, Director, Medical Student Education in Psychiatry

Charles W. Patterson, M. D., Associate Professor of
Clinical Psychiatry

Warren Procci, M.D., Associate Professor of Psychiatry,
Director, Consultation-Liaison Psychiatry Service

Sidney Russak, M. D., Assistant Professor of Psychiatry,
Director of the Division of Child & Adolescent
Psychiatry

John R. Snibbe, Ph.D., Assistant Clinical Professor of
Psychiatry, Staff Psychologist, Assessment Clinic,
Psychiatric Hospital

Beatrice A. Sommers, Ph.D., Associate Clinical Professor
of Psychiatry (Psychiatric Social Work)

Michael P. Ward, Ph.D., Associate Professor of Clinical
Psychiatry, Staff Psychologist, Assessment Clinic,
Psychiatric Hospital

All of the contributors are affiliated with the Los
Angeles County/University of Southern California Medical
Center and are members of the teaching faculty at the
University of Southern California School of Medicine.

Acknowledgments

We are indebted to many individuals for their assistance in the preparation of this book. In particular we are grateful to the staff, faculty and patients of the Los Angeles County/University of Southern California Medical Center and the University of Southern California School of Medicine. We are especially appreciative for the fine editorial assistance provided by Louis A. Gayle of the Department of Medical Education.

Introduction

The purpose of this second edition, as for the first,
is to enable practicing professionals and other students
of psychopathology, to acquire knowledge and skills in:

the systematic observation of patient behavior
the effective use of the mental status examination
the correct application of psychiatric terminology
  to patients
the recognition and classification of major
  syndromes of psychopathology

It has been five years since the first edition of
Basic Psychopathology was published, and the recent adoption by the American Psychiatric Association of the third
edition of Diagnostic and Statistical Manual of Mental
Disorders (DSM-III) dictates the need to update and significantly revise the book. The most important changes
involve incorporating into the text the terminology and
many of the diagnostic criteria of DSM-III. Additionally,
the chapter covering the Mental Status Examination and its
format have been substantially revised and two new chapters
have been added. The first new chapter deals with The
Psychopathology of Family, Marital and Pair Relationships,
and the second is devoted to Affective Disorders.

Each chapter contains information basic to the evaluation of patients with psychological problems. Commonly
used psychiatric terms are defined, and the major psychiatric syndromes are phenomenologically described in detail.
The reader is systematically taught to accurately identify,
describe and classify pertinent patient behaviors and
match these findings with established psychopathologic
syndromes. The book is designed to be used primarily for
the acquisition of diagnostic and observational skills,
and little information is included about psychodynamics,
etiology or treatment. All subject matter has been selected

to be of practical value to the reader with an interest in clinical psychopathology, irrespective of his theoretical orientation, discipline or previous training.

The format of this programed text facilitates learning and makes optimum use of the reader's time. Each chapter begins with an overview statement and objectives which specify the knowledge and skills that are most important to learn. Information needed to achieve the objectives follows next and is interspersed with evaluation exercises and feedback which will enable the learner to assess his progress. Supplementary reading references are included for each subject. Basic terminology and principles for the systematic observation of behavior are presented in Chapter 3, Mental Status Examination. We recommend that it be read as a preparation for later chapters.

Experimentation in the classroom has shown that the book can be used successfully either as a primary text or as a supplement to another one. Emphasis is placed on teaching the reader to apply to patients the knowledge which they have acquired

The instructional system applies modern educational principles and represents a joint effort by the Department of Psychiatry and the Department of Medical Education. The program design was the responsibility of the Department of Medical Education and the content of the curriculum was developed by the Department of Psychiatry. Both departments worked collaboratively to prepare teaching materials and to implement instruction. It may be of interest for the readers to learn about the way in which we used this text at the University of Southern California School of Medicine. Approximately forty hours were devoted to instruction in psychopathology during the second year of medical training. The year-long curriculum was begun with an orientation session that provided the students with an overview of the course content and design. A pre-test, which approximated the final examination, was administered. It allowed the students to see what was expected of them by the conclusion of the course and provided us with valuable planning information. The examination featured multiple choice questions about various psychiatric syndromes. The students were also required to perform a mental status examination based upon a videotaped patient interview. The students were given immediate feedback about their performance. A comparison of the pre-test and final examination results enabled us to evaluate student progress and course effectiveness. A detailed questionnaire about the format of presentation was completed by the students.

Both the faculty and medical students found the text to be an efficient and interesting means of presenting basic psychiatric information and no formal lectures were needed or given. The programmed text replaced traditional didactic presentations, and the students were asked to assimilate

the information contained in assigned readings before
coming to class. Weekly two-hour class sessions were devoted to faculty-led workshops designed to clarify and
expand upon the concepts presented in the programmed text
and to enable the student to apply them to patients. Each
session was patient-centered and a variety of learning
experiences were tried and evaluated. Some workshops used
a chalk board and live patient interviews, while others
utilized color videotape presentations and closed circuit
television. All instructors were carefully oriented to the
topic purpose and learning objectives prior to every session.
Each meeting centered upon a different syndrome and built
upon concepts presented in previous sessions. The students
were required to make observations and perform a partial
or complete mental status examination on all patients
presented. The small group sessions allowed the students
to freely ask questions and exchange ideas with their instructors. Overall, the substitution of a programmed text
for lectures and the patient-centered workshops were en-
thusiastically received by the students. The results of
achievement tests demonstrated a significant increase in
student knowledge and skill in formulating a psychiatric
diagnosis. Our method of using the text is only one of
many and we welcome the opportunity to exchange ideas and
experiences with others.

This newly-revised second edition when combined with
its companion text, Basic Psychotherapeutics, and the set
of videotaped psychiatric interviews--also developed at
the University of Southern California School of Medicine--
provides an effective and efficient instructional package
for learning psychopathology and its treatment.

Contents

Basic Psychopathology: A Programmed Text
2nd Edition

Chapter 1

Human Growth and Development
Part I: Infancy and Childhood
David B. Friedman

This chapter covers the first portion of Human Growth and Development, Infancy and Childhood (0-12 years). The information is presented as a baseline against which you can evaluate the level of maturation and the age-appropriateness of your patient's behavior.

LEARNING OBJECTIVES

At the conclusion of this chapter and after studying a written case history, be able to:

1. Describe a young patient in terms of:

    a. Physical and/or emotional traits: The characteristics of physical and emotional growth, perception and motor abilities.

    b. Developmental tasks: the physical, social and/or psychological "skills" which require a minimal degree of mastery if maturation is to proceed.

    c. Interpersonal relationships: the characteristics of interpersonal relationships that are typical to an age group.

    d. Implications for management: the typical developmental characteristics of an age group as related to psychological treatment.

2. Determine if the patient's behavior is age-appropriate for categories a, b, and c above.

OVERVIEW

Human growth and development are best conceptualized as an ongoing process of change. Many of these changes occur in an orderly, stepwise fashion and useful descriptions and comparisons of different levels of development can be made. Four age levels of development will be characterized and considered: infancy and childhood (0-12 years), adolescence (13-19 years), the middle years (20-64 years), and the later adult years (over 65 years). Some of these age groups will be subdivided further for review. The categories, as presented, will contain generalizations about age groups. The descriptions given will apply to most individuals of a designated group, but it is important to keep in mind that a number of persons can show deviations in their development and still be considered "normal." Human development is often an irregular process; the levels of psychological and physical attainment may not coincide. For example, an adolescent may become physically mature while remaining emotionally immature in areas of interpersonal relationships. To some extent each phase of development builds on preceding ones. If former stages are not sufficiently mastered, it may be more difficult to achieve success in later ones. At times of privation or stress, individuals may revert to behavior and emotional patterns typical of earlier stages of development. Therefore, it is useful to be able to distinguish the physiological and behavioral characteristics of types of pathological conditions other than those of normal development.

The child is not merely a miniature adult. He is a dynamic, growing organism with specific, but constantly changing, physical and emotional traits characterizing each developmental stage. Disease processes, response to medications, physiological and psychological reactions are all influenced by these developmental phenomena. A knowledge of these characteristic patterns and developmental landmarks is essential if one is to work effectively with children. The following outline describes areas of development which are important for gathering a data base and forming a management plan for children.

THE INFANT (0-1 year)

Physical and Emotional Traits

Newborn infants are physically helpless and yet they are emotionally agreeable if they are able to communicate their needs and if their cues are interpreted correctly. The newborn infant demonstrates the Moro or "startle" reflex in which the infant grasps symmetrically with both arms when startled. This primitive reflex disappears by four to six weeks. By six weeks, the young infant begins to develop a social smile which is a very important landmark. The young infant follows light with his eyes, and by two to three months he can follow the light past the midline and begins to develop midline activity. By four to five months, the infant can roll over and demonstrates active hand-to-mouth activity. By six to seven months, he can grasp a toy or an

object and transfer it from hand to hand. By seven to eight
months, the infant sits steadily and is able to feed himself
a cracker. He may have some identifiable words such as
"mama" and "da da," but this is variable.

Developmental Tasks

The newborn infant must adjust physiologically to extra-
uterine life. If he is to grow and develop, he needs food,
fondling, and physical care. The young infant appears to
have two basic tasks: to develop trust in his environment
and to recognize and differentiate himself from his mother
and the outside world.

Interpersonal Relationships

The early mother-infant interaction is characterized by
mutual gazing, touching, and verbalization. The mother
learns to interpret the infant's signals. The infant knows
his mother, but the bond is fragile. For the young infant
there is no object permanence, either in time or space. However, by the second six months the infant has often developed
"stranger anxiety," i.e., overt distress when in the presence of unfamiliar persons.

Implications for Management

The young infant needs consistent mothering and basic
family nurturing. While he is learning what and whom to
trust in his environment, his parents need to learn to interpret his needs. Illness or hospitalization tends to interfere with these processes. This is especially true of
long hospitalization in environments which cannot provide
adequate mothering; such situations should be avoided whenever possible. Parents should be allowed to participate in
the care of their young infants when they are hospitalized.

Now complete Self-Assessment Exercise #1 on the following page.

Self Assessment Exercise #1

1. Based on the nature of the mother-infant relationship, would surgery and short-term hospitalization best be performed at three months or twelve months of age? Why?

2. A family physician routinely scheduled "well-baby check-ups" at four-month intervals. At four months, one infant was responsive, smiled and cooed at the physician. Four months later the same infant burst into tears upon seeing the physician and cried throughout the examination. No physical abnormality was found. Explain this phenomenon.

3. What potential developmental problems may arise for an infant who requires prolonged hospitalization? How would you manage the case to minimize potential problems caused by separation of the infant and his family?

<u>Self Assessment Exercise #1 (continued)</u>

4. The following developmental history was obtained from
    the mother of an eleven-month-old infant: the infant
    crawled at five to six months, sat unaided at eight
    months, was able to stand with minimal help at eleven
    months of age. Is this baby developing "normally?"

        When you have completed this exercise to the best of
your ability, check your answers with those on the following page.

Self Assessment Exercise #1 - Feedback

1. Relative to the single factor of the infant-mother re-
    lationship, the surgery should be performed at three
    months. The infant-mother bond is less well established
    at three months than at twelve. Separation of the in-
    fant from the mother at the earlier time would evoke
    less anxiety in the infant.

2. The infant demonstrated "stranger anxiety." Infants
    are not able to distinguish clearly between familiar
    and unfamiliar persons until the sixth or seventh month.
    After that time the infant may respond with distress
    when confronted with persons who are strangers.

3. Basic nurturing, learning to interpret emotional and
    physical needs, and basic communication are develop-
    mental processes contingent upon a close interaction
    between mother (parents) and infant. A prolonged
    separation would seriously hinder development. The
    situation would be alleviated if the parents were allowed
    to visit and/or provide physical care for the infant as
    much as possible.

4. Yes, the child's developmental progress seems normal.
    Most infants begin to crawl at six months, sit unaided
    at seven to nine months and can stand with assistance
    around one year of age.

    If your answers correspond closely with those above,
please continue your reading on the following page; if not,
please reread the material in the section preceding until
you are confident you know the material.

THE TODDLER (1-2 years)

Physical and Emotional Traits
     The toddler, the child between about ten months and two years, is developing a sense of his own individuality and willpower. He vacillates between dependence and independence. By one year, many infants will walk when one hand is held. When presented with a block or a small cube and a cup, he will release the block into the cup if he is asked to do so. By fifteen months, he can usually walk alone and he vocalizes or points out his wants. By eighteen months, he turns pages of a book--usually two to three pages at once--and he can imitate a person making a horizontal pencil stroke. By two years, he can correctly make a vertical and circular pencil stroke, and he can also build a tower of six or seven blocks or cubes. He usually verbalizes his needs well and very vocally.

Developmental Tasks
     The toddler is becoming more complex. He needs muscular activity, and he needs to feel a sense of accomplishment. He appears to be negativistic because he is always testing physical and psychological limits. He tends to reinforce skills by repetition. The three basic developmental tasks of the toddler are: to develop a beginning sense of autonomy, to tolerate separations from the mother and to begin to assimilate and handle socialization.

Interpersonal Relationships
     By thirteen or fourteen months, objects begin to develop permanence for the infant; mother-infant attachment is virtually complete. The toddler can differentiate his mother from a stranger, and he practices letting his mother out of his sight by playing peek-a-boo. By two years of age, he is very much aware of his parents' leaving, and separation anxiety is at its height. The toddler may act out his anxieties in play and begins to use language (verbal labels) for communication. One begins to see early symbol formation and conceptual thought.

Implications for Medical Management
     The toddler needs both encouragement and limits; his parents need to accept his independent development and to encourage his emerging autonomy and personality. Parent-child separation, as a result of hospitalization, interferes with these processes and is difficult for both parent and child. The two year old is particularly vulnerable and prone to develop separation anxiety.

     Now complete Self-Assessment Exercise #2 on the following page.

Self Assessment Exercise #2

1.   A mother of a 22-month-old boy expressed worry about
     his behavior. She related that in eight months' time
     he had changed from a "sweet, lovable baby" into a
     self-willed, stubborn, bundle of energy who says "no"
     to everything she asks him to do. What is the most
     likely reason for the boy's behavioral change? How
     would you help the mother?

2.   A mother of a physically healthy, 27-month-old girl
     relates that her child becomes very tearful when left
     with the babysitter. The mother is worried that the
     girl's reaction is the result of some "psychological
     trauma." What is a likely explanation for the child's
     behavior? Based on your understanding of developmental
     stages, what would you suggest to the mother as a pos-
     sible remedy?

Self Assessment Exercise #2 (continued)

3. A concerned woman solicits your opinion about her 28-
    month-old girl. Developmentally, the girl could sit
    unaided at ten months, walk with assistance at sixteen
    months and could stand and walk unaided at twenty months.
    Her vocabulary consisted of two or three monosyllabic
    sounds. Is the woman's concern justified? Why?

When you have completed this exercise to the best of
your ability, check your answers with those on the following page.

Self Assessment Exercise #2 - Feedback

1. At this age the child becomes mobile, curious about
    his world and has a need for physical activity. His
    striving for autonomy may often overshoot the mark and
    appear to adults as negativism and willfulness. The
    mother can be reassured that this behavior is a sign of
    "normal" development and that it will moderate in time.
    It will help matters if she makes allowances for her
    son's behavior, but sets limits when needed.

2. This child is likely experiencing "separation anxiety,"
    which is characteristic of the two year old. This type
    of anxiety is usually transient and decreases as the
    child gets older. The mother should be encouraged not
    to leave the child for prolonged periods and to avoid
    making major life changes. The babysitter should be
    chosen for maturity and ability to establish rapport
    with the child. The child should become thoroughly
    acquainted with the sitter before being left with her.
    Periods of separation initially should be of short
    duration and gradually increased.

3. The woman's concern may be justified. Most infants can
    sit unaided by seven to nine months, stand by twelve to
    fourteen months and walk unaided soon thereafter. The
    girl described shows some developmental lag. She may
    be "normal" but deserves an evaluation by a competent
    pediatrician or other professional.

If your answers correspond closely with those above,
please continue your reading on the following page; if not,
please reread the material in the section preceding until
you are confident you know the material.

THE PRESCHOOLER (3-5 years)

Physical and Emotional Traits

The preschool child is more social and less concerned about independent rights. He or she imitates the important adults in his or her life and tends to admire and emulate adults of the same sex. The two- to three-year old child can walk and run very well. By three years, he can usually ride a tricycle and share it with others. He can draw more complicated figures, such as a circle and a cross, he can feed himself and, if presented with a picture book, he can identify the action in the book. By four years he is able to hop on one foot, draw a man characterized by two or more body parts, name colors and lace shoes (although he often has difficulty with his own). By five years, he can skip and he can draw a recognizable man. He copies more complicated objects, such as triangles, and he can name coins and ask the meaning of words.

Developmental Tasks

The preschool child needs room to expand, although he also needs to feel a sense of limits. He takes pleasure in mastering tasks such as working a new toy or coloring a design. The basic developmental tasks of the preschooler appear to be to gain skills in muscular activity (as in toilet training), to develop conceptual understanding, to learn to explore by trial and error, to make choices, and to develop a variety of coping mechanisms and ways of expressing feelings.

Interpersonal Relationships

By three years of age, the youngster has established memory representations of his mother to help sustain him when she is out of sight. Fantasy becomes a strong coping mechanism and the preschool child is better able to cope with separation, especially if the mother-child relationship is one of mutual trust. The favorite stories of the preschool child are fantasies involving loss and reunion, and these are often expressed symbolically as in many of the fairy tales. He or she learns what friends mean and how to relate to them.

Implications for Management

The preschooler is developing initiative, and his parents are learning to separate from him and to encourage independent growth and development. Illness interferes with the separation process and tends to threaten the developing coping mechanisms and expressions of feelings because family communication and interactions are disrupted.

Now complete Self-Assessment Exercise #3 on the following page.

Self-Assessment Exercise #3

1.   During a "well-baby" checkup, the mother of a 30-month-
     old girl asks when she can start her daughter in pre-
     school. Assuming that the child is physically healthy
     and developmentally "on schedule," what would you
     advise?

2.   The mother of an only child, a four-year-old girl, re-
     lates with pride that she and her daughter have a very
     close relationship. They go many places together and
     the girl seems to prefer her mother's company to that
     of some neighborhood children. The child relates satis-
     factorily to children who come to her house, but she
     will not go to their house for play. The child does
     not attend a preschool, but will be eligible for kin-
     dergarten in eight months. What recommendations, if
     any, would you make to the mother? Why?

Self Assessment Exercise #3 (continued)

3. Prolonged hospitalization and treatment are necessary
    for a five-year-old boy because of an automobile ac-
    cident. What type of developmental problems would you
    anticipate? How would you manage them?

When you have completed this exercise to the best of
your ability, check your answers with those on the following page.

Self Assessment Exercise #3 - Feedback

1.   Preschool experiences can be assimilated better after
     the age of three, unless the child shows special social
     precocity and self-assurance. By that age "separation
     anxiety" is less of a problem and the capacity for so-
     cialization has increased.

2.   The girl seems overly dependent upon her mother and de-
     ficient in peer relationships. She may have future
     trouble separating from her mother (and vice versa)
     when attendance at kindergarten is expected. Part-time
     attendance at a preschool will offer her an opportunity
     for gaining experience with peer relationships, a new
     environment and separation from her mother. It should
     be recommended.

3.   The restrictions imposed by illness and hospitalization
     would interfere with the development of initiative,
     autonomy, family identification, coordination of motor
     skills, coping mechanisms, socialization with peers
     and skills related to school. Regular, frequent family
     and peer visitation, opportunities for self-care and
     decision making should be encouraged. Arrangements
     for a visiting teacher, active physiotherapy, various
     craft projects and sensory experiences could be planned.
     Reinforcement of physical and personality strengths
     along with planning which implies future recovery should
     be implemented.

     If your answers correspond closely with those above,
please continue your reading on the following page; if not,
please reread the material in the section preceding until
you are confident you know the material.

THE SCHOOL-AGED CHILD (6-12 years)

Physical and Emotional Traits

The six- to seven-year-old child is capable of learning the three R's and continues to develop fine and coarse motor skills. He can tie his own shoes, ride a bicycle, roller skate and throw a ball. He understands abstract concepts. He begins to play games of skill, thought, and chance, and develops social relationships and concepts of sexuality. When asked to draw a person, he draws a figure with increasing detail and sophistication. As he progresses through the school-age years, he develops increasing awareness of clothes, appearance and social relationships.

Developmental Tasks

The school-aged child has a number of developmental tasks. He must learn to master greater physical prowess and to establish his self-identity more definitively. He must develop a conscience in order to adapt socially, and learn to fit into the outside world by developing peer and other relationships. In addition, he must acquire new learning skills and a sense of industry and accomplishment.

Interpersonal Relationships

By six years of age, the child can separate from his parents more comfortably except under situations of stress and anxiety. As the child develops self-mastery he begins to be able to tolerate frustration, control aggression, share, and delay gratification. Although the school-aged child still identifies strongly with his parents, he becomes free to develop relationships with teachers and friends and often appears to be rejecting his parents.

Implications for Management

The school-aged child is attempting to gain mastery over himself and his environment, and his parents are learning to accept independent behavior without rejecting him. Illness and hospitalization interfere with these processes. Hospitalization, painful procedures and the discomfort of illness threaten the youngster's feelings of mastery and tend to bring out feelings of guilt and inferiority. School-aged youngsters are particularly vulnerable to threats of pain and body mutilation.

Now complete Self-Assessment Exercise #4 on the following page.

Self Assessment Exercise #4

1. A six-year-old son of a successful businessman expressed
    regret that his father is "always away working so much."
    The father provides well for the family and is puzzled
    by the boy's statement. How can the boy's expression
    be understood in developmental terms?

2. An eight-year-old girl suffers from epilepsy. Keeping
    in mind her medical and developmental needs, what ad-
    vice would you give her parents regarding the girl's
    physical activity?

Self Assessment Exercise #4 (continued)

3. Some physicians perform a circumcision on school-aged
    boys when they have been hospitalized for a tonsillec-
    tomy. Usually the children are not told in advance
    about the additional surgical procedure. Comment on
    this practice using your knowledge of human develop-
    ment.

When you have completed this exercise to the best of
your ability, check your answers with those on the following page.

Self Assessment Exercise #4 - Feedback

1.   Children usually take the necessities of life for
     granted. The boy must learn a sex role model, to solve
     problems of living and to relate to others, etc. The
     most important source of this teaching comes from family
     members. The frequent absence of the boy's father inter-
     feres with the learning, and the boy is expressing his
     need for a model with whom to identify.

2.   A balance must be achieved between protecting the girl
     from possible physical harm and allowing opportunities
     that promote optimal development. Activities should be
     excluded that may either precipitate a seizure or which
     would endanger the girl if a seizure occurred, i.e.,
     climbing, swimming alone, etc. Aside from these con-
     siderations, the girl should be encouraged to participate
     fully in physical and social activities. Special physi-
     cal abilities should be openly complimented in order to
     enhance self-esteem.

3.   Failing to inform the child of the circumcision may under-
     mine the trust that he should feel toward adults impor-
     tant in his life. An inordinant fear of physicians, sur-
     gical procedures and illness in general may result.
     Strong anxiety about bodily injury and emerging sexuality
     may be evoked.

     If your answers correspond closely with those above,
please continue your reading on the following page; if not,
please reread the material in the section preceding until
you are confident you know the material.

SUMMARY

Charts summarizing the major points of this chapter are presented below and on the following pages:

	Physical and Emotional Traits	Developmental Tasks
I N F A N T (0-1)	physically helpless smiles at six weeks follows light with eyes past midline at two months transfers object from hand-to-hand at six months sits steadily by seven to eight months	to adjust physiologically to extrauterine life to develop basic trust in his environment to differentiate self from mother
T O D D L E R (1-3)	walks with hand held at one year developing sense of own individuality and willpower vocalizes or points out wants by fifteen months imitates horizontal pencil strokes at eighteen months	to develop sense of autonomy to tolerate separations from mother to assimilate and handle socialization

Interpersonal Relationships	Implications for Management
mutual gazing and touching in early months and mother interprets infant's signals infant knows mother but bond is fragile no "object permanence" in time or space by second six months, often "stranger anxiety"	infant needs consistent mothering parents need to learn to interpret needs illness or hospitalization interferes with both processes
by 13 or 14 months objects develop permanence and attachment is complete infant knows stranger from mother by two, separation anxiety at its height may act out anxieties in play and begins to use language for communication	toddler needs encouragement and limits parents need to accept development of independence hospitalization accentuates parent-child separation anxieties

	Physical and Emotional Traits	Developmental Tasks
P R E S C H O O L E R (3-5)	more social; imitates important adults rides tricycle; walks and runs well hops on one foot and draws man with two parts by four years skips, copies triangle and asks meaning of words by five years	to coordinate motor patterns, as in toilet training to develop conceptual understanding to learn by trial and error to develop a variety of mechanisms and means of expressing feelings
S C H O O L A G E R (5-12)	learns 3 R's and in-creasing fine and course motor skills by six to seven years plays games of skill, thought, chance by eight to nine years by ten to eleven years develops increasing awareness of clothes, appearance and social relationships	to master greater physical prowess to establish self-identity to develop a "conscience" to develop peer and other relationships to acquire new learning skills

Interpersonal Relationships	Implications for Management
by three years, develops memory representation of mother when out of sight fantasy is strong coping mechanism and child is better able to cope with separation socializing more	parents need to learn to separate from child and encourage independent growth illness interferes with separation process and threatens child's developing coping mechanisms
by age five or six, separation more comfortable except under situations of stress and anxiety able to tolerate frustration and control aggression develops relationships with teachers and friends imitates parents more	illness and hospitalization, painful procedures threaten youngster's feelings of mastery and tends to bring out feelings of guilt and inferiority vulnerable to pain and fears body mutilation

REFERENCES

Erickson, E.H.: Childhood and Society (2nd Ed.), New York: W.W. Norton & Co., Inc. 1963.

Friedman, A.S. and Friedman, D.B.: Parenting, A Developmental Process, Pediatric Annals, Sept. 77, Vol. 6, No. 9, pp. 10-22.

Lidz, Theodore: The Person, New York: Basic Books, 1968.

Lowrey, George: Growth and Development of Children, Chicago: Book Publishers, 1973.

Mahler, M.D., Pine, F. and Bergman, A.: The Psychological Birth of the Human Infant, New York: Basic Books, 1975.

Maier, H.W.: Three Theories of Child Development, New York, Harper and Row, 1969.

Rexford, Eveoleen N., et al.: Infant Psychiatry: New Synthesis, New Haven and London, Yale University Press, 1976.

Spock, Benjamin: Baby and Child Care, New York: Cardinal Press, 1964.

Thomas, A. and Chess, S.: Temperament and Development New York: Bruner/Mazel, 1977.

White, B.L. and Watts, J.C.: Experience and Environment, New Jersey: Prentice-Hall, 1973.

Chapter 2

Human Growth and Development
Part II: Adolescence Through The Later Adult Years
C. Warner Johnson

This chapter covers the latter portion of Human Growth and Development dealing with the years after age twelve. The information is presented as a baseline with which you can evaluate the maturation and the age-appropriateness of your patient's behavior.

By the conclusion of this chapter you should be able to:

1. After studying a written case history describe a teenage or adult patient in terms of:

   a. Physical and/or emotional traits: the characteristics of physical and emotional growth, perception and motor abilities.

   b. Developmental tasks: the physical, social and/or psychological "skills" which require a minimal degree of mastery if maturation is to proceed.

   c. Interpersonal relationships: the characteristics of interpersonal relationships that are typical to an age group.

   d. Implications for management: the typical developmental characteristics of an age group as related to medical treatment.

2. Determine if the patient's behavior is age-appropriate for categories a, b, and c above.

ADOLESCENCE

Adolescence encompasses that portion of the life cycle which extends from the end of childhood to adult maturity (13 to 19 years) and involves a complex interplay of biological, psychological and social forces. It is the period characterized by rapid growth and change. An understanding clinician, who is knowledgeable about this phase of life, can provide meaningful information and reassurance to teenagers and family members who perceive adolescence as a time of turmoil and distress.

Physical Traits

Dramatic physical changes are intrinsic to adolescence. The onset of adolescence typically coincides with a spurt of physical growth and/or the development of secondary sexual characteristics and the capacity to reproduce (puberty). Physical development and growth during this period is typified by variability--between the sexes and among individuals of the same sex. Many adolescents reach physical and sexual maturity by their midteen years, while others may show considerable, but normal, developmental lags.

Generally, females mature physically and emotionally earlier and more rapidly than males. For girls, the average age for the onset of puberty is ten or eleven, maximal growth occurs at twelve and the menarche occurs between eleven and thirteen. Both puberty and maximal growth for boys occur a full two years later. For either sex the typical growth of long bones, increase in body weight and changes in body contour may occur early, late or irregularly. The average ages and the typical sequence of pubertal change for males and females are listed below:

FEMALE
Onset of puberty (10-11)
Maximum physical growth (12)
1. Breast enlargement (10-11)
2. Pubic hair (10-11)
3. Maximum physical growth (12)
4. Menstruation (11-13)
5. Axillary hair (11-13)

MALE
Onset of puberty (12-16)
Maximum physical growth (14.8)
1.   Growth of testes (12-13)
2.   Pubic hair (12-14)
3.   Enlargement of penis (12-14)
4.   Early voice changes (13-17)
5.   First ejaculation (14-15)
6.   Maximum physical growth (14.8)
7.   Axillary hair (13-14)
8.   Marked voice changes (14-16)
9.   Development of beard (15-16)

Emotional Traits

Adolescence tests the adaptive capacity of teen-agers
because they must adjust to a body of changing proportions
and heightened sexual feelings. Physical and sexual development are simultaneously a welcomed sign of maturity
and a source of uncertainty and potential conflict. Since
their maturing sexuality cannot be easily avoided, much of
adolescent behavior, conversation and thought is under-
standably concerned with sexuality. It may be difficult for
adolescents to achieve an acceptable balance between their
personal need for sexual expression and cultural standards.
Misinformation, fear and guilt about sexual functioning and
maturation are widespread even in today's "enlightened age."
Indeed, establishing a sense of mature sexuality is rarely
accomplished without some feelings of worry, self-doubt
and guilt. Therapists can assuage much of the anxiety
about sexuality by giving tactful reassurance and information.

Many different coping mechanisms may be utilized as
adolescents attempt to master the various developmental
tasks of their age group. Transient mood swings, impulsive
behavior and alternating levels of activity are not unusual.
Although adolescence is a period of stress and change, these
changes are not necessarily to be equated with psychopathology and most teen-agers are able to successfully
navigate through this period of their lives without experiencing major psychological problems.

Now please complete Self-Assessment Exercise #1 on
the following page.

Self-Assessment Exercise #1

1. A thirteen-year-old girl was brought by her mother
    for consultation. The girl had allegedly refused to
    "suit up" for her physical education class and ex-
    pressed worry that she had not begun menstruating
    and "just wasn't developing physically" like her
    friends. She appeared to be somewhat physically
    immature for her age. A physical examination showed
    she was beginning to develop secondary sexual charac-
    teristics and was otherwise "normal." What is the
    most likely explanation for her condition?

    How would you manage this case?

2. You were asked to perform physical examinations for
    a Boy Scout Troop. Most of the boys were thirteen and
    fourteen years of age. Some of the boys were tall,
    well-muscled and demonstrated secondary sexual charac-
    teristics. Others showed no signs of pubescence and
    seemed "physically immature." They all seemed to be
    in good health and the physical examinations were
    "within normal limits." How can you explain this
    phenomenon?

Self-Assessment Exercise #1 (continued)

3.   A twelve-year-old boy comes to you for consultation and expresses his concern that his eleven-year-old sister and two of her girl friends are taller, heavier and stronger than he is. How can you explain this phenomenon?

What would you tell the boy that might reassure him?

When you have completed this exercise to the best of your ability, check your answers on the following page.

Self-A-sessment Exercise #1 - Feedback

1. The girl's delayed physical development is most likely
    a "normal" variation. Her concern should be acknowledged,
    but she should be actively reassured about her condi-
    tion. Educating the girl about the normal variations
    of physical and sexual development is indicated.

2. Human growth and development are characterized by
    variability. The normal range of the onset of puberty
    among boys is from twelve to sixteen. Some enter
    pubescence earlier than others and these boys illus-
    trate that fact.

3. The boy needs some education and reassurance. It
    would be comforting for him to know that girls usually
    develop physically earlier than boys, but that boys
    "catch up" in a few years. Generally boys become
    taller, stronger and more athletically able than
    their female counterparts.

    If your answers correspond closely with those above,
please continue your reading on the following page; if not,
please reread the preceding section until you are confident you know the material.

Developmental Tasks

Teen-agers must attain a modicum of mastery in certain developmental tasks if they are to achieve adult
maturity as defined by our culture. Some of the more
important tasks are: accepting physique and sexuality,
achieving a sense of emotional and financial independence
from the family, selecting and preparing for a life
vocation, developing skills to make meaningful social
relationships possible and establishing a sense of personal
"identity."

Interpersonal Relationships

As mentioned earlier, our culture expects adolescents
to eventually become financially and psychologically
autonomous. As the teen years draw to a close, teen-agers
are expected to be well on their way to selecting a life-
style and vocation and meet basic needs apart from the
family--in essence, to become self-sustaining individuals.
However, the need for extended training and education, the
scarcity of work and various cultural sanctions often
prolong their dependence upon the family.

The strivings for autonomy within the individual are
usually strong and persistent. In order to achieve meaningful independence teen-agers look more and more to their
peers for emotional support and need satisfactions. Their
improved communicative and social skills enable a mutual
sharing of feelings and ideas and enhance the capacity for
emotional intimacy. Close friendships and participation
in group activity become an important part of adolescence.
By the mid or late teen years, peer activities and standards
replace those of the family in importance. If peer relationships and self-assertiveness are impeded by adults,
the teen-ager will often respond by becoming argumentative,
challenging and defiant.

Implications for Management

It takes time for teen-agers to adapt to the changes
in bodily feelings, functions and proportions. It is not
surprising, then, that adolescents may become greatly
preoccupied with their body and very self-conscious about
their appearance. Many adolescents often feel threatened
by normal developmental changes, especially if they perceive themselves to be physically different from their
peers. Illness or injury may evoke strong feelings of
anxiety or depression at a time when their body image is
changing so rapidly.

Now complete Self-Assessment Exercise #2 on the
following page.

Self-Assessment Exercise #2

1.   A socially active sixteen-year-old girl was found to
     have diabetes. A regimen of twice daily urine testing,
     injections of insulin and a carbohydrate-restricted
     diet was prescribed. Several weeks later the girl
     became ill and was brought for consultation by her
     parents. She had symptoms of an incipient diabetic
     coma. Her parents related that the girl had stead-
     fastly refused to follow the prescribed regimen. How
     could the girl's behavior be understood in terms of
     her developmental stage?

2.   A worried mother confided that she "just can't under-
     stand" her sixteen-year-old daughter anymore. She
     related that formerly the family had enjoyed many
     activities and outings together. In recent months the
     girl had become sullen and disrespectful, and all but
     outrightly refused to go places with her family. She
     had little to say to family members but chatted end-
     lessly on the phone with school acquaintances. The
     mother expressed considerable distress and asked if
     her changed behavior might be due to a physical
     illness. What could you tell the mother about her
     daughter's behavior that might aid her understanding?

Self-Assessment Exercise #2 (continued)

3.   A fourteen-year-old boy must avoid strenuous physical
     activity because of a rheumatic heart condition.
     What potential developmental problems may occur?

     What action might you take to manage them?

     What would you advise the boy and his family about
     managing his condition?

          When you have completed this exercise to the best of
     your ability, check your answers on the following page.

Self-Assessment Exercise #2 - Feedback

1. Serious physical illness poses a threat to adolescents
    who are trying to adjust to a body of new proportions.
    They frequently deny their disease by resisting treat-
    ment measures that remind them of it. In this case,
    the special diet and treatment would cause the girl
    to feel apart and different from her peers. The
    establishment of good doctor-patient rapport, educa-
    tion about the disease, ample encouragement and hope,
    and relaxing some of the dietary restrictions are
    needed. The girl should be encouraged to participate
    fully in the usual social and physical activities of
    her friends.

2. The mother needs both education and reassurance about
    her daughter. Developmentally, the daughter is striv-
    ing to become autonomous from her family. In the
    process of doing so, she may appear to be contrary,
    disrespectful, stubborn, etc. Simultaneously, peer
    relationships replace those of the family in importance.
    The mother needs help in realizing that her daughter
    is developing "normally" towards independent adult-
    hood. The parents may need assistance in gradually
    severing some of the emotional ties with their daugh-
    ter. It is likely that closer family relationships
    will be reestablished after the girl has established
    her own identity.

3. An impaired self-concept because of restricted physi-
    cal activity, altered peer relationships, accentuated
    bodily concerns and restricted autonomy may result.
    Active counseling with the boy and his family should
    be undertaken. He should be encouraged to pursue
    social and intellectual activities in keeping with
    his physical tolerance. Personal abilities and traits
    that liken him to his peer group should be reinforced
    and liabilities deemphasized. He can be encouraged
    to become a participant observer in athletic events.

If your answers correspond closely with those above,
please continue your reading on the following page; if not,
please reread the preceding section until you are confident you know the material.

THE EARLY AND MIDDLE ADULT YEARS
This period of life covers a span of years from the close of adolescence to the sixties. A large number of patients who may consult you will come from this group.

Physical Traits
During the early years of this phase of development, young adults typically enjoy good health. Although peak physical abilities pass with the teen years, for many it is a time of maximum physical vigor, stamina and activity. Age-related health problems are relatively rare.
During the thirties and forties a gradual decline of physiologic functions occurs. Typically, there is a gradual gain in body weight and a reduction of physical strength, stamina and perceptual acuity. Many adults for the first time find it necessary to seek health care. Fears of disease characteristic of middle age, e.g., cancer and coronary artery disease, become more prominent, and countermeasures such as exercise programs, special diets and so forth frequently are initiated. Involutional changes become more pronounced during the forties and fifties. Symptoms of irregular and infrequent menstrual periods, fatigability, tension and insomnia are common experiences among females. Males, also, may complain of increased fatigability, decreased physical stamina and nonspecific bodily symptoms. Chronic diseases frequently associated with middle life, such as diabetes, arthritis and hypertension, may develop.

Emotional Traits
Many of the intense emotional responses of early adult life are related to the adjustments required in interpersonal relationships, marriage and one's life work. The exaggerated self-expectations of adolescence are gradually revised into more realistic life goals; but usually not without experiencing some degree of anxiety or depression. Adapting to responsibilities and problems associated with self-sufficiency, marriage, parenthood and choice of a life work make heavy demands upon coping mechanisms. The onset of psychoses is greatest during this time of life. However, good physical health, flexible adaptive capacities, and growing confidence in being able to handle life problems help to offset psychopathology.
After the mid-thirties, personal and family changes again alter the emotional equilibrium. It is a time for reappraising life and matching past expectations with actual accomplishments and an awareness develops that life and time are finite. Decisions about how to use the remaining years of life, establishing priorities and managing remaining resources become more important. Existential

preoccupations and involutional changes may result in feelings of depression and anxiety. Impulsive and maladaptive behavior, such as extramarital escapades, alcoholism, and sudden decisions to divorce or find a new life work may occur. The suicide rate increases, but the incidence of new psychoses is lower than in earlier years. Life responsibilities usually decrease as does the concomitant lessening of the emotional burden associated with them.

Developmental Tasks

For young adults, being self-sufficient, selecting a suitable life occupation and developing the capacity for close interpersonal relationships are important goals. The majority of persons within this age group achieve these goals by means of marriage, parenthood and gaining work skills.

In middle life it becomes important to reconcile past achievements and hopes with realistic, future capabilities. Changes in health, the family constellation, work and life purpose must be assimilated. Plans for the remaining years of life need careful formulation in order to make the most of the physical, social and financial resources available.

Interpersonal Relationships

The interpersonal relationships of young adults are characterized by more stability than those of the teen years. Friendships become closer and more selective. A closer relationship with members of both sexes is typical. For many, this capacity for closeness leads to marriage and other long-lasting relationships. The relationship between marriage partners supercedes in importance those of family members and peer groups. The deepening relationship allows a mutual satisfaction of emotional, sexual and dependency needs to a degree not achieved before. Family relationships become more exclusive with the birth of children and the responsibilities and activities of parenthood replace those outside the family.

As children grow and parents develop experience in their roles, leisure time and energy again are directed toward relationships outside the family group. In time, relationships with "important others" are accepted and more realistically appraised and provide a great resource in dealing with the vicissitudes of life.

Implications for Management

Most young adults have few health problems and therapists are consulted more often to help with the education of individuals in preparation for marriage and parenthood than because of illness. However, professionals should be alert to the presence of physical complaints which can be secondary to marital, sexual and occupational dissatisfactions.

As patients enter middle age, the increased incidence of pathology, both physical and emotional, requires careful evaluation. Medical examinations should be scheduled with greater frequency. Patients, for the first time, may develop diseases which only can be controlled, not cured. Patients will need support and education as they accustom themselves to physical decline. Symptoms of depression, tension, insomnia or overweight may require medical intervention.

Now please complete Self-Assessment Exercise #3 on the following page.

Self-Assessment Exercise #3

1.   A 24-year-old woman, married for one year, sought
     medical consultation because of tension, fitful
     sleep, irritability and recurring headaches. A physi-
     cal examination and routine laboratory tests were
     normal. Assuming that the etiology of her symptoms
     may be emotional and that she is typical of many
     young adults of comparable age, into which areas of
     her life would you inquire to find the source of her
     trouble?

2.   The zenith of physical ability is usually attained
     during:

     a.   early adolescence (12-15 years)
     b.   late adolescence (15-20 years)
     c.   the early adult years (21-35 years)
     d.   the middle adult years (36-65 years)

Self-Assessment Exercise #3 (continued)

3. You are asked to present a lecture to a group of
    student nurses entitled "Characteristics of the
    Middle Adult Years." From the list below, circle
    each statement that would be pertinent to your talk:

    greater incidence of psychoses

    life reappraisal

    optimum physical fitness

    noticeable decline in physical fitness

    limitation of relationships almost exclusively
    to immediate family

    need for clinician to help educate for
    parenthood

    typical concerns with "existential" problems

    increasing feelings of depression

When you have completed this exercise to the best
of your ability, check your answers with those on the
following page.

Self-Assessment Exercise #3 - Feedback

1. She is likely having problems in one or more of the
    following areas:

        marital adjustment
        sexual adjustment
        interpersonal relationships
        vocational adjustment

2. The prime years relative to physical fitness are
    during late adolescence--15 to 20 years of age.

3. You should have circled the following:

        time for a life reappraisal
        noticeable decline in physical fitness
        typical concerns with "existential" problems
        increasing feelings of depression

    It is the young adult years that are typified by the
    greatest incidence of psychoses, limitation of rela-
    tionships mostly to the immediate family, and need
    for clinician to help educate for parenthood.

    Optimum physical fitness occurs in late adolescence.

        If your answers correspond closely with those above,
    please continue your reading on the following page; if not,
    please reread the preceding section until you are confident
    you know the material.

THE LATER ADULT YEARS

For purposes of this section the "later adult years" begin at age 65. Many persons of 65 or older have changed little from their middle years and are mature, capable, productive and confident. The elderly comprise a spectrum of individuals with varying characteristics and personality traits. Therefore, it is useful to distinguish persons with signs of "senescence" (normal aging without significant loss of function) from those with signs of "senility" (aging accompanied by considerable physical and psychological deterioration). Only when changes in health or life circumstances force an individual to depend greatly on others for physical care and emotional well-being are elderly persons correctly termed "senile."

At the present time ten percent of our population are over 65, and physicians and other professionals are faced daily with providing adequate care for an ever increasing number of elderly persons. This task can most effectively be accomplished by thoroughly understanding the aging process. As with other stages of human development, a knowledge of the physical, emotional and mental changes that occur during aging will enable therapists to distinguish normal changes from pathological ones.

Physical Traits

The exact cause of aging is not yet known. It has been determined that the aging process is normal and not pathological. Current theories suggest that aging may result from diverse causes such as an auto-immune disease, a disturbance in the RNA-DNA metabolism, and/or the influence of genetic and other factors, including exposure to radiation, nutrition, intercurrent disease, etc.

Common signs of aging include the development of gray hair, wrinkling of skin and increased skin pigmentation. More subtle and significant changes become manifest as a gradual, but variable, decline in function within most organ systems. In some organ systems aging is imperceptible; in others there is a marked decrement of function. For example, glucose tolerance tests usually stay normal throughout a lifetime, yet pulmonary and renal functions decrease significantly.

There is a reduction in acuity of perceptual abilities, e.g., vision, hearing, and taste, and in psychomotor performance, e.g., coordination, strength and reaction time. Recovery from illness and injury proceeds at a slower rate, and hospitalization and surgical procedures are not tolerated as well as in earlier years. Homeostatic mechanisms that regulate blood pressure, cardiac rate, and other vital functions, become increasingly vulnerable to physical and emotional stress.

Emotional Traits

The loss of physical stamina, mobility and acuity of the sense organs affects each individual differently. But in spite of these losses, maturity can be a comfortable and broadening experience.

Individual emotional response to growing older is mostly learned. Some families "age well" generation after generation, not only because of genetic factors, but also because of the attitudes developed during earlier years. Many older persons remain cheerful and philosophically optimistic about their advancing years and these individuals adjust well to the aging process.

Generally, an accentuation of previous personality traits occurs. Transient symptoms of depression and/or anxiety are so universally experienced by the elderly as to be considered "normal" phenomena. Depression may result when former methods of coping are no longer satisfactory, and newer ways are difficult to cultivate. For some, sensory impairment and decreased mobility may lead to a feeling of social isolation, heightened suspiciousness and withdrawal from the mainstream of social activity. These responses may lead to greater depression, and a downward cycle begins. Egocentricity frequently accompanies a constriction of activity and loss of meaningful interpersonal relationships. Verbalized concerns about health, finances, creature comforts and the "good old days" become themes more common than in former years. Although many of the elderly experience a generalized decline in their intellectual functions with respect to new-learning ability and recent memory, it is untrue that brain damage is an inevitable outcome of aging. Only ten to fifteen percent of the elderly develop significant mental impairment. However, Organic Mental Disorders, both acute and chronic, occur with greater frequency in the elderly. It is most important to remember that the elderly retain the same human needs that they possessed during earlier years... to be wanted, useful and productive.

Developmental Tasks

The major task of aging persons is to establish a new psychological and physical equilibrium that is in keeping with the reality of physical decline and social and environmental change. It is necessary, for personal well-being, to maintain self-esteem and social interactions in spite of decreased capacity and productivity.

There are many compensations and pleasant anticipations associated with becoming older. Many persons maintain their personal and social skills throughout their lifetime. With pensions and increased leisure time, many can now pursue special interests, travel and recreation that was deferred during earlier years. Many older persons maintain and share their capabilities by serving as volunteers or consultants. Others pursue education or enter second careers. The elderly may experience relief at being able to set aside, with the sanctions of society, the responsibilities and strivings of earlier years, i.e., the raising of a family and the need to compete socially and in business. Life becomes simpler and less hectic. Satisfactions from various achievements and from having lived a full life cycle bring a sense of inner fulfillment and "integrity." Most of the aged perceive their physical and other changes as more of an inconvenience than a true handicap.

Interpersonal Relationships

All but five percent of "senior citizens" are able to maintain themselves in the community. The presence (or absence) of meaningful relationships during the later years of life plays a central role in determining emotional stability. New relationships become harder to establish, but an interested family, a caring spouse and friends can soften the impact of losses of physical capability. The mutual support and satisfactions provided through peer relationships help bind the elderly to involvement with the present. Without the stimulation of social interaction, older persons tend to become more preoccupied with themselves and withdrawn from life. The loss of loved ones through death and separation is tolerated better when other relationships are readily available. Active participation with people from both similar and younger generations provides an advantageous mix of experiences for the elderly and is conducive to an extended and satisfying longevity.

Implications for Management

Routine medical treatment requires modification to meet the special needs of elderly patients. In order to compensate for the decreased perceptual acuity and "forgetfulness" of some older persons, a physician should make prescription directions and medical explanations explicit. For many older persons, a visit to a doctor is a rare opportunity to converse with an interested listener; consequently, more time should be alloted for them. Physiological changes associated with aging often make older persons more sensitive to the effects of medication, and drug dosages should be reduced accordingly. Physiologic homeostatic mechanisms are less stable, and patients recover more slowly from illness and surgery. Hospitalization, with its attendant separation from family, isolation from familiar surroundings and inactivity, may precipitate symptoms of depression or an Organic Mental Disorder. It is important to take appropriate preventive measures.

Now complete Self-Assessment Exercise #4 on the following page.

Self-Assessment Exercise #4

Please answer the following questions:

1.   Most elderly patients develop mental impairment.

         True_____   False_____

2.   A 55-year-old woman states that she sees "nothing good about growing older." What positive comments could you make to counter her statement?

3.   A majority of elderly persons eventually end up in rest homes.

         True_____   False_____

Self-Assessment Exercise #4 (continued)

4.   A 67-year-old man is admitted to the hospital for an
      elective prostatectomy. Which age-related physical
      characteristics require a specialized medical approach?

When you have completed this exercise to the best
of your ability, check your answers on the following page.

Self-Assessment Exercies #4 - Feedback

1.   False--only ten to fifteen percent of the elderly
     become significantly senile.

2.   Some positive aspects of being older are:

     (a) decreased responsibility and strivings
     (b) satisfaction from life achievements, family, etc.
     (c) more time for interpersonal relationships, i.e.,
         family, friends
     (d) leisure time for the pursuit of hobbies, special
         interests, travel, etc.
     (e) for many, a degree of financial security
     (f) a simpler, less hectic life

3.   False--all but five percent of the elderly are able
     to maintain themselves in the community.

4.   Medically important, age-related characteristics are:

     (a) increased sensitivity to medication--reduce dosage
     (b) homeostatic mechanisms relatively unstable--
         closely monitor vital signs (heart rate, blood
         pressure, etc.) for an extended time post-
         operatively
     (c) tendency to develop an Organic Mental Disorder--
         reduce sedatives, allow frequent family visits,
         don't isolate the patient
     (d) slowed recovery time--initiate early rehabilita-
         tive efforts, plan for a prolonged convalescence

     If your answers correspond closely with those above,
please continue your reading on the following page; if not,
please reread the preceding section until you are confident
you know the material.

SUMMARY

Human life is characterized by continual change. Disease or maladjustment should be considered in the context of the patient's life cycle, because responses to illness plus life stresses are influenced by age and developmental characteristics. It is important for health care professionals to distinguish between patient symptoms which reflect normal developmental changes and those indicative of true pathology. A knowledge of human growth and development will enable you to provide better care. A chart summarizing this chapter is found on pages 48 and 49.

REFERENCES

Bowden, C. and Burstein, A., Psychosocial Basis of Medical Practice, Second Edition, Baltimore: The Williams & Wilkins Co., 1979.

Butler, R. N., Why Survive? Being Old in America, New York: Harper and Row, 1975.

Erikson, E., "The Eight Stages of Man," Childhood and Society, Second Edition, New York: W. W. Norton, Inc. 1963.

Lidz, T., The Person, New York: Basic Books, 1968.

Usdin, G. and Hofling, C., Aging: The Process and the People, New York: Brunner/Mazel, 1978.

Usdin, G. and Lewis, G., Psychiatry in General Medical Practice, New York, McGraw-Hill Book Co., 1979.

	Physical and Emotional Traits	Developmental Tasks
T E E N Y E A R S	girls develop physically and emotionally more rapidly than boys growth patterns variable preoccupied with physical changes and sexuality transient mood swings typical	developing a sense of "identity" developing social relationships coping with sexual development and physique becoming autonomous choosing life vocation
M I D D L E Y E A R S	Early: generally good health emotional symptoms due to marital, family or occupational stress Middle: onset of involutional changes, menopause, decreased stamina and strength onset of some chronic disease, e.g., diabetes, arthritis, etc. existential preoccupations may lead to depression and/or anxiety	Early: becoming self-sufficient, selecting a life occupation, developing relationships Middle: reconciling self-expectations with achievements making realistic plans for remaining years
L A T E R Y E A R S	general decline of functioning in all organ systems accentuation of existing personality traits sensory impairment homeostatic mechanisms less stable	adapting to decline of physical and mental functions adjusting to change in life style, i.e., "retirement," remaining autonomous and "involved"

Interpersonal Relationships	Implications for Management
better able to live independently but still needs support and limits develops ability to relate intimately with significant others peer relationships and activities replace those of the family	illness and hospitaliza- and fears of body mutilation especially threatening needs education and reassurance about bodily changes
Early: friendships more stable, selective and intimate most marry and begin families many of activities and relationships family centered Middle: less preoccupation with child raising; more involvement with relationships out-side immediate family relationships more stable and selective	Early: relatively few health problems, but needs education for marriage, sexual and family problems Middle: need for more regular physical examinations support needed for patients to accommodate to physical decline patients may become more dependent on physician
greater reliance upon the family and others continuing relation-ships become increas-ingly important more need and time for socialization less adaptable to change	increased susceptibility to organic brain syn-dromes and chronic disease greater need for emotional support slowing of recovery from illness more sensitive to medica-tions; and dosage adjustment needed

Chapter 3
Mental Status Examination
William G. Crary
C. Warner Johnson

This chapter presents a rationale for, and an explanation of, the Mental Status Examination (M.S.E.). It also describes and explains the broad observational categories and specific descriptors which are used when performing a Mental Status Examination. The Mental Status Examination is necessary for the evaluation and diagnosis of a patient's psychological state.

LEARNING OBJECTIVES
By the time you complete this chapter you should be able to do the following:

1. List four purposes served by doing a Mental Status Examination.

2. List and define the five major categories of the Mental Status Examination.

3. Correctly define the following terms and be able to place each term in the appropriate major category of the Mental Status Examination:

    orientation   mood
    level of consciousness   associational disturbance
    thought content   ideas of influence
    stream of thought   judgment
    depersonalization   phobia
    affect   ideas of reference
    hallucination   immediate memory
    illusion   insight

labile affect   blunted affect
obsession   compulsion
delusion   recent memory
remote memory

By the conclusion of this chapter and with supervised clinical experience, you should be able to do the
following:

1.   Accurately observe and record a patient's behavior
      within each of the M.S.E. behavior descriptors.

OVERVIEW

Accurate diagnosis and effective treatment are dependent upon the collection and systematic organization of observations about a patient's mental and physical state. These data then can be grouped into meaningful combinations, i.e., syndromes. Knowledge about the particular syndrome manifested by a patient (the nature of the pathology involved, course of the disease, etc.) can be utilized in designing the therapeutic approach.

When a medical evaluation of a patient is to be made, pertinent information is derived by taking a history, performing a physical examination, and doing appropriate laboratory tests. A similar process of data collection is followed when a psychological assessment of the patient is to be done. A history is taken, and a Mental Status Examination is performed.

A Mental Status Examination is both a descriptive inventory of behavior and a method by which to systematically organize and record observations which describe a patient's behavior. From these observations inferences about the mental and emotional condition of that patient can be made. From these inferences a working diagnosis and a therapeutic approach can be formulated.

To understand the patient's psychological condition, many high order inferences must be made by the interview. For example, it is not possible to see the depressed feelings of a patient. One can only infer their presence by noting what is said and the patient's overt behavior. Thus, objectivity is important and the behavior should be described accurately. Other persons concomitantly evaluating the patient should be able to duplicate the observations with a high degree of consistency.

It takes less time and activity on the part of the examiner to perform a Mental Status Examination than to do a physical examination. It is not necessary to question the patient extensively or drastically change interviewing techniques. Aside from asking a few pertinent questions, the interviewer needs only to observe carefully the responses of the patient. This is because the observed behaviors upon which the Mental Status Examination is based are spontaneously revealed by the patient as he speaks and responds to the interviewer. The observations should be transformed into a written record. This record reflects, then, the psychological condition of the person at the time that the interview was held.

Thus, the Mental Status Examination findings serve four important functions:

a. they aid in understanding the patient's psychological state at a point in time
b. they help to establish a diagnosis
c. they serve as a base-line against which future assessments of the patient's psychological state can be compared
d. they become part of a written, descriptive record of the patient.

Now complete Self-Assessment Exercise #1 on the following page.

Self-Assessment Exercise #1

1.   The Mental Status Examination is both:

     a.

     b.

2.   What are four important functions served by the
     Mental Status Examination findings?

     a.

     b.

     c.

     d.

     When you have completed this exercise to the best of
your ability, check your answers on the following page.

Self-Assessment Exercise #1 - Feedback

1.   The Mental Status Examination is both:

   a.   A method for systematically observing and record-
        ing a patient's psychological and physical
        behavior during an interview.

   b.   A descriptive inventory of behavior for re-
        cording the observations referred to above.

2.   The four important functions served by the Mental
     Status Examination findings are:

   a.   They aid in understanding the patient's psycho-
        logical state at a point in time.

   b.   They help to establish a diagnosis.

   c.   They serve as a base-line against which future
        assessments of the patient's psychological
        state can be compared.

   d.   They become a part of a written, descriptive
        record of the patient.

   If your answers correspond closely with those above,
please continue your reading on the following page;
if not, please reread the preceding section until you
are confident you know the material.

MENTAL STATUS CATEGORIES AND DESCRIPTORS

A Mental Status Examination, as indicated previously, is an evaluation of a patient's mental condition based upon careful observation of the patient during an interview.

Accurate observation of human behavior must be made over a large number of behavioral descriptors. This requires that therapists (1) become familiar with and use a common vocabulary of behavioral descriptors, and (2) be able to recognize when a patient has or has not exhibited a particular behavior.

The Mental Status Examination procedures described below and the M.S.E. form shown on the next two pages, will help you to observe and systematically record patient behaviors pertinent to establishing a psychiatric diagnosis. They are divided into five major categories--appearance, behavior, feelings, perception, and thinking--with an additional section for diagnosis.

Within each major category are numbered descriptors which define patient behaviors more specifically. Three vertical columns are located to the right of the descriptors. It is important to the learning process that you make a judgment for each descriptor on every patient evaluated and record your opinion in one of the three columns. For easier evaluation, all descriptors are worded to indicate the presence of abnormal behavior. Each descriptor for which, in your judgment, no abnormality is present, should be marked in the column headed "Absent." A check mark opposite that descriptor item signifies that no such pathology was observed in or described by the interviewed patient. If psychopathology is noted, then "Present" should be recorded. Furthermore, it is useful to distinguish between psychopathology as experienced by the patient in the past, from that which is present during the interview. If the patient demonstrates a current abnormality, a check should be placed in the column headed "Present."

Name_____ Observer's Name_____

		No Data	Present	Absent
APPEARANCE	1. unkempt, unclean, disheveled............			
	2. clothing and/or grooming atypical.......			
	3. unusual physical characteristics........			

COMMENTS RE APPEARANCE:

			No Data	Present	Absent
BEHAVIOR	Posture	4. slumped.................................			
		5. rigid, tense...........................			
	Facial Expression Suggests	6. anxiety, fear, apprehension.............			
		7. depression, sadness.....................			
		8. anger, hostility........................			
		9. absence of feeling, blandness...........			
		10. atypical, unusualness...................			
	General Body Movements	11. accelerated, increased speed...........			
		12. decreased, slowed......................			
		13. atypical, unusual......................			
		14. restlessness, fidgetyness..............			
	Speech	15. rapid speech...........................			
		16. slowed speech..........................			
		17. loud speech............................			
		18. soft speech............................			
		19. mute...................................			
		20. atypical quality, slurring, stammer.....			

Observer's Name_____

			No Data	Present	Absent
BEHAVIOR	Therapist-Patient Relationship	21. domineering, controlling...............			
		22. submissive, overly compliant,dependent..			
		23. provocative, hostile, challenging.......			
		24. suspicious, guarded, evasive...........			
		25. uncooperative, non-compliant............			

COMMENTS RE BEHAVIOR:

		No Data	Present	Absent
FEELING (AFFECT AND MOOD)	26. inappropriate to thought content........			
	27. increased lability of affect............			
	predominant mood is:			
	28. blunted, dulled, bland..................			
	29. euphoria, elation.......................			
	30. anger, hostility........................			
	31. anxiety, fear,apprehension..............			
	32. depression, sadness.....................			

COMMENTS RE FEELING:

			No Data	Present	Absent
PERCEPTION		33. illusions...............................			
		34. auditory hallucinations..................			
		35. visual hallucinations...................			
		36. other type of hallucinations............			

COMMENTS RE PERCEPTION:

			No Data	Present	Absent
THINKING	Intellectual Functioning	37. impaired level of consciousness.........			
		38. impaired attention span, distractible...			
		39. impaired abstract thinking..............			
		40. impaired calculation ability............			
		41. impaired intelligence...................			
	Orientation	42. disoriented to person...................			
		43. disoriented to place....................			
		44. disoriented to time.....................			
	Memory	45. impaired recent memory..................			
		46. impaired remote memory..................			
	Insight	47. denies presence of psychological problems...............................			
		48. blames others or circumstances for problems............................			
	Judgment	49. impaired ability to make routine decisions............................			
		50. impaired impulse control................			

			No Data	Present	Absent
THINKING	Thought Content	51. obsessions..............................			
		52. compulsions.............................			
		53. phobias.................................			
		54. depersonalization.......................			
		55. suicidal ideation.......................			
		56. homicidal ideation......................			
		57. delusions...............................			
	Stream of Thought	58. associational disturbance...............			

COMMENTS RE THINKING:

DIAGNOSIS:_____

as manifested by the following M.S.E. items

_____ _____ _____ _____ _____

_____ _____ _____ _____ _____

Finally, if a test of mental functioning is omitted during the interview, and if the findings cannot be inferred from other data obtained from the patient, place a check mark in the column headed "No Data." In this way, the need for future, specific evaluations can be indicated.

Below each of the major categories is a space allowed for comments. You may frequently find it necessary to qualify your comments about patient behaviors. You can do so by writing the descriptor item number following your comments in the space provided. Using check marks or letters on this form will allow you to quickly record observations about patients and at the same time give an opportunity to specifically qualify your observations.

The final section on the Mental Status Examination form is for diagnosis. Here, you are to write in the most appropriate diagnosis; in the spaces provided list the key item numbers which enabled you to make the diagnosis.

Expect some uneasiness as you attempt to quantify some of your patient observations. For example, there are few absolute standards by which to measure whether the patient is unkempt, to a normal, slight, or marked degree. The same problem will be encountered when making determinations about the patient's posture, affective state, intellectual functioning, etc. As you gain experience and compare your findings with the observations of others, you will establish workable standards of your own with which to evaluate patient behavior. Initially, many of the observations may seem somewhat subjective and reflect various biases of yourself and others. Nevertheless, it is important to begin to make the judgments, and then qualify and test them when indicated. Often you will be making judgments in terms of "shades of gray" and not "black and white." This is one of the ever-present problems when dealing with complex human behavior.

When evaluating most categories, recorded observations should reflect both <u>predominant patterns</u> of behavior and <u>highly atypical responses</u>, even if the latter occurs only once. For example, individuals who are somewhat depressed may momentarily smile during the course of an interview. In that instance, it is the pervading mood of depression that is to be recorded. On the other hand, it is diagnostically significant for a patient to describe a single, delusional belief during an otherwise "normal" interview. The delusion should be recorded. This determination will become clearer as you read further.

In the content material which follows, emphasis is placed on the definition of terms, a description of some of the behaviors which are important to observe and the diagnostic significance of findings. Various diagnostic categories will be mentioned, but it is not necessary to know or understand them in depth at this time.

When performing a Mental Status Examination, it is important to look for the unusual, the atypical, and the unexpected. If the unusual is detected, try to obtain clarifications from the individual as to why things are that way. (But remain open to data which may NOT confirm your initial impressions.)

Each of the major categories will be reviewed individually to enable you to become familiar with the subcategories and the descriptors which make them up.

Appearance

Appearance refers to how the person looked during the interview. You are asked to judge whether the patient is normal (i.e., listed findings are "Absent") or exhibits some degree of abnormality (i.e., indicated findings are "Present") in terms of the following descriptors:

1. unkempt, unclean, disheveled
2. clothing and/or grooming atypical
3. unusual physical characteristics (e.g., marked weight problem, deformity, disfiguration, etc.)

In making the necessary judgments, observe the general body build, state of nutrition, and physical defects and carriage. Also, note the manner of dress--whether it is neat, casual, slovenly, etc. Look for special adornments or absence of items of clothing. Consider the patient's general cleanliness and, for women, the presence and appropriateness of makeup. Is the appearance generally consistent with the person's age, social, education, economic and cultural background? "Unusual," "atypical," etc. are subjective and relative terms. If you have doubts about your judgments, make descriptive comments supporting them in the "comments" section.

Observations about patients' appearances may yield clues about their relationship to society at large, how they perceive themselves, and their awareness of social expectations. The diagnostic significance of the patient's appearance should be considered in relationship to other findings. In severe psychological disorders one often finds an inattentiveness to appearance. Occasionally a person seems to be severely disturbed and yet is neatly dressed. The interviewer should attempt to solve this apparent paradox. The person may be less disturbed than it first seems, or he may have an interested family caring for him.

Now complete Self-Assessment Exercise #2 on the following page.

Self-Assessment Exercise #2

Using the data taken from the history below, complete the "Appearance" section on the sample Mental Status Examination form below. Enter any comments you may deem necessary or significant.

HISTORY

Late one evening, the local police brought an elderly woman into the hospital emergency room for evaluation. She was found wandering at a busy intersection in a state of bewilderment. She wore no makeup and her hair was matted and uncombed. Her dress, while only slightly out of fashion, was tattered and smeared with dirt. She was not wearing shoes and her toe-nails extended almost three-fourths of an inch beyond her toes. No physical abnormalities were apparent.

Now complete the Mental Status Examination below:

		No Data	Present	Absent
APPEARANCE	1. unkempt, unclean, disheveled...........			
	2. clothing and/or grooming atypical......			
	3. unusual physical characteristics.......			

COMMENTS RE APPEARANCE:

When you have completed this exercise to the best of your ability, check your answers with those on the following page.

Self-Assessment Exercise #2 - Feedback

Based on the history, you should have marked the Mental Status Examination (M.S.E.) form accordingly:

		No Data	Present	Absent
APPEARANCE	1. unkempt, unclean, disheveled...........		✓	
	2. clothing and/or grooming atypical......		✓	
	3. unusual physical characteristics.......			✓

COMMENTS RE APPEARANCE:

1. hair matted and uncombed; long toe nails.
2. dress tattered and smeared with dirt, clothing out of fashion; shoes absent.

If your answers correspond closely with those above, please continue your reading on the following page; if not, please reread the preceding section until you are confident you know the material.

Behavior
     This category of the M.S.E. is concerned with the
person's general conduct during the interview. As you
can see on the sample Mental Status Examination form, this
category has many more descriptors than the Appearance
category. For this reason they have been grouped into
subcategories in an attempt to make the form more easily
usable. For example, on the sample form the descriptors
(4) slumped and (5) rigid, tense, are in the subcategory
Posture. The remaining descriptors are in four additional
subcategories. Here, as with the Appearance category,
each of the descriptors must be checked so that the
patient's profile may be objectively developed.
     Only practice and experience will enable you to re-
liably describe a patient. In making your judgments for
this category, consider all verbal and nonverbal behavior,
including the therapist-patient relationship. Difficulties in speaking, unusual amplitude or speed of speech
and atypical use of words may have diagnostic implications.
In appraising the patient's nonverbal behavior, the general
level of motor activity, posture, facial expressions and
general body movements should be noted and compared to
that expected of most persons in a similar setting.
     Patient responses and actions during the interview
yield information about the patient's ability to direct
his behavior and to express himself effectively. Behavioral observations may help to clarify motivational
and emotional states. Bizarre behavior, or disordered
communication, is generally a sign of severe psychological impairment.
     The Therapist-Patient Relationship subcategory is of
particular importance; some additional comments about it
are in order. An attempt should be made to succinctly
characterize the relationship between the therapist and
patient during each interview. Was the patient friendly,
cooperative, suspicious or evasive? What did the patient
seem to want from the interviewer? What methods were
used by the patient to achieve his goals? The interviewer
should note his own personal and emotional reactions that
he felt towards the patient. The patient's prevailing
attitude toward the therapist may influence the relationship profoundly. Five descriptors which may characterize
the patient's attitude toward the evaluator are listed on
the Mental Status Examination sample form. Some additional
explanatory words and phrases are added here to define
them for you more precisely:

          domineering - persistently tries to control and
                        direct the interview
          submissive - agrees with almost everything that is
                        said; excessively dependent
          provocative - hostile, clearly uncooperative, in-
                        sulting or challenging
          suspicious - guarded, unusually evasive and cautious
                        in responses

uncooperative - makes little or no effort to verbalize
and explain the problem, unreceptive
to recommendations

An ability to form a meaningful relationship is
important in order to "get along" in our society. The
relationship between the therapist and his patient is
a special one; a close working relationship is desirable.
Unresolved emotional conflicts between the therapist and
the patient can lead to problems in treatment. A markedly
positive or negative relationship may set a precedent for
future interactions. The patient may evoke emotional
responses within the clinician which may aid in assigning
a diagnosis. Individuals with schizophrenia may cause
a sense of puzzlement, strangeness, or a vague uneasiness
within their therapist. The affect of a truly depressed
or manic patient is often "contagious" and this feeling
may be evoked briefly in the therapist during the
interview.

Now please complete Self-Assessment Exercise #3
beginning on the following page.

Self-Assessment Exercise #3

Using information abstracted from the history below, complete the "Behavior" section on the Mental Status Examination form below.

HISTORY

Mr. Wright, a man in his mid 50's, was brought for psychological evaluation by his wife and son. He had allegedly become progressively apathetic, anorexic and sleepless during the past three months. He crossed the room moving slowly, partly leaning on his wife for support. His face was deeply lined, and the corners of his eyes and mouth were down-turned. Mr. Wright sat hunched in the chair, rarely moving. Generally, he ignored questions. When he did speak a word or two, it was in a slow barely audible monotone. Occasionally he would sigh deeply.

			No Data	Present	Absent
BEHAVIOR	Posture	4. slumped......................................			
		5. rigid, tense................................			
	Facial Expression Suggests	6. anxiety, fear, apprehension................			
		7. depression, sadness.........................			
		8. anger, hostility............................			
		9. absence of feeling, blandness..............			
		10. atypical, unusualness......................			
	General Body Movements	11. accelerated, increased speed..............			
		12. decreased, slowed..........................			
		13. atypical, unusual..........................			
		14. restlessness, fidgetyness.................			
	Speech	15. rapid speech...............................			
		16. slowed speech..............................			
		17. loud speech................................			
		18. soft speech................................			
		19. mute.......................................			
		20. atypical quality, slurring, stammer.......			
	Therapist-Patient Relationship	21. domineering, controlling...................			
		22. submissive, overly compliant, dependent....			
		23. provocative, hostile, challenging.........			
		24. suspicious, guarded, evasive..............			
		25. uncooperative, non-compliant..............			

COMMENTS RE BEHAVIOR:

When you have completed this exercise to the best of your ability, check your answers with those on the following page.

Self-Assessment Exercise #3 - Feedback

Based on the history, you should have marked the Mental Status Examination form accordingly:

			No Data	Present	Absent
BEHAVIOR	Posture	4. slumped...................................		✓	
		5. rigid, tense.............................			✓
	Facial Expression Suggests	6. anxiety, fear, apprehension.............			✓
		7. depression, sadness.....................		✓	
		8. anger, hostility........................			✓
		9. absence of feeling, blandness..........			✓
		10. atypical, unusualness...................			✓
	General Body Movements	11. accelerated, increased speed............			✓
		12. decreased, slowed.......................		✓	
		13. atypical, unusual.......................			✓
		14. restlessness, fidgetyness...............			✓
	Speech	15. rapid speech............................			✓
		16. slowed speech...........................		✓	
		17. loud speech.............................			✓
		18. soft speech.............................		✓	
		19. mute....................................			✓
		20. atypical quality, slurring, stammer.....			✓
	Therapist-Patient Relationship	21. domineering, controlling................			✓
		22. submissive, overly compliant, dependent.			✓
		23. provocative, hostile, challenging.......			✓
		24. suspicious, guarded, evasive............			✓
		25. uncooperative, non-compliant............		✓	

COMMENTS RE BEHAVIOR

    4. sat hunched in chair
    7. corners of eyes and mouth downturned;
        face deeply lined.
   12. moved slowly; rarely moved.
16 and 18. rarely spoke; slow barely audible
        monotone; deep sighs.
   25. generally ignored questions; when
        did respond, could barely be heard.

If your answers correspond closely with those above, please continue your reading on the following page; if not, please reread the preceding section until you are confident you know the material.

Feeling (Affect and Mood)

This is the third category indicated on the sample
Mental Status Examination form. It contains seven behavior descriptors which are important to observe and
check during the psychiatric interview.

Feeling (affect and mood) refers to the various
emotions which the patient demonstrates during the interview. Affect pertains to the variable feeling state associated with expressed, individual ideas. The affective
state of the patient is inferred from his behavior and
comments. Mood designates the predominant and pervasive
feeling tones of the interview. These feelings include
anger, elation, anxiety, fear, depression, apathy and
others.

The following determinations should be made by the
interviewer about each patient:

a. the appropriateness of the affect shown relative
to the circumstances of the interview and the
ideas being expressed.
b. the degree of affect lability, i.e., the extent
to which expressed affects reflect a rapidly
shifting state of feeling with a minimal stimulus.
c. the predominant type of mood(s) expressed, such
as elation depression, anger, etc.

Adaptive behavior is more probable if an individual
can experience emotions in some strength and yet not be
dominated by them. A persistent, unpleasant affective
state may point to a psychological disorder. If the
manifest affect of anxiety or depression is not a reasonable response to a real life situation, and if the mental
status examination is otherwise normal, the presence of
a neurosis is likely. An affective psychosis is diagnosed
in many patients who show very disturbed behavior which
is associated with greatly intensified feelings. If
a patient demonstrates an unexpected absence of affect, or
if the feelings shown are inappropriate to the thought
content, a schizophrenic condition may be present.

Now please complete Self-Assessment Exercise #4
on the following page.

Self-Assessment Exercise #4

1. Read the following description and then check each descriptor within the "Feeling/Affect and Mood" category in the appropriate column of the sample Mental Status Examination form below:

> A somewhat confused, elderly man began to weep openly when asked about his wife who died eight years previously. The crying abruptly stopped when the topic was changed. He became highly irritable when pressed to supply information which he could not easily remember. He spoke repeatedly about his loneliness and sadness.

		No Data	Present	Absent
FEELING (AFFECT AND MOOD)	26. inappropriate to thought content.........			
	27. increased lability of affect.............			
	predominant mood is:			
	28. blunted, dulled, bland...................			
	29. euphoria, elation........................			
	30. anger, hostility.........................			
	31. anxiety, fear, apprehension.............			
	32. depression, sadness.....................			

COMMENTS RE FEELING:

2. Select the best answer(s) for the following:

> A teen-aged patient with a schizophrenic disorder relates a fear that the world will be destroyed by her thoughts within the hour. She describes feeling terrified by her vast powers. While telling her story, the patient shows no change of facial expression. She speaks in a dull monotone without inflection. This patient is demonstrating:

a. an inappropriate affect
b. "blunting" of affect
c. emotional lability

When you have completed this exercise to the best of your ability, check your answers on the following page.

Self-Assessment Exercise #4 - Feedback

1.   You should have placed check marks in the following columns.

		No Data	Present	Absent
	26. inappropriate to thought content........			✓
	27. increased lability of affect.............		✓	
FEELING (AFFECT AND MOOD)	predominant mood is:			
	28. blunted, dulled, bland...................			✓
	29. euphoria, elation........................			✓
	30. anger, hostility.........................			✓
	31. anxiety, fear, apprehension.............			✓
	32. depression, sadness.-...................		✓	

COMMENTS RE FEELING:

 27.   affect quickly changes with different topic, is intense.

 32.   recurrent theme of loneliness and sadness; tearfulness at times.

2.   The patient with a schizophrenic disorder demonstrates both:

   a.   an inappropriate affect--her affective state is not in keeping with verbalized terror, and
   b.   a restricted range or "blunting" of affect is present.

   If your answers correspond closely with those above, please continue your reading on the following page; if not, please reread the preceding section until you are confident you know the material.

Perception
        This category concerns the way in which the patient
perceives the world and himself via his five senses
(vision, hearing, touch, smell and taste), as judged
during the interview.
        On the sample Mental Status Examination form please
note that examples of abnormal perceptions are illusions
and hallucinations.   Illusions are brief misinterpreta-
tions of actual stimuli.   Hallucinations represent a perceptual experience in the absence of any real, external
stimuli.   Illusions are typically visual or auditory
while hallucinations may involve perceptions from any
sensory organ.
        One must have intact perceptual processes in order to
accurately receive and process information about people
and the environment.   Normal individuals may experience
illusions from time to time, however, the presence of
hallucinations is indicative of a more serious condition,
usually psychosis.   Gustatory (taste), olfactory (smell),
and tactile (touch) hallucinations are usually limited to
persons with organic brain syndromes.   Visual and auditory
hallucinations are found in individuals with organic
brain syndromes and functional psychoses.   The hallucinations which are experienced during an organic brain syndrome are likely to be visual, unusually vivid and
frightening.   Auditory hallucinations are more characteristic of a functional psychosis, i.e. schizophrenia or
a major affective disorder.

        Now complete Self-Assessment Exercise #5 on the
following page.

Self-Assessment Exercise #5

1.   Read the following description and then check each descriptor within the "Perception" category in the appropriate column of the sample Mental Status Examination form below:

HISTORY
   A diabetic was brought to the hospital suffering from metabolic acidosis, ketosis and dehydration. She stated that God had told her to go on a fast. During the interview she would occasionally pause and nod her head as if responding to some stimuli. When questioned about her behavior she responded by saying that God was giving instructions to her. She suddenly pointed to a towel which lay crumpled on the floor and said, "I just saw that thing move, is it alive?"

		No Data	Present	Absent
PERCEPTION	33. illusions...............................			
	34. auditory hallucinations.................			
	35. visual hallucinations...................			
	36. other type of hallucinations............			

COMMENTS RE PERCEPTION:

   When you have completed this exercise to the best of your ability, check your answers with those on the following page.

Self-Assessment Exercise #5 - Feedback

Based on the history, you should have marked the Mental Status Examination form accordingly:

		No Data	Present	Absent
PERCEPTION	33. illusions..		✓	
	34. auditory hallucinations....................		✓	
	35. visual hallucinations......................			✓
	36. other type of hallucinations............			✓

COMMENTS RE PERCEPTION:

33. movement was misperceived in a real, but inanimate object, i.e., the towel
34. the patient described hearing God's instructions.

Be sure that you clearly understand the difference between an illusion and a hallucination. The patient demonstrated both. She was experiencing a hallucination (auditory) when she was "getting instructions from God." She experienced an illusion (visual) when she misperceived movement by the towel.

If your answers correspond closely with those above, please continue your reading on the following page; if not, please reread the preceding section until you are confident you know the material.

Thinking

Thinking is the final category on the Mental Status Examination form. In this category you must consider the intactness and level of functioning of the"higher" thinking (cognitive) processes. Abnormalities occurring in one or more of the areas under this heading may indicate the presence of a mental disorder of some type.

This category, like the one on Behavior, is a complex one; therefore, it is divided conceptually into several subcategories in order to make the form more easily usable.

A.   The first subcategory is entitled "Intellectual Functioning" and is composed of five descriptors as they appear on the sample form. Additional explanation is necessary to define more precisely each of the descriptors within this broad category.

Level of consciousness (Sensorium). The term "level of consciousness" refers to an individual's ability to perceive sensory stimuli and varies from a state of coma to hypervigilance. This function depends upon the intactness of various sensory receptive organs (sight, hearing, touch, etc.), and an ability to use higher thinking processes. Look for disturbances in attention or concentration not due to discernible external events. The patient may manifest responses such as a mental confusion with respect to people and the environment. An example of this is the following case study:

> During a bedside consultation the patient mumbled a few incoherent words in response to persistent questioning. Sometimes the patient did not acknowledge the presence of the therapist and appeared to be staring at some distant fixed object. The patient's level of consciousness seemed impaired.

Accurate perception and integration of the sensory input from the external world are vital for adaptation and goal-directed behavior. Impairment of alertness and concentration is frequently associated with the presence of an organic brain syndrome.

Attention span. This intellectual function has to do with a person's ability to concentrate his thought on a particular topic for a period of time. It is a function that may be easily lost in the presence of even a mild degree of organic brain impairment or emotional stress.

Abstract thinking. Abstract thinking is the ability to develop concepts from supplied information and to make useful generalizations from subtle data when necessary. This capacity may be tested by asking for an interpretation of a common proverb, such as, "It's no use crying over spilled milk."

Calculation ability. This function is defined as the ability to perform arithmetical problems without the aid of visual or motor cues. It is a skill which evaluates a person's intelligence, concentration and abstract thinking ability. It may be tested by asking the patient to perform simple arithmetic problems. This ability is easily compromised by organic or functional causes.

Intelligence. Intelligence includes a variety of intellectual abilities which, in combined form, allow one to perceive and respond discriminately to the world. The higher the intelligence the greater the potential for discriminating action. (In our country, intelligence is measured in terms valued by the middle class. Examples of these capacities include the store of general information, the ability to use abstract thinking, vocabulary, visual-motor coordination, etc. This is a culturally-bound way to define intelligence.) During an interview intelligence can be estimated by assessing the individual's verbal ability, school attainment, income and job status. These factors should be considered in relation to the person's cultural background. One can be very intelligent yet not have achieved socially or economically.

It is important for the interviewer not to assume that he himself is of "average" intelligence. The level of intelligence for most professional people is considerably above "average." To use the examiner's intelligence as the norm would result in an inaccurate appraisal of the patient.

A minimum degree of intelligence is necessary in order for persons to successfully cope in our increasingly complex society. Corroborative mental status findings and a history of persistent functioning at low intellectual level would justify a diagnosis of mental retardation. If a patient is functioning intellectually at a level considerable below that which he has maintained before, the presence of an organic brain syndrome or psychotic state should be suspected.

B.   The second subcategory within the "Thinking" category is "Orientation," which refers to an individual's ability to identify himself in relationship to others, to time and to place. To estimate this capacity, it may be necessary to ask questions such as, "Who are you?" or "What is this place?". The pertinent information will generally be revealed spontaneously during the interview. The disoriented patient is likely to demonstrate some uncertainty about time, place and person as he relates his history. Misidentifying strangers for friends and family members may be indicative of disorientation. Ask specific questions about the patient's state of orientation in those cases where significant doubt exists.

Adaptive behavior depends on being able to devine one's self in terms of space and time and person. True disorientation is most commonly found in organic brain syndromes. The more extensive the disorientation the more severe the brain syndrome.

C.   The third subcategory of "Thinking" is "Memory," as indicated on your sample Mental Status Examination form. There are many aspects to memory; however, the focus is mostly on the patient's ability to recall events which occurred at various times in the past.
    Recent memory designates the ability to recall things which occurred in the immediate and fairly recent past, i.e. within minutes to a few weeks. Memory covering the past few months can be considered "recent." Does the patient recall with consistency his recent behavior, that is, how and why he came to the hospital, his daily activities, etc.?
    Remote memory refers to the capacity to recall events from the distant past. The events should be significant ones for the individual. Does the person recall with consistency past relationships, previous employment and illnesses? In order to evaluate the accuracy of remote memory it may be helpful to obtain information from other sources. If a memory deficit is suspected, it is important to determine when it began.
    You should make judgments concerning each of these descriptors when completing the mental status examination.
    The ability to recall the past is vital for present, goal-directed behavior and in planning for the future. Memory is an integral part of intelligence. Real or apparent memory loss can be due to one or more of the following:

    a.   the effects of anxiety, pain, psychosis or other stressful psychological events (either in the past or during the time of the interview)
    b.   the presence of repression (an automatic "forgetting" which is outside of the control or awareness of the patient)
    c.   intentional deception by the patient
    d.   organic impairment of brain functioning

D.   The fourth subcategory is "Insight." The term "insight" refers to an individual's capacity to understand and accept responsibility for his problems. Evaluate the patient's ability to observe and offer logical explanations for changes in his behavior and feeling states. Insight may be present in varying degrees. It is important to determine which of the following best exemplifies the patient's capacity for insight:

    a.   the individual does not acknowledge having
        any problems
    b.   the individual acknowledges having problems
        but blames them on fate or others.

Accurate understanding of behavioral determinants is
necessary for self-corrective action and adaptation.
Failure to recognize the nature of grossly inappropriate
behavior may signify the presence of psychosis or an
organic brain syndrome. The level and quality of insight
tell something about the person's ability to deal with
psychological concepts.

E.   The fifth subcategory of "Thinking" is "Judgment,"
which is the ability to make realistic decisions. Assessment of this attribute can be based on the patient's
proposed solutions to hypothetical problems and/or the way
in which he handles real life situations. In evaluating
judgment it is important to consider the circumstances
and context in which the patient lives. Was the behavior
goal-oriented? Adaptive? Unrealistic? Also, what reasoning does the individual give for having behaved as he did?
An example of impaired judgment follows:

    A middle-aged man recounts spending his disability
    check for a bus ticket. He traveled from Iowa and
    now finds himself in Los Angeles without funds,
    lodging, or other resources. When asked to explain
    his actions, he replied, "I always wanted to see
    California and it seemed like a good idea at the
    time."

Sound judgment is important for coping with the
complexities of daily living. If judgment is unrealistic
or otherwise impaired, the individual is likely to experience difficulty in achieving his goals. Judgment is
usually impaired during states of psychosis or an organic
brain syndrome. Persons with low intelligence characteristically manifest poor judgment in complex or new situations.

Now complete Self-Assessment Exercise #6 on the
following page.

Self-Assessment Exercise #6

Read the following case history. Then, using the data collected from the case, complete the first five categories ("Intellectual Functioning" through "Judgment") under the heading of "Thinking" on the Mental Status Examination form which follows.

HISTORY

A 37-year-old man, Bert Dixon, was admitted to a local hospital for observation after receiving a head injury in an automobile accident. A psychological consultation was requested after he attempted to leave the hospital against medical advice. At the time of the consultation, Mr. Dixon was tied to the bed with soft restraints.

Mr. Dixon was fully awake, responded to his name and readily gave information about himself. But he often rambled on in a disconnected way. On several occasions he requested a restatement of the questions, saying, "Now what was it you wanted to know, doctor?" He tended to repeat out loud the questions asked of him before responding. It was difficult for him to remember the name of the interviewer and concentrate on what was being asked of him. Mr. Dixon was unable to provide specific details about his background or early life.

Mr. Dixon related information which indicated that he had attended college and had held a responsible job for several years. He deduced that he was in a hospital but could not name it or the city in which it was located. His "guess" at the day and date was incorrect by several months. Mr. Dixon could not subtract accurately serial sevens from 100. With a good deal of irritation he refused to attempt further arithmetical problems. He demanded to be released from his restraints, saying, "I want to go home; there's nothing wrong with me!"

Complete the Mental Status Examination below:

			No Data	Present	Absent
THINKING	Intellectual Functioning	37. impaired level of consciousness............			
		38. impaired attention span, distractible......			
		39. impaired abstract thinking.................			
		40. impaired calculation ability..............			
		41. impaired intelligence......................			
	Orientation	42. disoriented to person......................			
		43. disoriented to place.......................			
		44. disoriented to time........................			
	Memory	45. impaired recent memory.....................			
		46. impaired remote memory.....................			
	Insight	47. denies presence of psychological problems..			
		48. blames others or circumstances for problems.................................			
	Judgment	49. impaired ability to make routine decisions.................................			
		50. impaired impulse control...................			

When you have completed this exercise to the best of your ability, check your answers with those on the following page.

Self-Assessment Exercise #6 - Feedback

Your answers should correspond to the ones noted below:

			No Data	Present	Absent
THINKING	Intellectual Functioning	37. impaired level of consciousness............			✓
		38. impaired attention span, distractible......		✓	
		39. impaired abstract thinking.................	✓		
		40. impaired calculation ability..............		✓	
		41. impaired intelligence......................			✓
	Orientation	42. disoriented to person.....................			✓
		43. disoriented to place......................		✓	
		44. disoriented to time.......................		✓	
	Memory	45. impaired recent memory....................		✓	
		46. impaired remote memory....................		✓	
	Insight	47. denies presence of psychological problems..		✓	
		48. blames others or circumstances for problems.................................			✓
	Judgment	49. impaired ability to make routine decisions................................		✓	
		50. impaired impulse control..................		✓	

38.	decreased ability to concentrate on questions asked
39.	no data given
40.	trouble with subtracting seven from 100
41.	attended college; held responsible job; likely not retarded
43.	could not accurately state his location
44.	incorrect time orientation
45. & 46.	couldn't remember questions asked, doctor's name, or provide information about his early life
47.	"nothing wrong with me"--no awareness of mental problems
49. & 50.	confused and wants to go home in spite of head injury and doctor's advice

If your answers correspond closely with those above, please continue your reading on the following page; if not, please reread the preceding section until you are confident you know the material.

Thinking (continued)

F.   The sixth subcategory of "Thinking" is "Thought
Content," which pertains to what the individual wants to
discuss, his interests and preoccupations. Various types
of pathological thought content are described below.
Singly or in combination, they carry special diagnostic
significance.

   a.   obsession: a fixed or repetitive idea which
        the individual cannot voluntarily exclude from
        his thinking;
   b.   compulsion: a repetitive unwanted performance of
        an act contrary to the person's ordinary wishes
        or standards;
   c.   phobia: intense and usually unrealistic fear of
        an object or situation;
   d.   depersonalization: feelings of unreality (de-
        realization), strangeness or change in either
        the environment or the self (depersonalization)
        or both;
   e.   suicidal or homicidal ideation: thoughts of
        killing oneself or others;
   f.   delusion: a fixed, false belief which cannot be in-
        fluenced by logical intervention and which is
        not culturally approved.

   Unusual or pathological preoccupations of thought
restrict the individual's adaptive capacities. The occurrence of one or more of the above preoccupations is indicative of psychopathology. The presence of a delusion
is a sign of psychosis.

G.   The final subcategory of "thinking" to be considered
is "Stream of Thought." This category evaluates the
nature of the thinking process. The stream of thought is
usually revealed indirectly as a person speaks. Normally,
ideas flow in a logical, sequential fashion. Disorders
in the stream of thought are exemplified by an associational disturbance. This particular condition represents
a disordered continuity and/or continuity of ideas and
emotions. The following serves to demonstrate a marked
associational disturbance:

When a patient was asked what brought her to the hospital she responded with the following statements: "A car. It was my mother's car. It's old and blue. I feel blue, too, and scared. I could use a candy bar now, or a smoke, if you have one. Are you a real doctor?"

A different type of associational disturbance is exemplified by thought-blocking, the sudden obstruction and interruption in the train of thought. The speed of the thought-flow should be noted and recorded, e.g., increased thought-flow (rapid speech) or decreased thought-flow (slowed speech).

Intact thought processes are needed for effective communication, problem solving, etc. Impairment of the stream of thought is usually associated with high levels of tension and anxiety. The condition occurs in functional or organically caused psychological disorders.

Now complete Self-Assessment Exercise #7 on the following page.

Self-Assessment Exercise #7

For this exercise a different evaluation procedure will be followed. Sample statements of patients (Column B) are to be matched with the descriptors listed in Column A. The listing of items in Column A corresponds with that found in the Mental Status Examination form.

COLUMN A   COLUMN B

_____51. obsessions   a. "I know it's ridiculous, but I won't ride on the elevator. What if it should fall or get stuck? I get scared just thinking about it."

_____52. compulsions

_____53. phobias   b. "I know that the nurse is really a member of the Mafia. They are out to kill me. I'm a marked man."

_____54. depersonali-
        zation
                             c. "Whenever I shake hands with someone, I've just got to wash my hands at least three times. I get very tense if I can't wash them."

_____55. suicidal ideation

_____56. homocidal
        ideation   d. "Why are we here? Is it the navy? On the otherhand the sun is shining. But the son of the king is lost in the forest. We are all lost in mathematics."

_____57. delusions

_____58. associational   e. "Life's not worth living any-more."
        disturbance

                             f. "Everything seems changed. My hands look and feel strange to me. It's almost as if they didn't belong to me."

                             g. "The thoughts keep coming back over and over again. I just can't get them out of my mind."

                             h. "I'm going to fix him so he'll never bother me or anybody again, and I've got a gun to do it with."

When you have completed this exercise to the best of your ability, check your answers with those on the following page.

Self-Assessment Exercise #7 - Feedback

51. obsessions   _g_

52. compulsions   _c_

53. phobias   a

54. depersonalization   _f_

55. suicidal ideation   e

56. homicidal
     ideation   h

57. delusions   b

58. associational
     disturbance   d

If your answers correspond closely with those above, please continue your reading on the following page; if not, please reread the preceding section until your are confident you know the material.

SUMMARY

No single finding of the Mental Status Examination
should be used as the sole criterion for any diagnostic
conclusion. Delusions and hallucinations may be found in
psychotic states of either organic or functional etiology.
Findings of the Mental Status Examination should be considered in a probablistic sense. In forming a diagnostic
impression, one must carefully weigh all the observations
that have been made. A diagnosis should be selected which
is based upon the presence of many confirming and few non-
confirming, or contradictory, observations. For example,
to diagnose mental deficiency one should find indications
of a limited vocabulary, low intellectual ability, and
limited insight in routine living situations. The flow of
thought should be intact and no major affectual disturbance
should be evident.

Before reaching a definitive diagnostic conclusion, it
may be well to obtain additional information from relatives
and documents such as the medical history and police reports.
It is important to realize that many "abnormal" findings may
occur transiently in normal individuals who are experiencing
acute, situational problems; for example, temporary failure
of immediate and recent memory and the loose association of
thoughts that are frequently demonstrated by students on
their examination papers.

These considerations should be kept in mind when speci-
fying the diagnosis. Thus far, the current instructional
unit has focused mainly on the method and instrument for
collecting observational data. In subsequent chapters, the
observations of patient behavior will be organized in terms
of diagnostic categories.

REFERENCES

Enelow, A. J., and Swisher, S.: Interviewing and Patient
Care. New York: Oxford University Press, 1979.

Froelich, R. E., and Bishop, F. M.: Clinical Interviewing
Skills: A Programmed Manual for Data Gathering, Evaluation,
and Patient Management. St. Louis: C. V. Mosby Co., 1977.

MacKinnon, R.,"Psychiatric History and Mental Status Examination" in Comprehensive Textbook of Psychiatry III,
Baltimore, Williams and Wilkins, 1980.

MacKinnon, R., and Michels, R.: The Psychiatric Interview
in Clinical Practice. Philadelphia: W. B. Saunders Co.,
1971.

Strub, Richard L., and F. William Black: The Mental Status
Examination in Neurology, Philadelphia: F. A. Davis, 1977.

Chapter 4
Psychopathology in Childhood
Brian P. Jacks

This chapter presents information regarding the psychopathology of childhood. It will enable you to assess a child's behavior and determine if it is normal or pathological. It may be useful to review the table in Chapter 1, Human Growth and Development, before proceeding further.

LEARNING OBJECTIVES

By the time you complete the material in this chapter you should be able to:

1. List the developmental tasks and associated behavioral manifestations of the school-aged child in our culture.

2. List three age-related differences between children and adults that need consideration when assessing a child psychologically.

3. Compare and contrast significant differences between children and adults relative to:

   a. typical mental status findings
   b. the incidence of common psychiatric syndromes

4. List the four areas of history and two of examination in which to obtain data when evaluating a child's emotional problems.

5. Pertinent to the criteria used when evaluating psychopathology in children:

     a. briefly describe three special considerations to keep in mind when applying developmental criteria
     b. list three aspects of stress needing assessment
     c. list three sources of stress

6. Outline characteristics of a child's response to stress that suggest:

     a. normalcy
     b. abnormality

7. Given case vignettes of two children, assess the presence of abnormal findings, summarizing the data in appropriate outline form.

By the conclusion of this chapter and supervised clinical experience you should be able to:

1. Accurately observe and record a child's behavior within each of the M.S.E. behavior descriptors.

2. Determine whether psychopathology is present in a child given necessary M.S.E. information.

3. Indicate the history and M.S.E. findings which enabled you to make a diagnosis.

OVERVIEW

Children's emotional difficulties are more common than is often assumed. Also, much adult psychopathology, when traced back, can be found to originate in childhood. To assess psychopathology in those under twelve years of age, three significant differences between adults and children should be considered. First, the child typically is more sensitive to change of all types than is the adult. Alterations in a child's body, feeling and thinking take place continuously. Orderly maturation provides the foundation for all later growth; problems and interruptions in any area of physical or emotional development may produce far-reaching effects. For example, minimal anoxia at birth may cause later behavioral difficulties such as hyperactivity. What may seem to an adult a small shift in the external environment, i.e., people and surroundings, may result in significant emotional alterations in children. For infants, a prolonged absence of the mother figure may result in marked depression. Generally speaking, the younger a child is the more sensitive he will be to external changes. It is not unusual for normal children to react markedly to environmental changes which would little affect adults.

Secondly, whereas adults think logically, adult logic is not typical of young children and their thinking is influenced more by feelings and wishes. In a sense, young children believe in "magic" where, if you wish, elephants can fly and monsters stalk darkened bedrooms. Forgetting this, parents who have carefully explained to their child about his upcoming tonsillectomy may be surprised to find that at the time of surgery he expresses worries that a goblin might kill him while he is asleep in the hospital. It is "normal" for a child to accept an adult's rational explanations but simultaneously to experience the world in terms of his inner feelings. Although feelings influence thought and perception in children much more than in adults, by age five healthy children should begin to separate their inner impulses from the outer world and their own make-believe from reality.

Thirdly, <u>the life context of the child must be</u> <u>assessed.</u> No young child can be evaluated adequately without also considering his family. The child is more completely dependent upon his parents and family in all respects than is the adult. No other species is born so ultimately helpless and needful of others for survival than is the human infant. This dependency only gradually diminishes with the passage of time.

Consequently, with a child, more than with an adult, information from many sources must be gathered in order to evaluate adequately any problem. Table I represents an outline for organizing the pertinent data to be obtained when evaluating a child psychologically. The evaluator should have access to as much of this information as possible before attempting to make a diagnosis.

The format presented in Table I on the following pages will be used in later Self-Assessment Exercises.

TABLE I

EVALUATION OUTLINE FOR CHILDREN

A.   HISTORY: (from parents and other significant adults)

   I.   Presenting Problems:

      (Details of the child's behaviors which
      concern the parents or referring persons.)

   II.   Past Developmental History:

      a.   birth history
      b.   early feeding and sleep patterns
      c.   age at which walking and talking began
         and toilet training achieved

   III.   Social History:

      a.   school progress
      b.   nature and number of peer relationships
      c.   special interests (hobbies, activities)

   IV.   Family History:

      a.   family members (ages and relationship)
      b.   characteristics of the relationships

B.   EXAMINATION: (of the child)

   I.   Physical:

      a.   height, weight and size relative to age
      b.   presence of atypical physical findings
      c.   neurological findings (coordination, etc.)

   II.   Psychological: (mental status examination)

      (Note especially manifestations of Behavior)

C.   SUMMARY OF ABNORMAL FINDINGS:

      (List significant findings which you judge to
      be abnormal based on criteria to be presented
      later in this chapter.)

D.   DIAGNOSIS:

      (Should be evident after reviewing the
      summary.)

A reliable and complete history rarely can be obtained directly from the child and should be taken from parents and other significant persons (such as teachers). This is because most young children are not aware of "having problems" and do not regard their behavior as troublesome. They become concerned only when those they love are upset with them. When questioned, a child may say that he is "bad" but is unable to explain further. He only knows that his parents are angry or disappointed with him. At the same time that the history is obtained from the parents, it is useful to observe the family's unique ways of talking and interacting with one another.

In summary, then, it is important to remember that children are hypersensitive to external changes, that their perceptions and thinking are influenced greatly by inner feelings rather than logic and that a family evaluation and external sources of history must be included in your assessment of the child.

MENTAL STATUS EXAMINATION FINDINGS

Although the history is usually taken from others, the psychological (mental status) and physical examinations obviously involve the child directly. Since children more naturally express their feelings through activity rather than words, special techniques are needed to elicit data for the mental status examination. The descriptor headings of the M.S.E. are the same for children as adults, but greater emphasis is placed on observing the child's behavior. For example, careful observation of the child's actions during self-directed play with puppets, drawings and family dolls may be more revealing than what the child expresses verbally. An evaluation of what the child does under these circumstances often may reflect what the child feels and thinks. For instance, one child living with his divorced mother and three sisters played only with the male family dolls, and thereby indirectly expressed his yearning for his absent father. Another young child showed his anxiety about his mother's death by becoming very active and running around the room every time she was mentioned.

Data about the other descriptor categories also can be derived from observations of the child's play activities. (Since they often require special training to interpret they will not be further dealt with here.) Diagnosing children is based not so much on etiological factors as on evaluating the duration and characteristics of clusters of behaviors. Hallucinations in adults mean psychosis, but in children from age four to six imaginary companions (like a six-foot "Harvey the Rabbit") are not at all unusual. However, if the hallucinations in children persist or occur at a later stage of development, for example at age ten, they then may indicate psychopathology. In children, disconnected thinking, impaired orientation, illogical beliefs, etc. do not necessarily imply psychopathology as such findings would indicate in adults. Most diagnoses

are assigned according to the predominating type of
behaviors shown, e.g., overactivity, withdrawing tendency,
temper tantrums, etc. The behaviors are then classified
under a single descriptive heading such as Attention
Deficit Disorder-Hyperactivity, Unsocialized Conduct Disorder, Pervasive Developmental Disorders, Autism and
others.

THE INCIDENCE OF PSYCHIATRIC SYNDROMES

Although several types of emotional disorders have
similar symptoms and findings in adults and children, some
behavioral scientists believe that the psychopathological
states are not comparable with respect to etiology, course,
etc. In any case, there appear to be definite differences
in the frequency of occurrence of emotional disorders.
Both anxiety disorders (neuroses) and psychosis, fairly
common emotional afflictions of adults, occur less often
in children. Much more common in childhood are problems
in behavior. These behavioral manifestations may represent either transient disturbances or the first signs of
later adolescent and adult psychopathology, i.e., personality disorders, psychoses, etc.

Now complete Self-Assessment Exercise #1 on the
following page.

Self-Assessment Exercises #1

1. A seven-year-old girl was brought for consultation by
    her parents because when the lights were turned off
    at night she often experienced "visions," became
    tearful, and feared that prowlers were going to break
    into her bedroom to kidnap her. These symptoms began
    after the girl observed a loud argument between her
    parents, during which the mother threatened to leave
    the father.

    a. List three age-related differences between children
        and adults important to consider when evaluating
        psychopathology in children and give examples for
        each from the case presented.

        Difference #1:

        Example from case:

        Difference #2:

        Example from case:

        Difference #3:

        Example from case:

    b. Would you consider the "visions" indicative of
        serious psychopathology in the girl? Yes___ No___

        Why?

        If the "visions" occurred in an adult would it be
        a sign of serious psychopathology? Yes___ No___

Self-Assessment Exercise #1 (continued)

2. Describe the important difference between adults and
    children regarding:

    a. Mental status findings useful in diagnosis:

    b. Indidence of psychosis, anxiety (neurosis) and
        behavior disorders:

         When you have completed this exercise to the best of
    your ability, check your answers with those on the follow-
    ing pages.

Self-Assessment Exercise #1 - Feedback

1.   a.   Difference #1:
            Children are hypersensitive to environmental
          changes.

          Example from case:
            The parental altercation and threatened dis-
          ruption of her family life likely precipitated
          the girl's "visions" and fears.

          Difference #2:
            In children thinking and perception are
          greatly influenced by inner feeling rather than
          adult logic.

          Example from case:
            The girl's judgment and rational thinking
          have been overwhelmed by her intense fears of the
          mother leaving, and hence the "visions" and
          worries about kidnappers.

          Difference #3:
            To assess psychopathology in children, their
          family must also be evaluated.

          Example from case:
            Without learning of the parents' argument,
          the girl's complaints might have proved confusing
          and been misunderstood. The symptoms might have
          appeared unduly complicated and more ominous than
          the simple overreaction to a threatening environ-
          mental situation.

     b.   No, the girl's "visions" are not psychopathological.

          Why?
            The "visions" probably represent a child's
          overreaction to the external situation created by
          the parents' arguments.
            Similar perceptual experiences in an adult
          are manifestations of psychopathology and strongly
          suggest the presence of a psychosis.

Self-Assessment Exercise #1 - Feedback (continued)

2. a. Mental status findings useful in diagnosis:
        Although the descriptor categories of the
        M.S.E. needing evaluation are the same for chil-
        dren and adults (i.e., Appearance, Behavior,
        Feeling, Perception and Thinking), in children
        special emphasis is placed on observations of
        "Behavior." Careful observation and description
        of what the child does in play gives more diag-
        nostically useful information than evaluating
        orientation, affect appropriateness, associational
        patterns, etc.

    b. Incidence of psychosis, anxiety (neurosis) and
        behavior disorders:
        There is a distinct difference in diagnostic
        types and the incidence of different emotional
        disorders when comparing children with adults.
        Anxiety Disorders (neurosis) and psychosis, more
        common in adults, are infrequent in children;
        whereas behavior disorders are more frequent in
        children.

        If your answers correspond closely with those above,
continue reading; if not, please reread the preceding
section until you are confident you know the material.

CRITERIA FOR DETERMINING PSYCHOPATHOLOGY IN CHILDREN

Developmental Criteria
Determinations of the timing and quality of the child's interpersonal relationships and physical and emotional development are useful criteria for judging whether psychopathology is present. Deviations from these developmental milestones may be significant. However, age-appropriateness of development represents only an approximate guideline for determining the presence of psychopathology, since such chronological standards apply to only 90% of children. Five percent of children may be slower in achieving these milestones and five percent faster and still be "normal."

Just as describing only its trunk gives a false impression of what an elephant is like, so considering only one part of development by itself may also lead to erroneous conclusions. Thus, the balance in maturation and the interrelationships of various aspects of development should be examined. Development proceeds simultaneously along several planes (physical maturation, emotional traits and interpersonal relationships). These planes may be slightly out of phase with one another without signifying abnormality. For instance, a five-year-old boy, small for his age, may prefer playing with older boys eight and nine and still be "normal."

The extent of the developmental delay, if present, should also be appraised. It is less serious if development lags in one area than many. In the case of the five-year-old described above, other areas of development (such as emotional traits, coordination, etc.) need to be scrutinized before a judgment can be made about psychopathology. The most serious types of pathology are characterized not so much by a slowed rate of progress as a total cessation in development involving several areas.

Thus, the age-appropriateness of development (which provides only a rough guideline), the interrelationships of various aspects of development (physical and emotional traits and interpersonal relationships), and the extent of developmental lag, if present, are useful criteria for evaluating a child's psychological state.

Stress-Related Criteria
The relationship of "stress" (any factor which induces mental or bodily tension) to psychopathology is significant and deserves further consideration. Stress may arise from unpleasant external situations, e.g., the loss of a job, or from an individual's own maladaptive responses, e.g., excessive worry or unwanted thoughts. When an infant cries for his bottle, when a child worries about his poor report card or that his parents will divorce, in fact, whenever there are anxieties, worries or fears, then the presence of stress can be inferred. Although some people are exposed to more stresses than other, there is

no complete escape; sources of potential stress are
ubiquitous. Furthermore, no child can develop without
having to cope with stress in one form or another. Some
stress is probably necessary for normal development to
proceed. If a mother does not force her child to take his
first steps at the proper age (a stressful situation
indeed), then a child might never learn to walk. Not only
is stress inevitable and necessary, but its effects are
revealing. Success is usually easy to accept, but it is
when we are confronted with adversity or failure that we
show our strengths and weaknesses. Performance of any
task often involves both skill and the capacity to deal
with stress. For example, under the stress of the same
examination, different students show varying responses;
it is not only their knowledge that determines the final
grade but also how they perform when under stress.

In diagnosing psychopathology, the aspects of stress
which are most pertinent to evaluate are its source, duration and the child's response to it. When assessing
a child, information should be obtained about each of the
following potential sources of stress:

1. biological--any physical illness or defect, e.g.,
    an asthmatic attack, physical deformity
2. environmental--the presence of a situational
    stress (such as the first day of school) or
    familial stress, e.g., parental divorce
3. psychological--the presence of unpleasant inner
    feelings and thoughts, e.g., depression, fears
    of the dark, etc.

The duration of a stress frequently influences the
prognosis of a symptom. Transient stresses which are
easily discernable and environmental in origin are least
likely to cause permanent psychopathology. Examples of
environmental events that may cause transient symptoms in
a child are the effect of the birth of a new sibling or
moving into a new neighborhood. Most children adjust to
these new situations in a few weeks and their discomfort
and symptoms subside. However, even a mild stress, if it
lasts long enough and coping behaviors are inadequate, may
result in a permanent personality change or disorder. In
the instance above, if the child is not able to adjust to
the new sibling, he may develop a chronic feeling of inferiority or resentment that persists indefinitely as
a personality trait.

The child's individual response to stress also is
significant. All children will react adversely to stress
if it is of sufficient intensity. Depending on such
factors as age, the nature of the stress, support from
others, etc., the child may become withdrawn, experience
nightmares, tearfulness, tantrums, etc. However, "normal"
children, even when responding to stressful circumstances
still should be able to:

1. distinguish their inner feelings from external reality
2. be aware of their own feelings and to whom they are directed
3. delay gratification without great anxiety or anger
4. avoid feeling unwarranted self-blame, guilt or lowered self-confidence
5. try new ways of solving difficulties if their usual methods fail

Children differ in their "sensitivity" to stress. Some can tolerate major crises while others deteriorate under minor stress. Also, because of previous life experiences, some children will perceive a situation as stressful whereas others will not. It is "normal" to be fearful under dangerous or threatening circumstances and then make attempts to reduce that fear by whatever means are available. It is "abnormal" to continue to be anxious under circumstances which are not really dangerous but are perceived to be so because of past experiences. Also it is maladaptive to adhere rigidly to a single way of reacting without actively seeking out new solutions. Suppose for example a dog bit a young child. Later, while this same child is visiting a home, a puppy wags its tail and approaches. A "normal" response would be for the child to be fearful, but to cautiously approach the dog. As he learns that the dog is friendly, he would then play more and more with it. An "abnormal" response would be for the child to become very frightened of the dog, hide in the corner and stay there even when the dog is put outside.

In summary, when assessing psychopathology in children, it is necessary to consider:

the source of stress (environmental sources generally are least detrimental),
the duration of stress (transient stresses are least likely to cause pathology), and
the child's response to stress ("normal" children tend to be aware of their feelings, exhibit some control over them and approach a problem flexibly with different attempts at solution)

Evaluating pathology in children is no easy matter. Both developmental criteria and various characteristics of stress must be examined and the balance weighed on your own subjective scale. In the end, it depends greatly upon experience and clinical judgment.

Now complete Self-Assessment Exercise #2 on the following page.

Self-Assessment Exercise #2

1. A child is not talking by age three.

    a. Comment on whether this finding is indicative of abnormality.

    b. What additional criteria about development and stress should be used in the assessment of the child?

2. A child is first discovered to be a diabetic at age ten years. List the three <u>sources</u> of stress impinging on the child and give for <u>each</u> an example of a potential problem that this child might experience.

    <u>Source</u>:

    <u>Example</u>:

    <u>Source</u>:

    <u>Example</u>:

    <u>Source</u>:

    <u>Example</u>:

Self-Assessment Exercise #2 (continued)

3. A five-year-old boy is hospitalized to receive
    treatment for a burn. Although he was bladder trained
    at two, he begins to wet the bed again. The enuresis
    (bedwetting) stops after two weeks when the child
    grows attached to one of his nurses. Discuss whether
    this reaction to hospitalization is "normal."

    What kinds of behavior from such a child would
    suggest a more psychopathological response?

When you have completed this exercise to the best of your ability, check your answers with those on the following page.

Self-Assessment Exercise #2 - Feedback

1. a. According to usual standards, most children should
        be able to communicate verbally by age three.
        However, age-appropriateness of behavior should
        not be used as the sole criteria for judging
        normality in children. More information is needed.

    b. Additional information about development is needed
        including the interrelationships of various de-
        velopmental planes and the presence and degree of
        any maturational lags. An inquiry about possible
        sources (and duration) of stress should be made.

2. Three common sources of stress are:

    biological--decreased resistance to infections,
    fatigability (can he participate in athletic events,
    etc.?)

    environmental--the need for daily insulin injections,
    a special diet, his family's response to him, etc.

    psychological--a change in his self-concept now that
    he is "sick" and "different" from his peers; fears
    about his health, etc.

3. All children respond in some fashion to stressful
    situations (in this case the burn and separation from
    family because of hospitalization) and his transient
    bedwetting response is not necessarily "abnormal."

    If the child also showed delays and/or total cessation
    of development in other areas, the response then would
    be pathological. Other abnormal responses would in-
    clude the persistence of the bedwetting, the absence
    of other attempts by the child to cope with the stress
    of hospitalization, a past history of bedwetting as
    a usual response to many different stresses and an
    oversensitivity to slight stresses. Also, a lack of
    self-awareness of his fears and associating his burn
    with excessive guilt would be abnormal.

    If your answers correspond closely with those above,
continue with Exercise #3 on the following pages; if not,
please reread the preceding section until you are confident you know the material.

Self-Assessment Exercise #3

1.   Read carefully the history of "Jerry," age six,
below. As you read, record the information requested on
the Evaluation Outline for Children on the following page.

Case history #1:   Jerry, age 6

> Jerry is the first child of a mother age 30 years
> and a father age 31 years. The product of a full-
> term uncomplicated pregnancy, labor and delivery,
> Jerry weighed seven pounds at birth and went home
> two days later. He was bladder trained at one and
> a half years, began to walk at fourteen months,
> spoke his first words at fifteen to sixteen months
> and full sentences at twenty-four months.
>
> He is in grade one at school and achieves A's and B's
> on his report card. He has friends at school and is
> well liked by teachers and children.
>
> When his mother got pregnant for the second time,
> Jerry was very curious about the increasing size of
> his mother's "tummy." He asked questions about her
> condition and was very excited at the prospect of
> a new brother at home.
>
> When his new sister was brought home, Jerry could
> hardly wait to see her. A few days later, Jerry woke
> with a nightmare and went to his parents' bedroom.
> There he found his mother breastfeeding his new sister.
> Following this episode, Jerry's behavior changed. He
> began to wet his bed, refused food unless his mother
> fed him and complained that his mother didn't like
> him anymore. These symptoms continued for two months
> before he was brought to the doctor's office.
>
> On physical examination, **Jerry** appeared well-developed
> and nourished for his age, without detectable physical
> problems. Organic causes to account for his bed-
> wetting were ruled out. Psychological examination
> revealed a boy who was at first apprehensive about
> leaving his mother. However, after she left the room,
> Jerry picked up the family dolls, threw away the
> little girl doll and told the examiner in great detail
> of a family with two parents and one child. When
> asked about the little girl doll, Jerry insisted on
> leaving the room to go to the bathroom.

Self-Assessment Exercise #3 (continued)

EVALUATION OUTLINE FOR CHILDREN

A. HISTORY: (from parents)

   I. Presenting Problems:

   II. Past Developmental History:

   III. Social History: (school and peer relationships)

   IV. Family History: (family members and charac-
                        teristics)

B. EXAMINATION: (of the child)

    I. <u>Physical</u>:

    II. <u>Psychological</u>: (mental status examination)
        <u>(especially Behavior)</u>

C. SUMMARY OF ABNORMAL FINDINGS:

Self-Assessment Exercise #3 (continued)

2. a. Jerry's development to date has been normal/
        abnormal (circle one).

        Explain your answer.

    b. Jerry's response to stress has been normal/
        abnormal (circle one).

        Explain your answer.

3. The likely causes of Jerry's difficulties are:

When you have completed this exercise to the best
of your ability, check your answers with those on the
following pages.

Self-Assessment Exercise #3 - Feedback

EVALUATION OUTLINE FOR CHILDREN

A. HISTORY: (from parents)

  I. Presenting Problems:

      nocturnal enuresis, defiant behavior (food
      refusal and complaints about mother)

  II. Past Developmental History:

      milestones as presented are within normal
      chronological limits

  III. Social History:

      does well in school, good peer relations

  IV. Family History:

      father (31), mother (30), baby sister and
      Jerry; mother attentive to baby girl

B. EXAMINATION: (of the child)

  I. Physical:

      unremarkable; no physical problems to explain
      bedwetting

  II. Psychological: (mental status examination)

      difficulty separating from mother; anxiety
      expressed in play about sister (girl doll)
      in form of urge to go to bathroom

C. SUMMARY OF ABNORMAL FINDINGS:

      two months of bedwetting, defiant and complaining
      behavior with difficulty separating from mother
      and attempts to avoid talking about his new
      sister

Self-Assessment Exercise #3 - Feedback (continued)

2. a. Jerry is developing <u>normally</u>. His bedwetting,
        of course, was not age-appropriate but it was <u>not</u>
        affecting other areas of his development, which
        were progressing well, e.g., peer relations,
        school progress, etc.

    b. Jerry's response to stress has been an <u>abnormal</u>
        one. Jerry's behavioral problems persisted for
        two months before being brought for help. Also,
        Jerry seemed very reluctant to talk about his
        sister and adhered rigidly to maladaptive ways of
        coping with his feelings (the urge to leave the
        room and go to the bathroom). In short, then,
        Jerry's behavior is judged "abnormal" based on
        his lack of flexibility to adapt. However, the
        degree of pathology is "mild" based upon the
        minor effect of it upon his overall development,
        the easily understood origin (the birth of his
        sister) of a situational stress and the short
        duration (two months) of his response.

3. Ambivalent feelings about his new sister are the most
    likely cause of Jerry's difficulties. He is probably
    upset about losing his mother's attention to his
    sister. Jerry was the only child for six years prior
    to the birth of his sister. His behavior may reflect
    his need to regain the attention of his mother (to be
    fed by her, "babied" by her, etc.), while at the same
    time expressing his resentment towards his mother for
    "leaving" him.

    Note: An acute reaction to environmental stress (such
    as the birth of a new baby) without apparent underlying,
    more severe mental disorder is known as an "Adjustment
    Disorder."

        If your answers correspond closely with those above,
continue with Exercise #4 on the following page. If not;
please reread the preceding section until you are
confident you know the material.

Self-Assessment Exercise #4

1.   Read carefully the history of "Thomas." As you read,
     record the information requested on the Evaluation
     Outline for Children on the following pages.

Case history #2:   Thomas, age 10

     Although of above average intelligence, Thomas is
     a poor student, and it is at the teacher's insistence
     that Thomas is referred for evaluation. The teacher
     describes Thomas as being constantly active in the
     classroom where he "squirms like a worm," does not
     attend to a single task for very long, won't com-
     plete his assignments and seems easily distractible.
     At the present time, he is two years behind his peers
     in reading and often writes "d" for "b." His mother
     reveals that at home Thomas becomes tearful when
     told to do most chores. He does not play well with
     children his age and repeatedly fights with them.

     Thomas was one month premature and weighed only four
     pounds at birth. He had convergent strabismus
     (crossed eyes) which later required operative correc-
     tion and prescription glasses. Although his develop-
     mental milestones were within normal limits, Thomas
     was "always into things, a bundle of energy"
     according to his mother. Thomas had colic as an
     infant and constantly had difficulty falling asleep
     or sleeping for only a few hours.

     Thomas has an older brother twelve and an older
     sister thirteen. His parents, mother age 39 and
     father age 42 have a basically sound marriage but
     can come to no agreement about Thomas' discipline.
     In any case, nothing either parent does seems to
     change Thomas' overly active behavior.

     Physical examination reveals a boy who, when compared
     to age-mates, is small for his age and grossly un-
     coordinated in his gait, in his posture and with such
     activities as throwing and catching a ball and drawing.
     All other physical findings are "unremarkable."

     On mental status examination, Thomas is found to feel
     badly about himself and inclined to "give up" before
     completing simple tasks if frustrated. His behavior
     is erratic and very active. No other unusual
     findings are noted relative to affect, perception
     or thinking.

Self-Assessment Exercise #4 (continued)

A. HISTORY: (From parents)

    I. Presenting Problems:

    II. Past Developmental History:

    III. Social History: (school and peer relationships)

    IV. Family History: (family members and characteristics)

Self-Assessment Exercise #4 (continued)

B. EXAMINATION: (of the child)

    I. Physical:

    II. Psychological: (mental status examination)

C. SUMMARY OF ABNORMAL FINDINGS

Self-Assessment Exercise #4 (continued)

2. a. Thomas' development has been normal/abnormal
        (circle one).

        Explain your answer.

    b. Thomas' behavior is clearly related to a discern-
        able stress. True____   False____

3. The likely cause of Thomas' difficulties are:

    When you have completed this exercise to the best of
your ability, check your answers with those on the
following page.

Self-Assessment Exercise #4 - Feedback

EVALUATION OUTLINE FOR CHILDREN

A. HISTORY: (from parents)

   I. Presenting Problems:

      overactivity, short attention span, distractibility

  II. Past Developmental History:

      prematurity, convergent strabismus; high activity level; sleep and gastrointestinal disturbance during infancy

 III. Social History;

      underachievement in school despite average intelligence; letter reversals ("d" for "b") and reading lag; constant fights with peers

  IV. Family History:

      father (42), mother (39), brother (12), sister (13), overt parental disagreement over Thomas' discipline

B. EXAMINATION: (of the child)

   I. Physical:

      small for age, uncoordinated

  II. Psychological: (mental status examination)

      overactive, low self-esteem, easily frustrated; all else "unremarkable"

C. SUMMARY OF ABNORMAL FINDINGS:

    overactivity (lifelong), short attention span, distractibility, frequent fighting with peers, poor school performance with specific learning disabilities (letter reversals)

Self-Assessment Exercise #4 - Feedback (continued)

2. a. Thomas' development has been <u>abnormal</u> in terms of
        congenital difficulties (prematurity, strabismus,
        etc.), high activity levels and recurrent sleep
        and gastrointestinal disturbances.

    b. False. His behavior cannot be attributed to any
        readily discerned stress.

3. No single cause is readily apparent to account for
    the symptoms. There are <u>biological</u> elements (pre-
    maturity, strabismus and uncoordination) which some
    investigators believe may be due to neurological
    dysfunction. There are <u>environmental</u> stresses in the
    family (disagreement over discipline) and at school
    (social) but these, as well as the low self-esteem,
    may be end results rather than the cause of the
    problem. <u>Psychologically</u>, Thomas lacks self-confidence
    and is easily frustrated, but these characteristics
    may also be a product of his past poor performances
    rather than the cause of them.

    Note: A maladjustment of childhood that is longer
lasting and more resistant to treatment than an "Adjustment Disorder" but less so than an Anxiety Disorder, is
called a "Conduct Disorder." A behavior disorder characterized by overactivity, restlessness, distractibility
and short attention span without known cause is called
"Attention Deficit Disorder with Hyperactivity."

    If your answers correspond closely with those above,
continue your reading; if not, please reread the preceding section until you are confident you know the
material.

SUMMARY

Children are different in important ways from adults. These differences along with an assessment of development and response to stress need consideration when psychologically evaluating children under twelve years of age. An organized and systematic approach which includes specific information in four areas of history and two from direct examination is necessary for analyzing psychological problems in children.

REFERENCES

Diagnostic and Statistical Manual of Mental Disorders, Second Edition, American Psychiatric Association, 1968.

Freedman, A., Kaplan, H., Sadock, B., Modern Synopsis of Comprehensive Textbook of Psychiatry, Williams and Wilkins: Baltimore, 1972, Chapters 32, 33, 34, 35 and 36.

Freud, A.: Normality and Pathology in Childhood: Assessments of Development. New York: International Universities Press, 1966.

Harrison, S., and McDermott, J.: Childhood Psychopathology. New York: International Universities Press, 1972.

Johnson, D. J., and Myklebut, H. R.: Learning Disabilities. New York: Grune & Stratton, 1967.

Looff, D. H.: Getting to Know the Troubled Child, Knoxville: University of Tennessee Press, 1976.

Rexford, E. N. et al.: Infant Psychiatry: New Synthesis, New Haven and London: Yale University Press, 1976.

Rutter, M. and Hersov, L. (eds.): Child Psychiatry, Modern Approaches. Philadelphia: J. B. Lippincott, 1976.

Steinhauer, P. D. and Rae-Grant, Q. (eds.): Psychological Problems of the Child and His Family. Toronto: Macmillan, 1977.

Strauss, S.: Is It Well with the Child? Garden City, N. Y.: Doubleday, 1975.

Wender, P. H.: Minimal Brain Dysfunction in Children, Wiley Interscience: New York, 1971.

Wender, P. H.: The Hyperactive Child, New York: Crown Publishers, 1973

Wing, L.: Autistic Children, New York: Brunner/Mazel, 1972.

Chapter 5

Psychopathology in Adolescence
Brian P. Jacks
Sidney Russak

Adolescents represent a significant portion of the population. It is important to recognize that they possess unique characteristics that distinguish them from both adults and children. An awareness of these special features of adolescence will help in separating normal from psychopathological behavior.

This chapter presents information about psychopathology in adolescence. It will enable you to discriminate normal adolescent behavior from that which is indicative of psychopathology. It may be useful to review the section of the chapter on Human Growth and Development, before proceeding further.

LEARNING OBJECTIVES

By the time you complete the material in this chapter you should be able to:

1. List three developmental tasks emphasized in this chapter and other associated behavioral manifestations for the adolescent in our culture.

2. List the four areas of history and two of examination in which to obtain data when evaluating an adolescent's emotional problems.

3. Compare and contrast an outline for evaluating psychopathology in children with one for adolescents.

4. List three developmental, three stess-related and three social criteria for assessing psychopathology in adolescents.

5. Given case vignettes of two adolescents, assess the presence of abnormal findings, summarize the data in appropriate outline form.

By the conclusion of this chapter and supervised clinical experience you should be able to:

1. Accurately observe and record the adolescent's behavior within each of the M.S.E. behavior descriptors.

2. Determine whether psychopathology is present in the adolescent given necessary M.S.E. information.

3. Indicate the history and M.S.E. findings which enabled you to make a diagnosis.

DEVELOPMENTAL TASKS OF ADOLESCENCE
        One of the major tasks of adolescence is to integrate
and cope with the significant biological changes (such as
increased height, weight and sexual maturation) that are
typical of their age. These physical alterations require
a revision of behavior and of the teenager's perceptions
and feelings about himself and about how others see him.
Such readjustment can produce emotional uncertainty and
distress as attempts are made to harmonize a former self-
image with a newer one. It is normal for juveniles to
experience some discomfort while adapting emotionally to
their biological changes. However, it is abnormal for
them to show marked deviations in behavior because of
their distress. For example, it is not unusual for
a twelve-year-old girl, who is maturing physically, to
feel embarrassed when buying her first brassiere. However,
it would be abnormal if she felt so self-conscious about
her body that she refused to undress for her gym class.
It is important to evaluate adolescents' emotional response to their bodily changes.
        Secondly, an adolescent should show signs of becoming
more independent relative to family relationships. Whereas
young children are very dependent upon their families,
adolescents should gradually become more autonomous. If
the adolescent is to function later as an independent
adult, he must try to extricate himself from the social,
economic and psychological bonds of his family. This is not
to say that a teenager needs to completely reject every-
thing about his family, for to do so would be self-defeating.
However, "normal" teenagers should be able to disagree with
their parents, to criticize and question them, to begin
to earn their own money, and increasingly to seek relationships apart from the family.
        Finally, an adolescent must further develop a personal
identity, i.e., a sense of continuing "selfness." During
the teen years it is necessary for each individual to
gradually establish a set of philosophical, moral and
ethical values for himself.
        Parental standards and mores will not suffice as the
sole guideline for thought and behavior as they did formerly.
A teenager must decide for himself whether to join the
"athletes" or the "intellectuals." He should begin to
answer questions for himself about standards of drinking,
dating, scholastic achievement and vocation. In defining
himself as being separate from his family, the adolescent
outlines his chosen characteristics and affinities for one
group of people as opposed to another. During this time
the teenager "experiments" in his relationships with new
friends, joining them in selecting those activities and
relationships that best complement his needs and not
necessarily those of the family.
        When one attempts to assess the psychological state of
an adolescent, it is important to gain information about
his success in: coping emotionally with physical changes,
establishing a more independent status relative to his
family and forming a satisfactory personal identity.

TABLE I

EVALUATION OUTLINE FOR ADOLESCENTS

A. HISTORY: (from parents and teenager)

   I. Presenting Problems:
          (Details of the adolescent's behavior which
          concern him, the parents or referring person)

  II. Past Developmental History:
          a. birth history
          b. early feeding and sleep patterns
          c. age at which walking and talking began
             and toilet training achieved

 III. Social History:
          a. school progress
          b. nature and number of peer relationships
          c. special interests (hobbies, activities)

  IV. Family History:
          a. family members (ages and relationship)
          b. characteristics of the relationships

B. EXAMINATION: (of the adolescent)

   I. Physical:
          a. height, weight and size relative to age
          b. presence of atypical physical findings
          c. presence of secondary sexual character-
             istics

  II. Psychological: (mental status examination)
          (Use the same evaluation areas and criteria
          as are applicable to an adult)

C. SUMMARY OF ABNORMAL FINDINGS:

          (List significant findings which you judge
          to be abnormal based on criteria to be
          presented later in the chapter)

D. DIAGNOSIS:

          (Should be evident after reviewing the
          summary)

EVALUATING THE TEENAGER
     Information from many sources is needed to adequately
assess the psychological status of the adolescent.
Table I presents the areas of history and examination
needed for the evaluation of an adolescent. This table
represents an outline of pertinent data to be obtained
when evaluating an adolescent for the presence of psychopathology. The evaluator should have access to as much of
this information as possible before attempting to make
a diagnosis. This format for evaluation will be utilized
in the evaluation exercises which follow. The headings
essentially are the same as those used when assessing
a child (see the chapter on Childhood Psychopathology)
and only the points needing modification for adolescents
will be discussed

Findings of History
     Teenagers are better able than younger children to
articulate their ideas and feelings. Thus, adolescents
should be included along with their parents as sources of
important information. Data about developmental milestones should be obtained, but are of lesser diagnostic
significance than when incorporated in the evaluation of
younger children. Developmental information is important
mainly as an indicator for how long problems have been
present. For example, a carefully taken history may
reveal that a troubled teenager had earlier behavioral
difficulties adapting to school. Such findings suggest
that a psychological problem has been present for some
time.
     Of special value is the social history dealing with
school and peer activities. As mentioned earlier, adolescence is a time for establishing new individual and
group relations outside of the family. The quality and
number of these relationships should be noted. Participation in peer groups is as developmentally important for
teenagers as play is for children.
     Although the adolescent is in the process of becoming
more independent of his family, it is worthwhile to assess
familial relationships while the teenager still lives and
interacts with them. The importance of family evaluation
changes with the age of the adolescent. Whereas a thirteen-
year-old cannot be evaluated satisfactorily if family
relationships are not considered, an eighteen-year-old is
more adultlike and autonomous and the family evaluation
is less needed.

Findings of Physical Examination
     As with children, the physical examination plays
a significant part of the evaluation. It is especially
important to note the presence and development of secondary
sexual characteristics relative to age norms and the
adolescent's capacity to cope emotionally with personal
biological changes.

Findings of the Mental Status Examination
    The psychological examination (mental status examina-
tion) for adolescents utilizes the same category headings
as are applied to adults, namely Appearance, Behavior,
Feeling, Perception and Thinking. Generally, abnormal
findings such as disorientation, associational disturbances,
perceptual disorders, etc. carry the same implications of
psychopathology for adolescents as with adults. Although
children more naturally express their feelings and thoughts
through their actions (behavior), teenagers are more able
to express themselves through words. However, adolescents
frequently feel uncomfortable in discussing personal
feelings if the interview is conducted in a formal and
highly structured fashion. It is usually less threatening
for them to "rap" informally, if the interviewer can accomplish this without seeming insincere or stilted. A useful approach for interviewing an adolescent is to inquire
about his special interests such as music and outside
school activities. In speaking about his likes and dis-
likes, the teenager will also indirectly communicate
valuable data about himself.

INCIDENCE OF PSYCHIATRIC SYNDROMES
    Whereas anxiety disorders and psychoses occur infre-
quently in children, they are relatively common disturbances
with adolescents. The significance of mental status
findings, the type and incidence of some psychiatric syndromes (psychoses, anxiety, etc.) closely approximate
those of adults. Some psychoses, including schizophrenic
and affective disorders, typically begin in the teen and
early adult years. Although there are no accurate data
on the incidence of psychiatric disorders in adolescence,
the three most common psychiatric syndromes are substance
use disorders, conduct disorders and affective disorders,
especially depression.

    Now complete Self-Assessment Exercise #1 on the
following page.

Self-Assessment Exercise #1

1. The following statements reflect the concerns of
    a mother about her fifteen-year-old son. "He used to
    be such a good boy. He would stay around the house
    until his father came home and we would all have dinner
    together as a family. Now he only wants to be out
    with his friends and is never home except to eat and
    sleep. He criticizes us and says we are 'old
    fashioned.' That's wrong with him, anyhow?"

    a. What developmental task of adolescence does this
        case vignette illustrate?

    b. List two other developmental tasks of the
        teenager.

        (1)

        (2)

2. Using the chart on the following page, briefly
    characterize and contrast for children and adolescents
    the areas of history and examination needed to assess
    psychopathology. (It may be useful at this time to
    review the chapter on Psychopathology in Childhood.)

Self-Assessment Exercise #1 (continued)

	CHILDREN	ADOLESCENTS
HISTORY Source of history:		
Past history: (developmental milestones)		
Social history: (areas of special importance)		
Family history: (relative impor- tance of familial relationships)		
EXAMINATION Physical: (especially pertinent findings)		
Psychological: (best source of M.S.E. data)		

When you have completed this exercise to the best of
your ability, check your answers with those on the
following page.

Self-Assessment Exercise #1 - Feedback

1. a. A teenager needs to form a more independent rela-
      tionship with his family. This case illustrates
      an adolescent in the process of attempting to
      become independent of his parents by utilizing
      criticism of them and preferring to be with his
      age-mates.

   b. Two other developmental tasks of the adolescent are:

      (1) coping with biological changes

      (2) establishing a personal identity

2.

	CHILDREN	ADOLESCENTS
HISTORY		
Source of history:	many sources but not usually from the child	many sources but also from the adolescent
Past history:	developmental milestones-- important	developmental milestones--important to show problem's duration
Social history:	especially note school progress	especially note peer relation- ships and school progress
Family history:	familial rela- tionships very important	familial relation- ships less important
EXAMINATION		
Physical:	note especially neurological findings, co- ordination	note especially secondary sexual characteristics
Psychological:	observations of play activity	indirectly through the adolescent's own language and interests or by discussion

   If your answers correspond with those above, continue
reading; if not, reread the preceding section until you
know the material.

SPECIAL CRITERIA FOR EVALUATING ADOLESCENTS

Developmental Criteria

When evaluating adolescents, important criteria to note are the age-appropriateness of development and whether a discrepancy exists between attained levels of of physical and emotional development. Physical and psychological development may proceed at different rates for any one individual. Also, there is a high degree of variability when comparing the maturation levels of different individuals of the same age. Wide ranges of variability in development are to be expected during adolescence, and it is informative to assess the teenager's ability to cope emotionally with biological changes and discrepancies. Physical development which proceeds at a faster rate than emotional development may be problematic. For instance, a thirteen-year-old girl, physically mature and appearing eighteen, may feel and act much younger. It is important to determine how she feels about her development and that of her peers. Her physical maturation may be gratifying in some ways but the accompanying sexual impulses may frighten her, perhaps because she lacks experience to deal with them in a socially acceptable way.

Psychopathology does not inevitably follow from a discrepancy between physical and emotional development. Before such a determination can be made it is necessary first to assess the adolescent's response. In general, a "normal" response to maturational difference tends to be action- and people-oriented. An "abnormal" reaction would be suggested by social and emotional withdrawal. In the thirteen-year-old girl mentioned above, a normal reaction might be for her to become active in athletic events and/or share her feelings with peers. An abnormal response would be demonstrated if she stayed home from school, withdrew to her room and avoided personal relationships.

In summary, for adolescents it is important to evaluate the age-appropriateness of development, whether a discrepancy exists between emotional and physical maturity, and the adolescent's response to any difference between physical and emotional development. A more normal response leads to problem-solving activity rather than withdrawal.

Stress-Related Cirteria

When examining stress-related responses, many of the same criteria applied to children may be used with adolescents (see the chapter, Psychopathology in Childhood, Table I).

Both the source and duration of the stress should be considered. Stresses (usually environmental) which are transient and can be easily related to the onset of symptoms, generally are least pathological.

The adolescent's response to stress deserves attention. Teenagers are often characterized as being unpredictable in their response to stress. During a crisis they may reveal an adultlike maturity and perceptiveness only to demonstrate later a childish temper outburst at slight provocation. So long as these seemingly unpredictable mood swings are transient, they fall within the normal range of behavior. However, a diagnosis of psychopathology may be indicated if these reactions are long-lasting and unchanging. If the reactions persist and resemble difficulties experienced previously in early childhood, they are more likely psychopathological symptoms than variations of normal maturation processes. A defiant, rebellious teenager who takes pride in "never giving up" likely demonstrated similar behavior during earlier years.

When evaluating a teenager it is well to assess the source of stress present, its duration and whether it can be easily related to the onset of symptoms. As with younger children, the longer the stress lasts the more serious and permanent its effects are likely to be.

Social Criteria

In our culture, an adolescent's participation in activities outside of the immediate family circle represents an accurate barometer of his functioning. Healthy children, by their mid-teen years, are able to establish trusting relationships and share confidences with a few close friends. In addition, they may have casual acquaintances with many others of their age. Teenagers who shun peers, display extreme discomfort with people and regularly prefer to be alone may be emotionally troubled. In school and/or work, adolescents should perform at a level approaching their capabilities. They typically are eager to accept reasonable challenges and try new experiences. A teenager who "gives up" easily, has an I.Q. of 120 and yet is failing in school deserves careful evalu

Although cordial relations should still be maintained with their family, there should be definite evidence of the adolescent's move toward independence. A normal teenager should begin formulating plans for his future apart from the family. His ideas and activities, although family-related, should take on his own "stamp." It is not normal for a teenager always to agree with parental ideas and act as if he could not take care of himself apart from his family. However, it is equally maladaptive if the teenager finds it necessary to defy any and all reasonable attempts at guidance by his parents and others in authority.

Now complete Self-Assessment Exercise #2 on the following page.

Self-Assessment Exercise #2

1. A father brought his sixteen-year-old son for consul-
    tation expressing concern about his son's slowed
    physical development and emotional stability. He
    related that the boy recently confessed to taking
    PCP (phencyclidine) one week earlier and experienced
    frightening visual hallucinations. These hallucina-
    tions lasted for approximately four hours and then
    gradually decreased. The boy had not experienced
    similar aberrations before or since that time. A
    physical examination was done showing the boy to be
    thin and somewhat small for his age with sparse pubic
    and facial hair. The physical findings were other-
    wise unremarkable.

    a. Were the hallucinatory symptoms likely indicative
        of deep-seated psychopathology? Yes_____ No_____

        Briefly justify your judgment.

2. For each of the categories listed, briefly summarize
    any additional information which you would like to
    have in order to evaluate the boy more definitively:

    a. developmental criteria:

    b. stress:

    c. social history:

    When you have completed this exercise to the best of
your ability, check your answers with those on the
following page.

Self-Assessment Exercise #2 - Feedback

1. a. The hallucinations by themselves do not indicate
       deep-seated psychopathology. The stress causing
       them was most likely a biological one (the
       hallucinogen PCP), and is easily identifiable as
       the cause of the symptoms. The hallucinations
       lasted only a short time, had not been experienced
       previously or associated with other psychopathology.
       However, more information is needed before a de-
       finitive judgment can be made.

2. To achieve a more definitive evaluation of the boy,
   detailed information should be obtained in the
   following areas:

   a. developmental criteria:

       (1) age-appropriateness of physical and emotional
           development and whether any discrepancies be-
           tween them exist

       (2) the boy's response to any discrepancies between
           physical and emotional development

   b. stress:

       any other source of potential stress, its duration
       and the boy's response to it

   c. social history:

       evaluate peer and family relationships, school/
       work progress

    If your answers correspond closely with those above,
continue with Exercise #3 on the following page. If not,
please reread the preceding section until you are confident
you know the material.

Self-Assessment Exercise #3

1. Read carefully the history of "Mary", below. As you
    read, record the information requested on the
    Evaluation Outline for Adolescents on the following
    pages.

Case history #1: Mary, age 14

Fourteen-year-old Mary was brought for consultation by
her adoptive mother. Together they related the
following information. As far back as she could remember, Mary felt that she was "unwanted." Born out
of wedlock, her biological mother gave her up for
adoption at birth and never saw her again. Mary was
placed with a couple who eventually adopted her.
When Mary was two, her adoptive mother became pregnant
and later delivered a healthy son. Mary recalled
frequently being compared with her brother and felt
that she could never successfully compete with him
for parental approval and attention. She was described
by the adoptive mother as a "good girl, who always
tried to please and was very sensitive to criticism."

A developmental history was taken. Mary's present and
past physical and psychological development were within
age-appropriate limits.

Mary's adoptive father, an engineer, was portrayed as
a heavy drinker who, in former years, constantly argued
with his wife. Mary's parents divorced when she was
twelve years old. Mary's father had been involved
somewhat peripherally with the children during earlier
years. After the divorce was finalized, he periodically returned to the family home where he was regarded
by Mary with contempt and resentment. Mary felt
rejected by her father and wished that he would either
remain at home or stay away all together. She found
it difficult to tolerate the feelings and ambiguity
caused by her father's intermittent appearances.

School had always been easy for Mary. However, when
her parents separated, Mary's grades plummeted, and
she lost interest in academic activities. Mary, previously popular, became alienated from her old friends.
She began associating with the school trouble makers,
defying school authorities and often participating in
pranks. Her mother complained that recently Mary un-
predictably withdrew from family activities or demonstrated angry outbursts. Her mother stated that she
and Mary frequently argued and could no longer agree
on even simple matters. For her part, Mary described
feeling sad much of the time and recently experienced
episodes of tearfulness.

Self-Assessment Exercise #3 (continued)

A physical examination and medical history were done.
Mary showed signs of beginning breast development
(she started her menstrual periods at age thirteen,
one year before the consultation) and a physical
maturity appropriate for her age. She dressed in
jeans and a loose fitting flannel shirt giving the
impression of being tomboyish and unkempt. Her long
brown hair hung straight down over her face and she
spoke sparingly in a low monotone. She expressed
feelings of self-doubt, helplessness and hopelessness.
Mary rarely looked up, rarely moved or gestured. She
appeared depressed and expressed guilt for frequently
becoming angry with her mother. No other abnormal
findings were noted.

EVALUATION FOR ADOLESCENTS

A. HISTORY: (from parents and teenager)

  I. Presenting Problems:

  II. Past Developmental History:

  III. Social History: (school and peer relationships)

  IV. Family History: (family members and character-
      istics)

EVALUATION OUTLINE (continued)

B. EXAMINATION: (of the teenager)

I. Physical:

II. Psychological: (mental status examination)

C. SUMMARY OF ABNORMAL FINDINGS:

Self-Assessment Exercise #3 (continued)

2. Select which statement best characterizes Mary's behavior.

    ____a. Her behavior is indicative of psychopathology.

    ____b. Her behavior is only a manifestation of normal developmental changes.

    Briefly describe the basis for your judgment relative to her present developmental status, stress, school performance and peer relationships.

3. What diagnosis (if any) would you assign to Mary? Support your judgment in terms of M.S.E. findings and history.

    When you have completed this exercise to the best of your ability, check your answers with those on the following pages.

Self-Assessment Exercise #3 - Feedback

1. Case History #1: Mary

    EVALUATION OUTLINE FOR ADOLESCENTS

A. HISTORY: (from parents and teenager)

    I. Presenting Problems:

        impaired academic performance; behavior problems
        at home and school; irritability

    II. Past Developmental History:

        milestones up to the present are within normal
        chronological limits; her current tomboyish
        appearance is somewhat out of tune with her
        physical maturity and age

    III. Social History:

        marked change from good academic achievement and
        peer relationships to poor school performance and
        behavioral problems at school and home

    IV. Family History:

        parents divorced for two years; father uses alcohol
        to excess and appears ambivalent about divorce;
        mother unable to cope with Mary's behavior

B. EXAMINATION: (of the teenager)

    I. Physical:

        beginning breast development; physical maturity
        appropriate for her age; otherwise unremarkable

    II. Psychological: (mental status examination)

        tomboyish; unkempt; spoke in low monotone;
        appeared depressed; expressed feelings of guilt,
        depression, hopelessness

C. SUMMARY OF ABNORMAL FINDINGS

    poor grades; problem with behavior and peers; chronic
    depressive symptoms

Self-Assessment Exercise #3 - Feedback (continued)

2. Mary's behavior is abnormal and indicative of psycho-
    pathology. From a developmental standpoint, her
    tomboyish appearance is somewhat out of tune with her
    physical maturity and age. It appears that Mary is
    still responding adversely to her parents' separation
    (which she regards as a rejection) that occurred
    about two years previous to the consultation. Some of
    Mary's responses may carry over from earlier feelings
    of rejection, but in any case they seem prolonged
    and unchanging. There are definite disturbances in
    her school performance and relationships with friends
    and family.

3. Findings of history and mental status examination
    would be indicative of a Dysthymic Disorder (Depressive
    Neurosis). (Please refer to the chapter on Affective
    Disorders if you have any questions about this
    diagnosis.)

    Significant mental status examination findings in-
    clude her unkempt appearance, sad facial expression,
    low voice, decreased bodily movement, thought content
    of self-recriminations about angry feelings expressed
    toward her mother and a history of recurrent episodes
    of tearfulness and depression.

    If your answers correspond closely with those above,
continue with Self-Assessment Exercise #4 on the following
page.

Self-Assessment Exercise #4

1. Read carefully the history of "John," below. As you
    read, record the information requested on the Evalua-
    tion Outline for Adolescents on the following pages.

Case history #2:   John, age 16

John described his early life as an idyllic time spent
with his parents and younger sister in Chicago. John
had attended a private school and had ambitions to be
a musician like his father. He realized that his
vocational goals demanded work and discipline, but
John felt confident that he could do it. When he was
eleven, John's world abruptly changed because his
father died. John's mother began to drink heavily due
to the death of her husband and committed suicide one
year later. John, then twelve, and his sister (age 10)
went to live with maternal grandparents in Los Angeles.
Since both of his parents were deceased, little
specific information was known about John's early
development other than it seemed "normal."

John's grandparents, being much older, had been unac-
customed to caring for young children and set very few
rules for them. The new policy of discipline was
quite a change for John, who was accustomed to clear,
firm guidelines. In Chicago he was required to wear
a uniform while attending a private boys' school. In
Los Angeles the selection of clothes was left to his
individual choice and school was public and coeduca-
tional. His new friends were already interested in
girls and dared John to drink with them, which he did.

Within a few months of "freedom" John developed delinquent behavior. He was suspended from the football
team for stealing dangerous chemicals from the school
chemistry lab. In addition, a "friend" of John informed school authorities that John had stolen some
chemical weighing scales. John had used the scales to
market marijuana. John drank almost every weekend
and on one occasion was picked up by the police for
being intoxicated. A few days prior to the consultation, John was apprehended while attempting to break
into a liquor store and was placed on probation for
one year.

During these episodes it became apparent that John had
made little attempt to avoid being caught. Further
history revealed that although John had average intelligence his school grades were poor to failing. He had
a wide circle of friends, especially among the more
rebellious boys. John claimed an interest in dating
but had been unable to form lasting relationships with
any girl.

Self-Assessment Exercise #4 (continued)

A physical examination showed John to be a husky, blonde-haired boy who is physically and sexually developed appropriately for his age, sixteen. He was neatly and casually dressed. He related well to the therapist and was friendly and cooperative. He asked frequent questions about the personal life of the therapist and seemed interested in what the therapist thought about his behavior. He acknowledged that his actions had brought him into trouble repeatedly but was unable to explain the motivations behind his behavior. He stated that he was fascinated by being in dangerous situations. Other mental status examination findings were within normal limits.

EVALUATION OUTLINE FOR ADOLESCENTS

A. HISTORY: (from parents and teenager)

   I. Presenting Problems:

   II. Past Developmental History:

   III. Social History: (school and peer relationships)

   IV. Family History: (family members and characteristics)

EVALUATION OUTLINE (continued)

B. EXAMINATION: (of the teenager)

   I.   <u>Physical</u>:

   II. <u>Psychological</u>:   (mental status examination)

C. SUMMARY OF ABNORMAL FINDINGS:

Self-Assessment Exercise #4 (continued)

2. Which of the following diagnostic categories best fits John's case?

    a. Anxiety Disorder of adolescence

    b. Schizophrenic Disorder

    c. Conduct Disorder

    d. Schizoid Disorder of adolescence

3. Briefly discuss the major factors which contributed to John's troubles.

When you have completed this exercise to the best of your ability, check your answers with those on the following pages.

Self-Assessment Exercise #4 - Feedback

1. Case History #2:   John

EVALUATION OUTLINE FOR ADOLESCENTS

A. HISTORY: (from parents and teenager)

I.   Presenting Problems:

delinquent behavior; antisocial acts

II.   Past Developmental History:

not available

III.   Social History:

poor grades though of average intelligence; many friends; problems with authority figures

IV.   Family History:

parents both dead; elderly grandparents well-meaning but unable to set behavioral limits; sister (14)

B. EXAMINATION: (of the teenager)

I.   Physical:

husky; well-developed; physically and sexually mature for age

II.   Psychological:

aware of his problems but unsure of reasons behind them; describes fascination with danger; average intelligence; no other significant findings

C. SUMMARY OF ABNORMAL FINDINGS:

delinquent behavior; poor school performance; problems with authority figures

Self-Assessment Exercise #4 - Feedback (continued)

2. John's case exemplifies a Conduct Disorder in which occurs ongoing patterns of antisocial behavior, such as persistent verbal and/or physical aggressiveness, difficulty in maintaining social relationships, ego-centricity, callousness, defiance of authority, drug/alcohol abuse, truancy, poor scholastic performance, and vandalism. He demonstrated no symptoms of psychosis or significant overt anxiety.

3. With the death of John's parents, the orderliness and discipline of his life was destroyed. The move to Los Angeles, the developmental changes of adolescence, and the inability of his grandparents to set limits for behavior were too much for him. John was unable to control and direct his impulses into acceptable behavioral channels. Perhaps his delinquent behavior carried with it a plea to have limits set for him as his parents used to.

If your answers correspond closely with those above, continue reading; if not, please reread the preceding section until you are confident you know the material.

SUMMARY

Adolescents are in transit between childhood and adulthood and in our society the teen years can be a troubled and difficult period. Healthy teenagers may often feel awkward and uncomfortable with their biological and emotional changes. They need to establish a new and more independent relatinship with their family and form a personal identity. They should be able to accomplish these tasks without resorting to social withdrawal or self-defeating behaviors that are indicative of psychopathology. A careful evaluation of history and examination findings are needed in order to determine presence of psychopathology in adolescents.

REFERENCES

Diagnostic and Statistical Manual of Mental Disorders, Third Edition, American Psychiatric Association, 1979.

Erikson, E. H.: Identity, Youth and Crisis, New York: W. W. Norton & Co., 1968.

Hamburg, B. A.: Coping in Early Adolescence. In: American Handbook of Psychiatry. G. Caplan (Ed.), New York: Basic Books, 1974.

King, S. H.: Coping and Growth in Adolescence. In: Annual Progress in Child Psychiatry and Child Development. S. Chess and A. Thomas (Eds.), New York: Brunner/Mazel, 1974.

Nicholi, A. M., Jr.: The Adolescent. In: Harvard Guide to Modern Psychiatry. A. M. Nicholi, Jr. (Ed.), Cambridge: Belknap Press of Harvard University Press, 1978.

Offer, D. and Offer, J.: Normal Adolescence in Perspective. In: Current Issues in Adolescent Psychiatry, J. C. Schoolar (Ed.), New York: Brunner/Mazel, 1973.

Chapter 6

Psychopathology in Family, Marital and Pair Relationships
Beatrice Sommers
John R. Snibbe

It is important for professionals who work with troubled people to be able to identify signs of family and marital distress no matter how it is communicated. The task at hand, be it healing, teaching, advising, or legal representation, may be significantly affected by the existence of such problems. There is also the possibility that a client may be unaware of the existence of such distress and its significance to the very issues for which he seeks help. In many situations, the legal, medical, educational or vocational crisis itself may be a symptom of underlying emotional stress related to family relationships.

This chapter provides a beginning frame of reference by which some signals, causes and patterns of marital dysfunction can be recognized and used to improve ailing family relationships.

LEARNING OBJECTIVES
By the time you complete the material in this chapter you should be able to:

1. Correctly define the following terms as they pertain to interpersonal relationships:

   interpersonal expectations
   negotiation
   relationship stress
   overt expectations
   covert expectations

2. List the causes of unfulfilled expectations.

3. List the areas of a relationship which are commonly involved in marital dysfunction.

4. List and briefly describe the common symptoms of marital dysfunction.

By the time you complete the material in this chapter you should be able to list and/or describe:

1. The <u>overt</u> terms of the interpersonal and marital expectations.

2. The <u>cause</u> of unfulfilled marital expectations.

3. The <u>covert</u> terms of the interpersonal and marital expectations.

4. The common <u>areas</u> of the interpersonal and marital dysfunction.

5. The <u>symptoms</u> of the interpersonal and marital dysfunction.

OVERVIEW
    One of the most useful ways of understanding the nature
of conflict in relationships such as marriage, and other
significant interpersonal relationships, is to examine the
hopes that each person brings to the partnership. In all
relationships there is a basic understanding that if one
gives something, one will receive something in return. For
instance, a common assumption in a marriage is that if the
husband supports the family, the wife will be responsible
for housekeeping tasks and taking care of the children. A
common assumption between parent and child is that the parent will love and nurture the child who will, in turn, obey
and respect his parent.

    It may simplify matters to refer to these mutual hopes
as expectations. An expectation is an agreement between two
(or more) persons to do something or respond in a specific
way. All paired persons, whether parent and child, friends,
doctor and patient, employer and employee or husband and
wife, express with varying degrees of clarity what each expects to receive from the other in return for that which is
done or given.

    In marriages, as in all interpersonal relationships, the
terms of expectations and the ability of the partners to
meet them determine the nature and the quality of the interaction. Good relationships are those in which each partner
is able to meet the majority of needs and desires of the
other. Poor relationships develop when expectations are un-
met or in dispute.

MODES OF COMMUNICATING CONTRACTURAL EXPECTATIONS
    Some expectations may be verbalized; many others are
left unspoken or are assumed. For instance, the partners
may voice overt expectations of each other regarding role
functions; e.g., the male is the provider and the female
the homemaker. However, there may be covert expectations,
in that the role of each partner carries specific privileges,
i.e. only the husband decides how the money should be spent
or the wife alone decides how the home should be decorated
and what food is served.

    Sometimes the unspoken expectations of one partner are
unknown to the other. In the example above, the wife may be
surprised to discover that her husband bought a new T.V. without consulting her. Correspondingly, the husband may be
puzzled by his wife who uses colors to decorate the home
without regarding his preferences.

UNFULFILLED EXPECTATIONS
    It is when expectations are not met that partners ex-
perience difficulty and discomfort. This condition of discomfort is termed relationship stress. An example of this
is the husband who, after a difficult day at the office, as-
sumes that he will receive "tender loving care" from his
wife. If his wife is absorbed in her own problems and ignores

him, he then may become resentful (stressed) because of feeling cheated out of something he expected.

Sometimes agreements are formed between husband and wife early in their relationship to meet the particular needs of the time. Later one or the other may experience changes in responsibilities, health, economics, self-esteem, and so forth, which modify the conditions and appropriateness of the original expectations. Relationship stress and discomfort for the partnership may result. For example, at the beginning of a marriage the husband may have a small business with the wife functioning as a part-time bookkeeper and homemaker. If the business fails, the wife may be forced into a full-time job while the husband stays at home. These role changes, with their impact on the couple's daily life and self-esteem, can create tension between the partners or intensify existing tension.

Some causes of unfulfilled expectations are:

a.   Ignorance of the partner's expectation--One of the partners may be unaware of the other's expectations and fail to fulfill them out of ignorance.

b.   Inability--Partners, because of their personality structure, physical stamina, religious or ethical preferences, and so forth, may not be able to fulfill the overt and/or covert terms of the expectations. For example, one partner may be physically or emotionally disabled and unable to live as actively as the other expects.

c.   Unwillingness--One partner may be reluctant to meet the other's expectations (sexual, domestic, or social), or withhold stating his feelings clearly. He may resist clarifying his reasons perhaps out of fear of conflict. For example, if the overt expectation is that both the husband and wife work and share economic responsibilities, the wife may covertly expect that they will also share domestic ones. If the husband does not perform these functions voluntarily, the wife may become resentful but remain silent. She may fear that if they explore the matter, the husband, once aware of his wife's expectation, would declare himself unwilling to accept the role of part-time homemaker, and an argument would follow.

The ultimate success or failure of a marriage (or any partnership) depends upon the ability of the partners to cope effectively when expectations or assumptions are not met or are no longer appropriate. Ideally, the rules of the partnership allow for open discussions of feelings and thoughts about such agreement breakdowns. When this happens, the partners can confer, identify the troublesome issues, and openly state their differing points of view. Once these issues are clear to both partners, they can then explore their willingness to compromise or change their previous expectations. Through such discussion and sharing they may find

a mutually satisfactory solution to the problem. Each must
feel that the other possesses the capacity and desire to
fulfill his or her part of the compromise in daily living.

The process described above can be effective in the reso-
lution of differences between partners in that it allows
the partnership to deal with the facts at hand; to reinforce
positive feelings and to develop necessary mutual trust.
Sometimes this process is called the negotiation of differences. The ability to engage in such negotiations is essential to the healthy survival of all partnerships. For example, a wife may be secretly disappointed with certain sexual behaviors of her husband. As a result she has lessened
the frequency of her participation in intercourse. Her husband expresses concern and bewilderment about this change.
Instead of making up an excuse for her behavior, she dis-
cusses her concern in a frank and open manner. The husband,
upon considering the matter, may agree to alter some of his
practices, or discuss his reluctance to do so directly with
his wife.

Open discussion can lead to a modification of expectations
and more appropriate roles in the relationship which then may
relieve the stress and disappointment. When another breakdown in fulfillment of expectations occurs, partners could
again negotiate their differences and a new equilibrium can
be reached.

If, however, the nature of the partnership does not allow
for open, direct discussion of expectations and disappointment, then effective negotiations of differences are blocked.
Each partner then deals with discomfort, relationship stress,
disappointment and resentment in indirect ways, and marital
(or partnership) dysfunction begins.

Now complete Self-Assessment Exercise #1 on the following page.

Self Assessment Exercise #1

1.   In reference to this chapter, define the following terms:

   a.   expectation

   b.   negotiation of differences

   c.   relationship stress

   d.   overt expectations

   e.   covert expectations

2.   List three common causes of unfulfilled expectations:

     When you have completed this portion of Exercise #1,
check your answers with those on the following page.

Self Assessment Exercise #1 - Feedback

1. a.   An <u>expectation</u> is a verbalized or unspoken assumption between partners to do something.

    b.   <u>Negotiation of differences</u> is the process of openly discussing differences in a partnership and reaching a mutually acceptable compromise or change in expectations.

    c.   <u>Relationship stress</u> is the distress which arises between partners when expectations are not met.

    d.   <u>Overt expectations</u> are those which are explicit and verbalized.

    e.   <u>Covert expectations</u> are those which are unverbalized and may be out of conscious awareness.

2.   Three common causes of unfulfilled contractual expectations are <u>ignorance</u> of what is expected, <u>inability</u> to meet the expectation and <u>unwillingness</u> to satisfy the the expectations.

    If your answers correspond closely with those above, continue with Exercise #1 on the following page; if not, please reread the preceding section until you are confident you know the material.

<u>Self Assessment Exercise #1 (continued)</u>

Please read this case history and answer the questions which follow.

<u>Case History</u>:

> Seventeen-year-old Julie who experienced repeated con-
> flicts with her parents decided to marry her 19-year-
> old boyfriend, Bob, a premed student who lived at
> home with his parents. The couple planned to live
> with Bob's family who would continue to pay his edu-
> cational expenses and board the couple. Bob's parents
> expressed delight at having two children living at
> home again, since their only daughter had recently
> married and moved away. After the marriage, Julie
> agreed to work in order to meet the couple's expenses
> and save money for future needs.
>
> About three months after they were married, Julie im-
> pulsively purchased a hair dryer. She was shocked at
> the outrage and criticism expressed by her husband
> and his parents over her "extravagant, unnecessary
> purchase." All three criticized Julie as being "sel-
> fish and wasteful" and stated that the money should
> have been banked for the couple's future needs.

1. List the <u>overt</u> expectations for Bob, Julie and Bob's
    parents:

2. List the possible <u>covert</u> expectations for Bob, Julie and
    Bob's parents which caused discord:

Now check your answers with those on the following page.

Self-Assessment Exercise #1 - Feedback

1. The overt expectations are:

    a. Bob plans to pursue his premed studies in order to prepare for his profession.

    b. Julie will work temporarily and provide for their basic "incidental" expenses and savings for their future needs.

    c. The couple will live in the home of Bob's parents who will provide basic necessities such as shelter, food, and educational expenses for their son.

2. The covert expectations seem to be:

    Bob expects that Julie will consult with him and his parents about spending the money she earns.

    Julie expects that she can spend some of the money she earns as she chooses without consultation.

    Bob's parents may view Julie as a "second daughter" or replacement for their own absent "daughter" and expect to continue functioning with parental authority toward her.

    Bob's parents expect that they can express their disapproval of how Julie spends her money.

    Julie may have viewed her marriage as freeing her from parental authority and expects to live in Bob's home as an independent adult.

    Bob may view Julie in the same way as his parents and agree with their expectations.

    If your answers correspond closely with those above, continue your reading; if not, please reread the preceding section until you are confident you know the material.

AREAS OF MARITAL DYSFUNCTION
     Some partners resort to indirect ways of expressing their
resentment and disappointment with one another. They may
utilize a function requiring joint participation such as sex,
child-rearing practices or finances to communicate their distress. Problem areas that stand out in marital relationships
are outlined below.

Sexual Relationships
     Satisfactory sex relations presuppose an open, relaxed
and affectionate attitude between sex partners. Unexpressed
negative feelings can introduce tension and thereby affect
both the performance of the sex act and the feelings experienced by the partners. If this situation continues, sexual
problems develop within the partnership.

Financial Planning and Management
     Successful handling of finances within a marriage demands
cooperation involving self-discipline of both partners in relation to a common goal. Such cooperation may be withdrawn
if one partner harbors unexpressed resentment toward the
other; the origin, though, of the resentment may be completely unrelated to finances. A common instance of this is a
wife who reacts to her husband's unannounced "night out with
the boys" by making an impulsive, extravagant purchase which
throws off the monthly budget.

Child-Rearing Practices
     The constructive and positive discipline of children needs
an atmosphere of parental cooperation and respect for one another's disciplinary values. Child-rearing practices are
common areas in which marital partners conduct their struggle
over other issues, i.e. the breakdown of expectations.

Relationship to the Extended Family
     The attitude of one partner toward family members of the
other can indirectly reflect feelings toward the other partner. When there is resentment over a contractual disruption, an expression of criticism of the partner's family, or
reluctance or refusal to participate in social relationships
with them, may be shown.

Companionship
     The satisfactory use of leisure time is another area in-
volving compromise for the partners. From time to time one
partner may give up first choice of a movie, sport activity,
television program, and so forth, in order to meet the other's
needs or wishes. This is done in the belief that the other
partner will, in turn, allow a reciprocal first choice the
next time. When covert, negative feelings are present in a
partnership, it becomes more difficult to maintain the trust
which is basic to the act of compromise, or postponing one's
own pleasures. Problems involving use of recreational time
commonly develop as indirect expressions of resentment.

SYMPTOMS OF MARITAL DYSFUNCTION

When partners in a marriage utilize indirect means of communicating their distress and disappointment over breakdown in contractual expectations, their feelings may find expression by demonstrating one of the behaviors listed below. Counsellors and other professionals should be alert to the manifestation of such behaviors.

Excessive Criticism

Increasing irritability and excessive criticism by a partner over inconsequential issues. A point may be reached when only negative feelings are expressed, while positive feelings are left unspoken.

Obstructionism

One partner may actively block fulfillment of the spouses plans rather than helping attain it. For example, a husband may refuse to provide financial support for his wife's special education which would enable her to pursue a wished-for career.

Passive-Aggressiveness

One partner may be unwilling to openly express contrary suggestions for implementing the work of the partnership, i.e. financial planning, child-rearing issues, etc., and subtly avoid and/or procrastinate decision making.

Deliberate Withholding of Feeling

In the presence of anger and resentment which cannot be expressed directly, partners may withhold expression of feelings and create an emotional sterile atmosphere within the marriage which is discouraging.

Overt Psychopathology

At times, partners express their distress indirectly through problem behavior such as gambling, alcoholism, drug abuse, child abuse, sexual promiscuity, criminal behavior or vocational instability or other self-defeating behavior. Behaviors such as overeating, excessive complaints of physical ailments, and recurring anxiety may also be indirect ways of communicating contractual or expectancy breakdown. In such instances, it is important to differentiate how much pathology is related to marital stress and how much is a reflection of the individual's habitual method of coping with the problems of living.

Sexual Dysfunction

Sexual dysfunction such as premature ejaculation and impotence for the male; frigidity and decreasing sexual responses and interest for the female can be indirect ways of expressing anger and resentment toward the sexual partner.

Authoritarianism

One partner may dominate and make unilateral decisions without consulting the other partner.

Now complete Self-Assessment Exercise #2 on the following page.

Self-Assessment Exercise #2

Please read the case history below and answer the questions which follow:

Case History:

    Harry Smith consulted Dr. White, his family physician,
to obtain a renewal of medication for a bronchial infection. After renewing the prescription, Dr. White
asked casually about Harry's wife and family. Harry
responds with an automatic "fine" and then, almost as
an afterthought adds, "She's sure been getting crabby
lately and never wants to go anywhere or do anything."

    Dr. White asked about the specifics of Mrs. Smith's
irritability and learns that she was constantly critical
of Harry's social behavior at parties, his lax attitude
toward the discipline of the children, and his unwilling-
ness to help her with household chores. Dr. White also
learns that her irritability started about six months
earlier and was a marked change from her previous behavior. Further inquiry reveals that six months earlier,
without consulting his wife as he usually did, Harry had
refused a job promotion involving a large increase in
both job responsibilities and salary. He stated that he
was best qualified to make the decisions since he knew
the total picture. He also indicated that his wife was
not to interfere in his business affairs.

1. What are the <u>areas</u> of dysfunction in Mr. Smith's marriage?

2. What are the <u>symptoms</u> of dysfunction in Mr. Smith's mar-
    riage?

    When you have completed this exercise to the best of your
ability, check your answers with those on the following page.

Self-Assessment Exercise #2 - Feedback

1.   The areas of dysfunction are:

     companionship issues, child discipline, and financial
     matters

2.   The symptoms of dysfunction are:

     a.   Mrs. Smith seems overcritical and negativistic about
          inconsequential issues.

     b.   Mr. Smith made decisions affecting the family with-
          out consulting his wife.

     If your answers correspond closely with those above,
please continue with Exercise #2 on the following page; if
not, please reread the preceding section until you are confident you know the material.

Self-Assessment Exercise #2 (continued)

Please read this case history and answer the questions
which follow.

Case History:

Mrs. Anderson, a woman 35 years of age, had long been a
church goer. She requested a meeting with her clergyman to discuss a problem.

Mrs. Anderson related to the clergyman that over the
past few months she ate continuously and had gained
20 pounds. Mrs. Anderson recounted that her husband's
parents had divorced within the last year leaving her
mother-in-law distraught. The mother-in-law had turned
to her only child, Mrs. Anderson's husband, for emotional support and advice in handling everyday decisions.
Mr. Anderson spent much of his leisure time in attempting to help his mother during this difficult period. He
also invited his mother to spend considerable time at
the couple's home, thus reducing the couple's customary
recreational time together. He seemed to ignore his
wife's reaction to the change in their relationship and
criticized her weight gain.

Mrs. Anderson found it difficult to complain about this
arrangement, which she resented, because she felt that
her mother-in-law was in crisis. She asked for her
clergyman's advice.

1.   What is the area of dysfunction?

2.   What are the symptoms of dysfunction?

When you have completed this exercise to the best of your
ability, check your answers with those on the following page.

Self-Assessment Exercise #2 - Feedback (continued)

1. The area of dysfunction involved:

    companionship issues

2. The symptoms of dysfunction are:

    Mrs. Anderson, the wife, exhibited problem behavior in the form of overeating.

If your answers correspond closely with those above, continue reading; if not, please reread the preceding section until you are confident you know the material.

SUMMARY
    Many health care professionals are often called upon to
evaluate and ameliorate crises which are directly or indirectly related to problems in interpersonal relationships.
Marriage and pair relationships can be conceptualized as involving mutual expectations, e.g. contracts, on the part of
each partner. Each individual has an understanding about
how the details and daily life of a relationship will proceed. When contractual expectations are not met, or are
violated by one partner, stress and dysfunction in the relationship may result. The partners may not know how to
handle contractual problems. A therapist alert to these
factors can, by listening, be instrumental in helping the
couple develop awareness of the possible significance of
their problems and promote the negotiation process and facilitate important open communication. Through this process
compromise and discussion may be encouraged so that newer
and more mutually acceptable expectations may be developed.

    If the interventions, as outlined above, do not prove
sufficiently effective, then referral to a mental health
professional for more specialized treatment may be indicated.

REFERENCES

Bandler, R., Grindler, J., and Satir, V.: Changing with
Families. Palo Alto: Science and Behavior Books, 1976.

Berman, Ellen et al.: "The Two-Professional Marriage: A
New Conflict Syndrome," J. Sex & Marital Ther., 1:242-253,
1975.

Caplan, G.: The family as a support system. In: Support
Systems and Mutual Help: Multidisciplinary Explorations.
G. Caplan and M. Killilea (Eds.) New York: Grune & Stratton,
1976, pp. 19-36.

Charney, Israel: Marital Love and Hate, New York: Macmillan,
1972.

Dodson, L.: Family Counseling: A Systems Approach, New
York: Academic Press, 1977.

Herndon, C.M., and Nash, E.C.: "Marital Counseling," JAMA,
180:395, May 1962.

Jackson, Don: "Family Rules: The Marital Quid Pro Quo,"
Arch. Gen. Psychiatry, 12:589-94, 1965.

Mace, David R.: "Marital Intimacy and the Deadly Love-Anger
Cycle," J. Marr. Fam. Couns., 2:131-139, April 1976.

Pearlman, Thomas W.: "Domestic Relations--Advice for the
Physician," Rhode Island Med. J., 57:108-109, March 1974.

Silverman, H.: Marital Therapy, C.C. Thomas: Springfield,
1972.

Watzlawick, P., Beavin, J. and Jackson, D.: Pragmatics of Human Communication, W.W. Norton: New York, 1967.

Wittkower, E. and Lester, E.P.: "Marital Stress in Psycho-somatic Disorders," in D.W. Abse et. al. (eds.), Marital & Sexual Counseling in Medical Practice, 2d ed., Hagerstown, Md.: Harper & Row, 1974, pp. 218-230.

Chapter 7
Mental Retardation
Michael P. Ward

There are more people with primary or major secondary
problems of mental retardation and low intelligence than
any other psychiatric disorder.   Thus, on a purely statistical basis, a professional can expect to encounter
this condition with some frequency.
     While this chapter focuses on mental retardation, it
is also meant to orient the reader to the importance of
intellectual variability in the general population.   In
our society, at both lay and professional levels, if
a person is not "obviously" retarded (the common stereo-
type includes notions of drooling, incoherence, and physical deformity), then his intelligence is often of little
concern.   Such a conception is unfortunate and "unhealthy."
Other difficulties often mask problems of low intelligence.
For instance, a child not performing adequately in school
(academically or behaviorally) is often brought by the
parents to various professionals for consultation.   In
adults, some psychosomatic symptoms may be the direct
result of underlying coping deficits related to intellectual limitations.
     Low intelligence also complicates the diagnostic and
treatment process.   The professional must rely on the
client's report of symptomology in order to diagnose,
follow-up, and evaluate the effectiveness of treatment.
Clients are sometimes required to follow complicated
treatment programs. It is crucial that the professional
be able to assess the ability of his patients to report
accurately and reliably follow instructions.

LEARNING OBJECTIVES
     By the time you complete the material in this chapter
you should be able to:

  1.   Correctly define mental retardation using the
       three recommended criteria.

162

2. Define "I.Q.", and briefly describe:

    a. the distribution of I.Q.'s in the general
        population
    b. the prevalence of mental retardation

3. List two or more criteria for assessing adaptive
    impairment in each of the following age groups:

    a. infancy and early childhood
    b. later childhood and early adolescence
    c. late adolescence and adult life

4. List and briefly describe the four levels of mental
    retardation in terms of:

    a. I.Q. range
    b. probability of concomitant neurological
        damage
    c. ability to benefit from academic training
    d. need for life-long supervised care
    e. capability to live independently when of
        adult age

5. List six or more methods by which to assess
    a person's level of intellectual and adaptive
    functioning.

6. List the M.S.E. findings typical of a mildly
    retarded person.

By the conclusion of this chapter and supervised
clinical experience you should be able to:

    1. Accurately observe and record a client's behavior
        within each of the M.S.E. behavior descriptors.

    2. Determine whether mental retardation is present
        in a person given necessary M.S.E. information.

    3. Indicate the history and M.S.E. findings which
        enabled you to make a diagnosis.

MENTAL RETARDATION DEFINED
      In 1977, the American Association on Mental Deficiency
defined mental retardation as: <u>significantly subaverage</u>
<u>general intellectual functioning existing concurrently</u>
<u>with deficits in adaptive behavior, and manifested during</u>
<u>the developmental period.</u> This definition consists of
three essential requirements which must be present before
a diagnosis of mental retardation can be made.
      The first requirement for a diagnosis of mental re-
tardation is <u>significantly subaverage general intellectual</u>
functioning. General intellectual functioning is defined
and measured by performance on an individually administered,
standardized test of intelligence. Use of group tests of
intelligence is specifically excluded as an acceptable
measure on which to base the diagnosis. The most commonly
accepted tests that satisfy the requirement are the
Wechsler Adult Intelligence Scale (WAIS), the Wechsler
Intelligence Scale for Children-Revised (WISC-R), and
the Stanford-Binet. Each of these tests yields an I.Q.
(intelligence quotient) which is a quantitative summary
index that indicates the general intellectual functioning
of the individual. A consideration of the meaning and
distribution of I.Q. will be covered later in this chapter.
      An I.Q. of 100 represents average intellectual func-
tioning. "Significantly" subaverage general intellectual
functioning is operationally defined as two or more
"standard deviations" (a statistical measure of variation
in a distribution of scores) below the mean or average.
The standard deviations for the commonly employed tests
mentioned above are 15 (Wechsler Scales) or 16 (Stanford-
Binet) points. Thus, two standard deviations below the
mean (100) would be represented by I.Q.'s of 68 or 70,
depending on the standard deviation of the test used. I.Q.
scores below these points satisfy the criteria of significantly subaverage, general intellectual functioning.
      The second requirement for a diagnosis of mental re-
tardation is a <u>concurrent deficit in adaptive behavior</u>.
The addition of this dimension in the criteria for mental
retardation came about for several reasons. In the past,
it was assumed that the intellectual deficits measured by
a test of intelligence would be reflected in behavior by
an impaired ability to cope and adapt. However, empirical
studies demonstrated that there were numerous individuals
with I.Q.'s below 70 who were adapting to the demands of
their environments. It became apparent that a diagnosis of
mental retardation needed a behavioral component as well
as test validation if the concept was to have any real
meaning.
      Another related issue was the increasing recognition
of the cultural bias present in tests of intelligence.
Studies have shown that many persons of different cultural
and social backgrounds who scored low on I.Q. tests were
adapting in their own social and cultural milieus. Calling
them retarded on the basis of an I.Q. score in the absence
of manifest behavioral impairments was unjustified and
illogical.

These issues make apparent the cultural-relativity of mental retardation and the fact that, in its essence, mental retardation is a socially defined phenomenon. If a person has no difficulties adapting to the demands of his society, it is meaningless to consider him as having a problem solely on the basis of a test score.

Adaptive behavior is generally defined as the degree to which the individual meets the standards of personal independence and social responsibility expected for his age and cultural group. Since the normal development of adaptive skills is age-related, a classification of expectations and criteria according to age is needed. This classification will be considered in detail later in the chapter.

The third requirement for a diagnosis of mental retardation is that the condition be manifested during the developmental period. This requirement is added to differentiate mental retardation from other disorders, such as brain damage incurred as an adult or the temporary intellectual deficits secondary to emotional problems. The "developmental period" refers to the time during which the growth of intelligence presumably occurs and extends from birth to eighteen years of age.

In summary, there are three criteria that must be satisfied before a person can be diagnosed as mentally retarded. Most importantly, I.Q., in and of itself, no longer suffices as the sole factor in making such a diagnosis. Without demonstrating that the person with low I.Q. has manifest behavioral deficits, which also existed during the development period, the diagnosis cannot be applied.

In general, the new definition of mental retardation focuses on the current status of the individual. Mental retardation is not viewed as a single disease or syndrome. In fact, there are now known to be over 250 etiological conditions associated with mental retardation. It is a state of behavioral impairment that has many causes. Also, the focus on current status emphasizes that no prognostic statements are implied. In the past, a diagnosis of mental retardation carried with it the idea of incurability. With the present view of mental retardation, wherein the focus is on the developmental aspects of the genetic-environmental interaction, there is a greater recognition of the notion of modifiability. Prognosis is now more related to such factors as motivation, treatment and training opportunities.

Now complete Self-Assessments Exercise #1 on the following page.

Self-Assessment Exercise #1

1. Define mental retardation, using the three recommended criteria.

2. On the basis of the information given, indicate for each of the following individuals whether a diagnosis of mental retardation is appropriate. Briefly state reasons for your opinion.

   a. a 13-year-old boy, I.Q. 65, doing C- work in his regular grade

   b. a 13-year-old boy, I.Q. 75, doing B work in a grade two years behind his regular grade

   c. a 13-year-old boy, I.Q. 65

Self-Assessment Exercise #1 (continued)

  d. a former Rhodes scholar, with multiple head
      injuries after an automobile accident, now scoring
      I.Q. 65 on the WAIS

  e. an acutely disturbed paranoid schizophrenic with
      a 4th grade education, on welfare, scoring I.Q. 65
      on the WAIS

  f. a 25-year-old married male, one son, 2nd grade
      education, with I.Q. 60, supporting family on
      full-time janitorial job.

    When you have completed this exercise to the best of
your ability, check your answers with those on the
following page.

Self-Assessment Exercise #1 - Feedback

1. Mental retardation is significantly subaverage intellectual functioning existing concurrently with deficits
   in adaptive behavior, and manifested during the developmental period.

2. None of the case vignettes, as stated, would deserve
   the designation of mental retardation for the following reasons:

   a. Although doing C-work, he is not behind in grade
      level--thus, scholastically performing marginally.

   b. I.Q. above 70.

   c. No mention of adaptive deficit.

   d. Former Rhodes scholar functioned well during
      developmental period. Condition exists after
      this period.

   e. This is the most complex item. The lowered per-
      formance on the I.Q. test is most likely the tem-
      porary result of an acute psychiatric disability.
      It would be important to test the person in a more
      stable state. The 4th grade education suggests
      there may have been a problem during the develop-
      mental period. However, one would need to examine
      why he stopped at 4th grade. If he scored below
      70 at the time of retesting when he was emotionally
      more stable, and if he left the 4th grade because
      of an inability to handle academic material, the
      criteria for mental retardation would be satisfied.

   f. Adaptive impairment is not present and the man is
      working full-time supporting his family.

     If your answers correspond closely with those above,
continue your reading; if not, please reread the preceding
section until you are confident you know the material.

CONCEPT OF I.Q.

An I.Q. is a quantitative summary of a person's general intellectual functioning as measured by a test of intelligence. To properly understand the meaning of I.Q. a knowledge of the distribution of I.Q.'s in the population is required. Like many other human characteristics, intelligence is assumed to be distributed according to the normal curve or distribution as presented in Figure I. Empirical studies have demonstrated that the distribution of actual I.Q.'s closely approximates this curve. It can be seen that the normal or "bell-shaped" curve is symmetrical, and that the percentage and breakdown of cases is the same both above and below the mean of the distribution (I.Q. 100). It should be noted that almost 70% of the population falls within plus or minus one standard deviation from the mean (I.Q.'s 85 to 115), and that in moving away from the mean in either direction there is a progressive reduction in the number of cases.

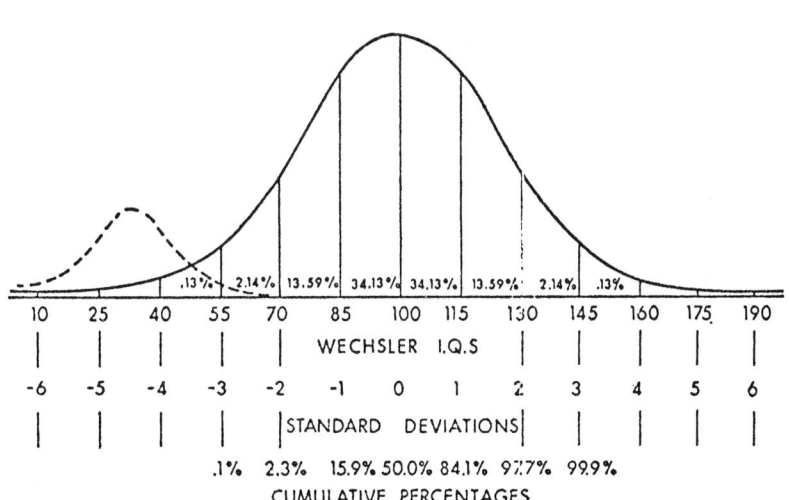

Figure I
A Distribution Curve of Intelligence

The figure gives the standard deviation units, the corresponding I.Q. scores for those units and the percentage of cases (rounded off) that fall within the various standard deviation units.

Generally, this "normal" distribution of intelligence
thus shows the number of cases that fall at each I.Q. score
level. Therein lies the real and only meaning of I.Q.
It is most easily understood where each I.Q. score level
has a corresponding percentile rank which indicates the
percentage of cases that fall above and below that point.
For instance, I.Q. of 100, which is the mean of the distribution of intelligence, indicates that 50% of the
population have I.Q.'s above this point and that 50% have
I.Q.'s below this point. Likewise, given an individual
with an I.Q. of 70, it can be determined from the shape
of this distribution that he or she is in the lowest 2%
of the population and that 98% of the population have
I.Q.'s greater than this individual.

Thus, an I.Q. is a relative measure which shows the
relative position of an individual (in terms of the normal
distribution of intelligence) compared to his age peers.
It is not an absolute measure of intellectual ability; it
is a relative indicator which compares an individual's
performance with that of his peers. In terms of mental
retardation, an I.Q. of 70 or lower does not indicate what
the person knows (how smart he is) in the same sense that
a yardstick measures how tall a person is. The only thing
that can be stated with certainty is that a person with
an I.Q. of 70 or below is in the bottom 2% of his age
group in terms of performance on an intelligence test.
Knowing that, one can then make probabilistic statements
about the kinds of abilities the person has or does not
have based on test content and experience with people of
similar low scores.

While the theoretical normal distribution of intelligence indicates that approximately 2% of the population
have I.Q.'s of 70 or below, actual sampling studies have
demonstrated that there are, in fact, many more cases than
theoretically expected in the extreme lower end of the
empirical distribution of intelligence. This situation is
graphically presented in exaggerated form by the dotted
line on the left tail of the normal distribution of intelligence in Figure I. The explanation for these empirical
findings is the presence of severe pathological conditions
that have pronounced effects on the normal expression of
intelligence. This is also the reason why the traditional
prevalent estimate of mental retardation is "around 3%."

Such data have led to a useful conceptual distinction
concerning the etiology of mental retardation. Persons in
the I.Q. range 0 to 50 constitute a group wherein mental
retardation is usually a concomitant symptom of a disordered
nervous system. Both the structural (organic) and functional (behavior impairment) reactions are manifest. Persons in the upper ranges of mental retardation (I.Q.'s 50
to 70) exhibit no obvious pathological condition and are
said to have only a functional reaction. They are considered to be either persons whose I.Q.'s are normal expressions of the distribution of intelligence or persons
whose potential intellectual expression has been hampered
by adverse sociocultural factors. Of course, there is

overlap between the two groups, i.e., some persons in the
0 to 50 range have no evident organic pathology and some
in the 50 to 70 range do. Nevertheless, there appears to
be two groups or kinds of mental retardation that are
conceptually distinguishable. The presence or absence of
neuropathology has obvious implications for treatment
possibilities and prognosis.

A final important feature about the distribution of
intelligence that needs to be emphasized is that 16% of
the population have I.Q.'s of 85 or below. (In the
United States population of 240,000,000 people, this would
amount to approximately 38 million people). The extent
of the problem as well as its implications for the practicing profession should be obvious.

Now complete Self-Assessment Exercise #2 on the
following page.

Self-Assessment Exercise #2

1. Define I.Q.

2. For each of the items below, designate whether it is true or false.

a. Theoretically one would expect a greater number of mentally retarded people with an I.Q. between 0 to 50 than 50 to 70.

True_____ False_____

b. I.Q. refers to the absolute level of intellectual capacity that a person possesses.

True_____ False_____

c. There is a high probability of neurological problems in the profound and severely retarded.

True_____ False_____

d. Approximately 70% of the population have I.Q.'s of 100 or above.

True_____ False_____

e. There are more people with I.Q.'s between 70 and 85 than all of the mentally retarded put together (I.Q. 0-70).

True_____ False_____

f. Neurological damage accounts for the greatest number of mentally retarded persons.

True_____ False_____

g. There are more mentally retarded persons than would be expected on the basis of the normal curve.

True_____ False_____

When you have completed this exercise to the best
of your ability, check your answers with those on the
following page.

Self-Assessment Exercise #2 - Feedback

1. An I.Q. (intelligence quotient) is a quantitative
    summary of an individual's general intellectual
    functioning as measured by an intelligence test.

2. a. False - There are more individuals with an I.Q.
        of 50 to 70 than 0 to 50 (see Figure I).

    b. False - An I.Q. states a _relative_ not an absolute
        level of intellectual capacity.

    c. True - There is a higher incidence of neurological
        problems among the profound and severely retarded
        individuals.

    d. False - Approximately 50% of the population has an
        I.Q. of 100 and above (see Figure I).

    e. True - There are more persons with I.Q.'s between
        70 and 85 than all of the combined mentally
        retarded (see Figure I).

    f. False - Manifest neuropathology is _not_ the main
        etiological factor for the majority of cases of
        mental retardation.

    g. True - There are more mentally retarded individuals
        than would be expected on the basis of the normal
        curve. The explanation for this phenomenon is
        the greater incidence of severe pathological
        conditions which affect intelligence.

        If your answers correspond closely with those above,
continue your reading; if not, please reread the preceding
section until you are confident you know the material.

THE ASSESSMENT OF ADAPTIVE IMPAIRMENT
        Manifest deficits in adaptive behavior, in addition
to an I.Q. of 70 or less, must be present to satisfy the
criteria for mental retardation. In general, adaptive
behavior refers to the individual's effectiveness in maintaining himself independently and in meeting the demands
of his environment. Since these demands vary with the
age of the individual, different criteria are applied at
the various age levels. There is an expectation for
increasing independence, self-mastery, and conformance to
societal demands and conventions as the person progresses
from one developmental stage to the next.
        During infancy and early childhood, the focus is on
the development of sensory-motor (crawling, walking,
running, eye-hand coordination, etc.), communication (receptive and expressive language), self-help (eating,
dressing, personal grooming and hygiene), and socializa-
tion (ability to deal and interact with adults and peers)
skills. Deficits in the "maturational" process or lags in
the appearance of developmental milestones constitute
evidence for an adaptive impairment at this age level.
        During later childhood and early adolescence, the
focus for adaptive behavior centers primarily on academic
pursuits, "learning process" and social skills. Difficulty in school, low achievement levels, and being "behind"
one or more grade levels are signs of potential adaptive
impairments. In addition to academic pursuits, the person
in this age group should be exhibiting the development of
more sophisticated social skills (e.g., participation in
group activities and the development of meaningful interpersonal relationships). Deficits in this area could also
suggest retardation.
        During late adolescence and adult life, the primary
focus is on the fulfillment of vocational and social
responsibilities and performances. The ability to obtain
and maintain employment, to handle financial matters with
some judgment and foresight, to meet the practical requirements of daily living, to develop close interpersonal
relationships, and to be cognizant of and abide by con-
ventional social mores are areas of particular concern.
In short, the ability of the person to conform to standards of the community and maintain an independent existence
is assessed and if deficits are found, mental retardation
should be suspected.
        Deficits in many of these areas can of course occur
for many reasons, particularly at the adult level (e.g.,
deficits associated with situational and psychiatric problems). As such, the deficits themselves do not indicate
mental retardation. It is only when these deficits occur
in a person with an I.Q. below 70 that they become criteria
for mental retardation. At that point, the adaptive impairments are considered to be the result and indication
of serious intellectual limitations.

        Now complete Self-Assessment Exercise #3 on the
following page.

Self-Assessment Exercise #3

1. List two major criteria for assessing adaptive impairments in each of the following three age levels:

   a. infancy and early childhood

   b. later childhood and early adolescence

   c. late adolescence and adulthood

When you have completed this exercise to the best of your ability, check your answers with those on the following page.

Self-Assessment Exercise #3 - Feedback

1. The criteria for assessing adaptive impairments for
   various age levels are:

   a. infancy and early childhood

      (1) lag in developmental milestones (standing,
          walking, talking, etc.)
      (2) deficits in areas of sensory-motor, communi-
          cation, self-help, and socialization skills

   b. later childhood and early adolescence

      (1) deficits in the "learning process" and
          academic pursuits
      (2) poor social skills relative to peers

   c. later adolescence and adulthood

      (1) inability to maintain self independently--
          have a job, support self, handle practical
          affairs of living
      (2) problems in conformance to societal standards,
          e.g., personal hygiene, social appropriateness

    If your answers correspond closely with those above,
continue your reading; if not, please reread the preceding
section until you are confident you know the material.

LEVELS OF MENTAL RETARDATION
    It is useful to categorize degrees of mental retarda-
tion according to its severity. Each of the four generally
accepted levels of retardation, i.e., profound, severe,
moderate and mild, imply a different prognosis and
management approach.
    Profoundly retarded persons upon becoming an adult
have an estimated mental age of three years and eight
months or lower. The probability of concomitant neurological damage is extremely high in this group, as well as
the presence of other physical handicaps. Many of them
are nonambulatory or restricted in their ability to move
about. If they do ambulate, it is often with considerable
awkwardness, a characteristic that tends to pervade all
of their movements. Many possess no speech, although some
can verbalize a few words. However, they can learn to
respond to simple verbal commands and recognize familiar
objects and persons. Until recently, most of these persons were unable to feed and toilet themselves. The
emerging use of "behavior modification" procedures has
been effective in increasing the number who have such
skills. Little learning beyond simple motor tasks is
possible, and they are essentially unable to protect and
care for themselves. Total supervision is required for
this group. The mortality rate tends to be high.
    Severely retarded persons have a mental age roughly
between three years and nine months to six years at adulthood. Although neurologic damage is common in this group,
they are more apt to be ambulatory than the profoundly
retarded. Also, unlike the case with profound retardation,
special training is effective in teaching these persons
to talk minimally and care for simple personal needs.
Academic training, however, is not effective. The chief
focus of training is on self-care skills, but little independent behavior occurs. These individuals need constant supervision and care.
    The moderately retarded adult has an approximate
mental age from six years and one month to eight years and
five months. Although the chief focus of training with
this group is still self-care, some of these individuals
do maintain full-time jobs and many others have part-time
or odd jobs. The majority do become fairly proficient in
self-care skills such as dressing, toileting, eating, etc.
The moderately retarded adult is roughly intellectually
equivalent to normal second or third grade children. Very
few of these persons marry or become independent; many
continue to live with their families. They have few
friends of their own. Any employment they obtain is usually
of a repetitive, unskilled nature, and often in a sheltered
setting where income is not dependent on production. Although possessing many skills, they are not capable of an
independent existence.
    Adults functioning in the mild range of mental re-
tardation typically have mental ages ranging from about
eight years and six months to ten years and ten months.

They are frequently able to maintain themselves in laboring positions, but often need supervision in social and financial affairs. Typically they have mastered only a fourth or fifth grade level of school work, and are comparable intellectually to a child in elementary school. They must be considered very vulnerable to occupational displacement by automation and economic factors. They are often said to be "the last hired and first fired." In our culture, mildly retarded women are more capable than men of successful marriage since the homemaking and social skills required of them are less demanding than the skills for public work required of men. Motor slowness and lack of reading skills make competitive employment an ever-increasing difficulty for them. Although capable of independent living in many respects, they require the assistance of "benefactors" who run interference for them in certain problematic situations. Thus, in general, they cannot be considered to be fully independent and self-sufficient.

Table I summarizes the range of I.Q. scores and standard deviation values for the four levels of mental retardation presented.

TABLE I

LEVELS OF MENTAL RETARDATION

Degree of Deficiency	I.Q. Range on WISC-R or WAIS	Range in Standard Deviation Values
Mild	55 - 69	-2.01 to -3.00
Moderate	40 - 54	-3.01 to -4.00
Severe	25 - 39	-4.01 to -5.00
Profound	0 - 25	-5.00

Now complete Self-Assessment Exercise #4 on the following page.

Self-Assessment Exercise #4

For each of the items in Column A, list the levels of mental retardation from Column B that apply. Any letter can be used more than once and each item may have more than one answer.

	COLUMN A	COLUMN B
1.	I.Q. below 20	A = Profound
2.	neurological damage often present	B = Severe
3.	may hold laboring jobs	C = Moderate
4.	can benefit from academic training	D = Mild
5.	can become proficient in self-help skills	
6.	can live fairly independent existence with minimal help	
7.	will need constant supervision and care	
8.	unlikely to marry	
9.	can carry on simple conversation	
10.	often nonambulatory	
11.	able to read and write at approximate 4th grade level	
12.	possess little or no speech	

When you have completed this exercise to the best of your ability, check your answers with those on the following page.

Self-Assessment Exercise #4 - Feedback

	COLUMN A	COLUMN B

COLUMN A

__A_1.   I.Q. below 20

_AB_2.   neurological damage
often present

_CD_3.   may hold laboring jobs

_CD_4.   can benefit from
academic training

_CD_5.   can become proficient
in self-help skills

__D_6.   can live fairly inde-
pendent existence
with minimal help

_AB_7.   will need constant
supervision and care

ABC_8.   unlikely to marry

_CD_9.   can carry on simple
conversation

_A_10.   often nonambulatory

_D_11.   able to read and
write at approximate
4th grade level

_A_12.   possess little or no
speech

COLUMN B

A = Profound

B = Severe

C = Moderate

D = Mild

If your answers correspond closely with those above,
continue your reading; if not, please reread the preceding
section until you are confident you know the material.

METHODS OF ASSESSING INTELLIGENCE

The average professional will rarely encounter persons of profound, severe, and low moderate mental retardation (I.Q.'s 0 to 50). These individuals will usually be taken care of by private and public institutions and social welfare agencies. When such persons are encountered, the degree of deficit is so obvious that the diagnosis is easy to make. It is the milder forms of mental retardation (I.Q.'s 50 to 70), especially the upper end of that range, that pose diagnostic problems.

When the presence of mental retardation is suspected, one must substantiate the diagnosis by utilizing the criteria included in the definition of mental retardation. In other words, the person's general intellectual function- ing as well as impairments in adaptive behavior must be considered.

Before presenting some assessment suggestions, another important issue must be considered. People in the mild range of retardation (I.Q.'s 50 to 70) are often acutely aware of their intellectual and adaptive impairments. They will go to great lengths to prevent the exposure of such deficiencies. This "defensive" reaction is quite understandable given the importance of intelligence to one's social status in our culture. The attempt to hide their retardation is a reasonable adaptation to a society that places high value on competencies they do not possess. In dealing with such a sensitive matter, tactfulness is of crucial importance. The methods suggested below utilize a rather direct approach and will need modification when examining someone who is very sensitive to such probing.

In tests of intelligence, scores on vocabulary sub- tests typically correlate the highest with the total test score. Accordingly, the interviewer should pay attention to vocabulary usage. Also, if a person's abstract thinking is at a simple, concrete (literal) level, it is important to determine whether he can deal with more complex mater- ial. This can be assessed in a direct manner by asking the person to give the meaning of some proverbs, such as: "Barking dogs seldom bite."

Keep in mind that even intelligent people use the face-saving nod and "Yes, I see," which is often hastily accepted as understanding. The mildly retarded are well aware of the advantages of such devices. Another method is to ask the person to read a magazine aloud and evaluate his comprehension (many people possess the mechanics of reading but fail to comprehend). A more indirect approach is to ask them to fill out some "forms" that would allow you to appraise their reading, writing, and comprehension skills. The person's fund of general information can be assessed by casually talking about current events and examining the breadth and depth of their knowledge about them.

The remaining suggestions relate both to intelligence and adaptive behavior. An excellent way of tapping a per- son's general functioning level is to examine their

educational history. For persons who admit to not gradu-
ating from high school, the reasons for leaving should be
explored. Statements such as, "I didn't like it; I was
kicked out for always fighting" and "I had to go to work"
cannot be accepted at face value. If the person states
he has graduated, determine whether he ever attended
special classes. If the diagnosis is still unclear, ask
detailed questions about the kinds of courses taken, the
ones liked and disliked, and the grades received. ("I got
C's and D's because I didn't like the course and wouldn't
study" needs further probing; "I took geography" leads to
questions about what he actually did in the course.)

Another way of assessing intelligence and adaptive
behavior is to inquire about the occupational history.
The types of jobs held, vocational skills, number of job
changes, promotions, layoffs, firing, etc., should be
explored.

Another area for examination is facility in handling
concepts of time and money. If the patient states, "I
graduated a long time ago" ask him to specify the exact
year or length of time since the event. Inquiry about
dates or time intervals for significant life events (e.g.,
deaths in family, illnesses, marriage, etc.) can be revealing. Questions about time raise an important interviewing caution with the mildly retarded. Responses such
as, "I don't remember" often lead the interviewer to
present the question in a multiple choice format (e.g.,
"Have you had these headaches for a month, a week, or
a couple of days?"). Persons with an impaired concept of
time will gladly pick one of the alternatives with little
concern for its correctness. The ability to make change
and use money should also be assessed. Ask the person to
change a half dollar or help in counting some assorted
coins. It is also instructive to see if the person knows
the approximate cost of such articles as a television set,
new car, gallon of milk, suit, and underwear.

There is one final caution that should be noted. If
the examination suggests serious intellectual deficit,
further assistance for the person may be warranted. In
that event, a referral to a mental health or rehabilita-
tion clinic is sometimes more desirable than one to a clinic
specifically designed for managing mental retardation. Such
clinics are often the last place these people want to go.
Communicate your impressions to the agency and allow them
to make the necessary arrangements.

Now complete Self-Assessment Exercise #5 on the
following page.

Self-Assessment Exercise #5

List six methods of assessing level of intellectual and adaptive functioning.

1.

2.

3.

4.

5.

6.

When you have completed this exercise to the best of your ability, check your answers with those on the following page.

Self-Assessment Exercise #5 - Feedback

Six methods of assessing level of intellectual and adaptive functioning are:

1. note vocabulary usage

2. test the abstract thinking (e.g., interpretation of proverbs)

3. test the ability to read, write and comprehend

4. evaluate the educational history

5. evaluate the occupational history

6. test the person's facility with time and money concepts

If your answers correspond closely with those above, continue your reading; if not, please reread the preceding section until you are confident you know the material.

MENTAL STATUS FINDINGS

In addition to intellectual and adaptive impairments, a mentally retarded person <u>can</u> manifest the symptomology associated with any other psychiatric disorder (psychosis, neurosis, etc.) presented in this text. To the extent that such is the case, the mental status examination would be similar to the M.S.E. for persons of normal intelligence who manifest the same psychiatric syndrome. However, there are some characteristics that are unique to mental retardation. These distinguishing features are best highlighted by comparing them to the results of a mental status examination for a person who is not mentally retarded.

The mental status examination categories of Appearance, Behavior, Feeling and Perception would be essentially the same as for persons of normal intelligence. Any abnormalities in these areas would reflect additional psychiatric impairments rather than anything inherent in the nature of mental retardation. The one possible exception would be in the "Behavior" category describing the quality of speech. A higher incidence of speech defects is found and the general quality of speech is somewhat lower. These differences would not be especially striking.

The category wherein major differences do occur is <u>Thinking</u>. By definition, the person has impaired intelligence and would <u>perform poorly on tasks of abstract thinking</u> (e.g., interpretation of proverbs) and <u>calculation</u>. There may be some disorientation to time in some of the mildly retarded, and many would have difficulty with precise time intervals and dates. Mildly retarded persons are not generally introspective and have <u>deficiencies in insight</u>. Those demonstrating some insight would do so in a limited way, lacking in sophistication. <u>Judgment</u> is not so much impaired as it is "limited" in decision making for more complex situations. Memory for specific events, both recent and remote, would be generally adequate, although there may be some difficulty in processing the time intervals involved. <u>Thought content may often be impoverished</u>, simple, and literal. Although associational disturbances are not inherent to mental retardation, the mildly retarded occasionally give this impression. Closer examination indicates that some of their supposedly rambling responses are actually an attempt to answer, just for the sake of answering, questions that are too complex for their comprehension. The answers given are often absurdly concrete or just nonsensical. They do not, however, indicate a thought disorder.

In summary, the deficits revealed in a mental status examination are primarily limited to areas of the "Thinking" category. The clinical impression one receives from the mildly retarded consists of limited intellectual ability, concrete thinking, impoverished thought content and a certain naivete.

Now complete Self Assessment Exercise #6 on the following page.

Self-Assessment Exercise #6

Place an "X" in front of the following mental status findings that are typically found with the mildly mentally retarded.

_____a.   low intelligence

_____b.   depression

_____c.   auditory hallucinations

_____d.   concrete (literal) thinking

_____e.   poor remote memory

_____f.   shabby appearance

_____g.   persistent associational disturbance

_____h.   labile affect

_____i.   impaired calculation ability

_____j.   impaired level of consciousness

_____k.   impaired abstract thinking

_____l.   impaired insight

_____m.   delusional thinking

When you have completed this exercise to the best of your ability, check your answers with those on the following page.

Self-Assessment Exercise #6 - Feedback

Mental status findings typical of an individual with mild retardation are:

a. low intelligence

d. concrete (literal) thinking

i. impaired calculation ability

k. impaired abstract thinking

1. impaired insight

If your answers correspond closely with those above, continue your reading; if not, please reread the preceding section until you are confident you know the material.

SUMMARY
The purpose of this chapter is to highlight the importance of low intelligence as a factor in clinical practice, both in terms of the number of people involved and the resulting problems and implications of their intellectual limitations. The pervasiveness of problematic low intelligence is graphically portrayed by the distribution of I.Q.'s in the general population. A diagnosis of mental retardation can only be made when there are manifest adaptive impairments along with low tested intelligence. The methods by which a professional might confirm a suspected intellectual deficit are presented. A general description of the four levels of mental retardation and the mental status examination findings of mildly retarded persons are also included. The mildly retarded and those of borderline intelligence are the most difficult to detect. Detection is only possible when the professional is aware of such a possibility and employs methods similar to the ones suggested in his overall clinical assessment.

REFERENCES

Bosco, J. J., Robin, S. S. (eds.), The Hyperactive Child and Stimulant Drugs, Chicago: University Press, 1977.

Crandall, B. F., "Genetic Disorders and Mental Retardation," J. Am. Acad. Child Psychiat, 16:88-108, Winter 1977.

Cruickshank, W. M., "Myths and Realities in Learning Disabilities," J. Learning Disabil., 10:51-58, January 1977.

Forness, S. R., "Educational Therapy," in (Cantwell and Tanguay, editors), Clinical Child Psychiatry, New York: Spectrum, 1979.

Grossman, H. D., Manual on Terminology and Classification in Mental Retardation, 1973 Revision, American Association on Mental Deficiency, Baltimore: Garamond/Pridemark Press, 1973.

Johnson, S. W., Morasky, R. L., Learning Disabilities, Boston: Allyn and Bacon, 1977.

MacMillan, D., Forness, S. R., "Applied Operant Programs in Mental Retardation," Monographs of the American Association on Mental Deficiency, No. 4, Washington, D. C.: American Association on Mental Deficiency, 1979.

MacMillan, D., Mental Retardation in School and Society, Boston: Little, Brown, 1977.

Maloney, M. P., Ward, M. P., Mental Retardation and Modern Society, New York: Oxford University Press, 1979.

Robinson, N. M., Robinson, H. B., The Mentally Retarded Child: A Psychological Approach, New York: McGraw-Hill Book Company, 1976.

Spring, C., Sandoval, J., "Food Additives and Hyperkinesis: Critical Evaluation of the Evidence," J. Learning Disabil., 9:560-569, November 1976.

Chapter 8

Substance Use Disorders
C. Warner Johnson

During the past decade there has occurred an unprece-
dented increase in the abuse of chemical intoxicants by
the American public to the extent that drug and alcohol
dependency presently constitutes a major health problem.
It is one of the roles of a health care professional to
diagnose and treat whatever disorders accompany the misuse
of drugs.

LEARNING OBJECTIVES
By the time you complete the material in this chapter
you should be able to:

1. Correctly define the following terms:

    physical dependence
    psychological dependence
    tolerance
    withdrawal (abstinence) syndrome
    Substance Use Disorder

2. List four or more behavioral traits common to
    individuals who are prone to develop drug or
    alcohol dependency.

3. List four or more "reasons" why individuals use
    drugs or alcohol.

4. List and briefly characterize four different
    theories of etiology for physical drug dependency.

5. List the M.S.E. findings characteristic of a mild
    drug induced intoxication.

6. List:

   a. common physical problems associated with long-term use, if any
   b. common psychological sequelae to periodic or continuous use
   c. potential for developing psychic dependency
   d. potential for developing physical dependency
   e. potential for developing a withdrawal (abstinence) syndrome

For each of the following substances:

alcohol
barbiturates
opiates
cocaine
marijuana
hallucinogens (L.S.D., Peyote, mescaline, etc.)
amphetamines
inhaled solvents

By the conclusion of this chapter and with supervised clinical experience you should be able to:

1. Accurately observe and record a patient's behavior within each of the M.S.E. behavior descriptors.

2. Determine whether drug dependency is present in a patient, given necessary M.S.E. behavior descriptors.

3. Indicate the history and M.S.E. findings which enabled you to make a diagnosis

OVERVIEW

So much has been said about substance (drug) abuse that many persons have either overreacted to the problem or closed their minds to it. But the problem is a very major one. Many of the complications of drug use rank among the most serious diseases encountered. Indeed, serum hepatitis, endocarditis, psychosis and organic brain disorders are not rare among drug abusers. It is likely that all therapists, regardless of their professional discipline, will be called upon to evaluate persons with drug related disorders.

It is of special importance for physicians to prescribe with care medications which may produce drug dependency in their patients. Clinicians should watch carefully for personality traits of patients which may make them particularly susceptible to drug abuse, because approximately five percent of narcotic addition is physician induced.

Present information shows that drug and alcohol abuse is no longer a problem confined to the ghettos, the poor or the "depraved." Drug dependency is increasingly prevalent among all ethnic, economic and social groups, especially the younger segments of the population. The deleterious effect of drugs on society and on the emotional and physical health of thousands has reached awesome proportions. Although the communication media have emphasized repeatedly the evils of heroin, marijuana and barbiturates, by far the most serious drug problem in the United States is that of alcohol abuse. In this chapter statements about drug abuse also apply to alcohol.

BASIC DEFINITIONS

In dealing with any complex disorder it is important that communications about it are accurate and understandable by others. Therefore, some definitions of commonly used terms referring to drug dependency are in order.

In the context of this chapter a substance will refer to any chemical which, if taken internally and because of its properties, may affect perception, feeling, behavior and physical functioning. It is more meaningful to use newer terms to describe drug-related behavior than the traditional labels of drug "addiction" and or "habituation." The term drug dependence implies a state of physical and/or psychic need resulting from a continuous or periodic use of drugs. Physical dependence (addiction) implies that actual physiological changes have occurred within the person as a consequence of drug use. Tolerance is the need for increased amounts of a drug in order to produce effects formerly brought about by smaller doses. Tolerance is characteristic of drugs causing physical dependency. However, not all drugs to which a tolerance develops cause physical dependency. When tolerance occurs as the drug is stopped, varying degrees and types of physical disturbances result. These symptoms comprise a withdrawal (abstinence) syndrome. The nature and severity of the symptoms depend upon the amount and type of drug taken.

Psychological dependence (habituation) refers to the impelling need to reexperience the pleasing and satisfying psychological state which accompanies the use of certain drugs. This type of dependence can be intensely felt and is often the most influential reinforcement leading to repetitive (and compulsive) use of the substance. Either physical or psychological dependence can develop without the other being present, or they may occur simultaneously.

A Substance Use Disorder is the new, DSM-III diagnosis designating the presence of a persistent drug problem. For this diagnosis to be used, a person must have used the substance (drugs or alcohol) for longer than one month which causes serious life consequences such as significantly impaired personal relationships, health or daily functioning and/or be psychologically dependent on the intoxicant. The diagnosis can be refined further by indicating the substance(s) involved and whether dependence (physical) has developed.

Now complete Self-Assessment Exercise #1 on the following page.

Self-Assessment Exercise #1

In your own words, define the following terms:

1. substance

2. Substance Use Disorder

3. physical dependence (addiction)

4. psychological dependence (habituation)

5. tolerance

6. withdrawal (abstinence) syndrome

When you have completed this exercise to the best of your ability, check your answers with those on the following page.

Self-Assessment Exercise #1 - Feedback

1. substance--any chemical which taken internally
    may affect a person's perception, feeling,
    behavior and physical functioning.

2. Substance Use Disorder--persistent substance
    taking behavior which lasts longer than one
    month and results in significant consequences
    such as impairment of relationships, health and
    daily functioning and is associated with psycho-
    logical dependency.

3. physical dependence (addiction)--this designation
    implies that physiological changes have resulted
    from drug use which require the continued ad-
    ministration of the drug in order to avoid
    a physical disturbance.

4. psychological dependence (habituation)--the
    impelling need to reexperience the satisfying
    psychological state which accompanies drug use.

5. tolerance--the need for increased doses of a drug
    in order to produce effects formerly brought
    about by smaller doses.

6. withdrawal (abstinence) syndrome--the symptoms
    resulting when the drug that has produced physical
    dependence is withdrawn.

    If your answers correspond closely with those above,
please continue reading; if not, please reread the preceding
section until you are confident you know the material.

THE DYNAMICS OF DRUG USE

Drug and alcohol dependency involve a complex interaction of motivations and behaviors. In order to understand better the drug-dependent person, it is necessary
to consider such things as the meaning and ends served (for
both society and the individual) by drug use, the particular effects (physical and psychic) of a particular drug
and the patterns and frequency of administration. Additional factors are the physical and psychological state of
the drug user, the speed of administration and the anticipated effects. Certainly then, no stereotyped generalizations about etiology or treatment will suffice when considering a particular drug dependent individual. However,
some general statements can be made about drug abusers as
a group.

TRAITS COMMON TO DRUG ABUSERS

Drug dependency occurs in all ethnic, economic and
cultural groups. Yet certain personality traits, singly
or in combination are found frequently in drug-dependent
persons. Physicians should be alert to these characteristics in patients for whom narcotics or sedatives are
prescribed. In many ways drug dependent individuals seem
emotionally immature, and are usually excessively dependent. They tend to be impulsive and have little ability
to tolerate tension or delay gratification. Rising tension
may lead to poorly thought-out behavior without regard to
the consequences. These persons have a low tolerance for
frustration and easily become discouraged. They are less
able than other persons to tolerate unpleasant feelings
such as pain, guilt or grief. It is especially difficult
for these individuals to solve problems by facing them,
or seek to change their unpleasant reality through con-
structive action. A more common response to problems is
to "get away," or act as if the trouble did not exist
(denial).

PERSONAL REASONS FOR DRUG ABUSE

Each drug produces unique physical and emotional
effects and carries special meanings for the user and
society. The selection of a "drug of choice" by the drug-
dependent person is rarely a fortuitous event and often
reflects important motivations. It is possible to get
a sense of the needs of the drug user by examining the
effects produced by the drug selected. Even the method
and attendant rituals of administration have psychological
implications which should be considered. Morphine, for
example, reduces tension, anxiety and drives such as sex
and hunger. Cocaine and marijuana react to lower inhibitions but do not greatly affect drives. Amphetamines
decrease feelings of fatigue and depression and give an
illusion of increased mental and physical competance.
Alcohol and bartiturates both act to reduce inhibitions
initially, only to reduce drives later. Behavior that
does not fill a need is rarely continued. To persist,

behavior must be reinforced. Drug use is powerfully reinforced in at least two ways: it provides instantaneous
gratification, and it simultaneously reduces present or
anticipated psychic pain. This source of rapid pleasure
and relief from tension is in sharp contrast to most
other patterns of problem solving behavior that take time
to achieve. Drug caused feelings of pleasure originate
from a chemically induced enhancement of self-esteem,
a release of inhibitions and/or a flush of physical
relaxation. The reduction of emotional tensions provide
a relief from anxiety and a temporary dulling of reality
problems. For some deeply troubled individuals, existence without the beneficial effects of drugs may be difficult or even impossible. Successful treatment or a "cure"
is difficult to achieve since it requires giving up an
instant source of pleasure and relief from suffering.

GENERAL THEORIES OF DRUG DEPENDENCY
At least four different hypotheses concerning the
etiology of drug dependency have been proposed and they
may be present singly or in combination. An understanding
of these etiological considerations is useful when treating
drug-dependent persons. It should be noted that the
etiological factors presented can be closely interrelated.
The pharmacodynamic theory proposes that it is the
intrinsic effects of the drug acting upon the organism
which perpetuate drug dependency. The tendency for the
drug to inhibit or stimulate drives, to alter perception
or produce euphoria is considered the most significant
mechanism.
The psychodynamic hypothesis states that substance
dependent persons have experienced severe psychic trauma
during their formative years which has resulted in continuing emotional conflicts. The use of drugs helps to
alleviate these conflicts.
The physiological hypothesis affirms that the drug-
dependent persons have an inborn or acquired metabolic
deficit which makes them more psychically and/or physically susceptible to beginning and maintaining drug use.
For learning theorists the conditioning aspects of
drug-taking behavior is of great importance. It is believed that the immediate tension relief and feelings of
gratification following the use of drugs provide a powerful incentive (reinforcement) to repeat the behavior.

Now complete Self-Assessment Exercise #2 on the
following page.

Self-Assessment Exercise #2

1. List four or more behavioral traits common to individuals who are prone to develop drug dependency.

2. List four or more personal reasons why an individual uses drugs.

3. List and characterize briefly the four hypotheses proposing an etiology of drug dependency.

When you have completed this exercise to the best of your ability, check your answers with those on the following page.

Self-Assessment Exercise #2 - Feedback

1. The traits of an individual prone to develop drug
    dependency are:

    emotional immaturity
    excessive dependency
    impulsiveness
    impaired capacity to tolerate tension
    impaired capacity to delay gratification
    low tolerance for frustration
    limited problem solving ability
    inability to tolerate painful or unpleasant
        feelings

2. The personal reasons why an individual uses drugs
    may be to:

    reduce psychic tension, anxiety, depression, etc.
    reduce drives--aggressive and sexual
    increase pleasure--euphoria, well being
    increase drives--sexual and aggressive
    avoid reality problems
    reduce inhibitions

3. The four hypotheses proposing an etiology for drug
    dependency are:

    a. pharmacodynamic - the basic effects of the drug
        upon the organism
    b. psychodynamic - to relieve psychic conflicts
    c. physiological - inborn and/or acquired metabolic
        defects
    d. conditioning - strong reinforcement leads to
        repetition of drug taking behavior

    If your answers correspond closely with those above,
please continue reading; if not, please reread the preceding section until you are confident you know the
material.

M.S.E. FINDINGS OF MILD DRUG INDUCED INTOXICATION
     The mental status findings typical of a moderate to
severe Organic Mental Disorder can be readily detected
and include impairment of recent memory, disorientation,
impairment of intellectual functioning (the ability to
perform calculations or think abstractly), compromised
judgment and emotional lability.
     It is also useful to identify in drug users the
presence of intoxication when the presenting signs may be
much less obvious. Intoxicated persons may show decreased
coordination, indistinct speech, fine tremors, and an un-
steadiness of gait and balance. Feelings of depression,
euphoria, or irritability often are labile and intense
and intoxicated persons are inclined to react more emotionally. Perception is rarely disordered. Intellectual
functioning is impaired in proportion to the amount and
type of medication taken. Stimulants usually accelerate
the speed of thought while depressants slow down the
thinking processes. In both cases the ability to think
clearly and abstractly is impaired. Memory and orientation usually remain intact while judgment may be compromised.
Attention span and the ability to concentrate are often
impaired.

     Now complete Self-Assessment Exercise #3 on the
following page.

Self-Assessment Exercise #3

1. List the M.S.E. findings characteristic of a <u>mild</u>
    drug induced intoxication.

BEHAVIOR:

FEELING (AFFECT
AND MOOD:

PERCEPTION:

THINKING:

When you have completed this exercise to the best of your ability, check your answers with those on the following page.

Self-Assessment Exercise #3 - Feedback

1. M.S.E. findings characteristic of a <u>mild</u> drug induced
    intoxication are:

BEHAVIOR: decreased coordination and balance,
                             indistinct speech, fine tremors,
                             unsteady gait

FEELING (AFFECT   exaggerated--euphoria, irritability,
AND MOOD)   depression, lability

PERCEPTION: little change except with
                             hallucinogens in which case
                             illusions or hallucinations
                             may occur

THINKING: generalized impairment of:
                                intellectual functioning
                                abstract thinking
                                attention span
                                concentration
                                judgment
                                memory and orientation intact

If your answers correspond closely with those above,
please continue reading; if not, please reread the preceding section until you are confident you know the
material.

GENERAL CHARACTERISTICS OF SPECIFIC DRUG DEPENDENCIES

It is well for health care professionals to be familiar with the characteristic effects of different types of drugs. We will not present information about the most commonly used intoxicants.

Alcohol

Alcohol is by far the most commonly used cerebral intoxicant, and excessive alcohol intake among teen-agers greatly surpasses their use of all other drugs combined. For all age groups there is more personal disability and economic loss due to alcohol abuse than from all other intoxicants. Paradoxically, alcohol remains a socially sanctioned intoxicant.

Psychological dependency of varying degrees may be readily established in susceptible persons. Some tolerance may occur and physical dependency develops when alcohol is ingested in large amounts over an extended period of time. In such situations, abstention may result in a severe withdrawal syndrome (withdrawal delirium), more commonly known as delirium tremens. A unique feature of alcohol dependency is that it may cause tissue pathology. Medical problems which are frequently associated with prolonged and excessive alcohol intake are cirrhosis, gastritis, pancreatitis, malnutrition and chronic organic brain disorders. While alcohol acts primarily as a central nervous system depressant, its initial effect is to reduce inhibitions. Depressive symptoms result within an hour. After consuming alcohol an individual is more likely to act out psychological conflict. After this brief release of inhibitions a depressant effect follows.

Barbiturates (and related sedatives)

In many respects dependency upon this group of drugs is comparable to that of alcohol. Psychological dependence is often quite strong, and if barbiturates are taken over an extended period of time, physical dependency and tolerance may also develop. Then the drug intake is reduced below a critical level, a withdrawal syndrome of severe proportions may cause grand mal seizures, mental confusion and delirium. Barbiturates and related sedatives are considered "downers;" that is, they cause relaxation, physical and psychological depression, a diminution of drives and in general act as central nervous system depressants. An overdose (O.D.) can lead to coma and respiratory arrest.

Opioids (morphine, Demerol, heroin, etc.)

These drugs are characterized by a marked degree of psychological dependence which is due to the profound euphoria and relief from physical and emotional tension which they produce. Early development of physical dependence occurs, the intensity of which corresponds to the dosage used. Tolerance to the drug usually develops rapidly and is also dose related. A withdrawal syndrome follows the cessation of the drug. Opioids rapidly reduce all physiological drives. The medical complications which commonly are associated with use of the opioides are serum hepatitis, endocarditis and thrombophlebitis. Respiratory depression is a serious complication associated with an overdose.

Cocaine

This drug produces a strong psychological dependence because of its euphoric and pleasurably stimulating effects. Its use may mask hunger and fatigue but tends to accentuate temporarily both sexual and aggressive drives. Tolerance may occur, but physical dependence or withdrawal syndrome do not. Repeated use of the drug may lead to unpredictable and assaultive behavior of psychotic proportions. The reasons for such aggressive behavior are unknown.

Cannabis (marijuana)

When taken in large quantities cannabis may produce a moderate to strong degree of psychological dependence, but there is no evidence that either tolerance or physical dependence develops, even with prolonged use. There is little tendency to increase the amount taken. Cannabis generally produces feelings of mild euphoria and well-being. Perceptual disturbances may occur. Marijuana usage is widespread and second only to that of alcohol in the United States. There is growing scientific evidence that significant physical and psychological changes may occur secondary to regular use. Marijuana does not seem to be the benign intoxicant which it was once thought to be.

Hallucinogens (L.S.D., mescaline, peyote, P.C.P., etc.)

Individuals who use drugs of this group typically do so periodically rather than continuously. Psychological dependence is variable and no physical dependence or abstinence syndrome usually occurs. Tolerance to these drugs varies and is unpredictable. Marked changes in the intensity and quality of perceptual sensations and feelings are common. Vivid hallucinations may be accompanied by dramatic and unpredictable shifts of feeling tone and disordered behavior. P.C.P. usage, in particular frequently causes grossly inappropriate and markedly assaultive behavior. Generally, all thinking processes and intellectual functioning are impaired to some degree. Delusions of a grandiose or paranoid type are common but transient. Occasionally, "bad trips" may be experienced, during which great anxiety occurs and is associated with frightening delusions and hallucinations. "Flashbacks" or recurring bad trips may begin long after the drug is stopped. Functional psychoses, which are not always reversible with treatment, may be precipitated by the use of this class of drugs.

Amphetamines (benzadrine, methylphenidate, etc.)

Amphetamines and related drugs act primarily as central nervous system stimulants and cause feelings of

euphoria. Drugs from this class tend to decrease appetite,
reduce feelings of depression and fatigue, and provide
the user with a sense of increased energy and physical
and mental capability. Insomnia and physical restlessness are typically present. A variable degree of psychological dependence may occur. There is no significant
degree of physical dependence or withdrawal syndrome
associated with the persistent use of use of amphetamine-
like drugs. However, a state of depression and physical
exhaustion may follow discontinuance of the drug. Functional psychosis, particularly of a paranoid type, may
accompany persistent use of the drugs from this class.
Hypertension and cardiac arrhythmias are medical complications regularly associated with use of central nervous
system stimulants.

Solvents (inhalation of airplane glue, gasoline,
acetone. etc.)
    Varying degrees of psychological dependence may
occur with inhalation of various solvents, but no physical
dependence has been noted. Serious and irreversible
organic pathology involving the heart, brain, liver, and
kidneys are regularly found in individuals dependent upon
inhalation of solvents. Chronic brain damage is commonly
associated with the persistent inhalation of solvents.

    Now complete Self-Assessment Exercise #4, including
the case histories, on the following pages.

Self-Assessment Exercise #4

On the blank charts provided, for each of the drugs named, list:
a. the physical problems associated with the use of the drug
b. any psychological symptoms associated with the drug
c. the degree to which psychic dependence occurs
    +(least)   ++++(most)
d. the degree to which physical dependence occurs
    +(least)   ++++(most)
e. whether or not a withdrawal syndrome can occur

DRUG CLASS	PHYSICAL PROBLEMS	PSYCHOLOGICAL SYMPTOMS
ALCOHOL		
BARBITURATES		
OPIOIDS		
COCAINE		
MARIJUANA		
HALLUCINOGENS		
AMPHETAMINES		
INHALED SOLVENTS		

Self-Assessment Exercise #4 (continued)

PSYCHOLOGICAL DEPENDENCY	PHYSICAL DEPENDENCY	WITHDRAWAL SYNDROME

Self-Assessment Exercise #4 (continued)

CASE HISTORIES

1. A somewhat disheveled, middle-aged housewife is re-
    ferred for evaluation of depression and generalized
    weakness. During her workup she volunteers informa-
    tion that she has been consuming fifteen to twenty
    "reds (secobarbital) a day for over six months.

    From the following terms, check all that may have
    relevance to her case:

    a. physical dependence
    b. psychological dependence
    c. tolerance
    d. withdrawal syndrome

2. A young man is brought to your office for evalutaion.
    He appears to be very apprehensive and describes
    delusional beliefs and auditory hallucinations. He
    states that he had taken many drugs in the past, but
    has not used any for six to eight months.

    If his statements are true, and if his symptoms are
    drug related, which of the following might be responsible
    for his condition now?

    a. opioids
    b. hallucinogens (L.S.D., P.C.P., etc.)
    c. stimulants (amphetamines, cocaine)
    d. barbiturates

3. An 18-year-old man who regularly inhaled various sol-
    vents over a 3-year period was hospitalized for medical
    evaluation. Check all of the following items which
    would likely apply to his case:

    a. an abstinence syndrome
    b. he would likely show some evidence of an O.B.D.
    c. he would likely show some evidence of major
        organ system pathology

Self-Assessment Exercise #4 (continued)

4. A middle-aged man was admitted to the hospital for
    a suspected O.D. (overdose) of an undertermined type.
    He was comatose, did not respond to painful stimuli
    and had a depressed blood pressure and respiratory
    rate. Check one or more of the following drugs which
    are least likely to have caused the symptoms described:

    a. alcohol
    b. opioids
    c. barbiturates
    d. amphetamines
    e. hallucinogens
    f. cocaine

    When you have completed this exercise to the best of
your ability, check your answers with those on the
following page.

Self-Assessment Exercise #4 - Feedback

DRUG CLASS	PHYSICAL PROBLEMS	PSYCHOLOGICAL SYMPTOMS
ALCOHOL	cirrhosis, gastritis, malnutrition	organic brain disorder; intoxication
BARBITURATES	seizures, delirium, respiratory depression	depression
OPIOIDS	thrombophlebitis, endocarditis, respiratory depression,hepatitis	depression
COCAINE	few	unpredictable behavior; hostility
MARIJUANA	none	few
HALLUCINOGENS	none	psychosis
AMPHETAMINES	insomnia, hypertension arrhythmias	paranoid psychosis
INHALED SOLVENTS	generalized organ system damage	chronic organic mental disorder

Self-Assessment Exercise #4 - Feedback (continued)

PSYCHOLOGICAL DEPENDENCY	PHYSICAL DEPENDENCY	WITHDRAWAL SYNDROME
+ to ++++	+	Yes
+ to ++++	+ to ++++	Yes
++++	++++	Yes
++++	None	None
+ to ++	None	None
+ to ++++	None	None
+ to ++++	None	None
+ to ++++	None	None

Self-Assessment Exercise #4 - Feedback (continued)

CASE HISTORIES

1. The woman is very likely to have both a physical
    and psychological dependence on secobarbital. She
    is physically dependent and has developed a tolerance
    to the drug. An abrupt cessation of the drug will
    result in a withdrawal syndrome.

    Items a, b, c, and d should have been checked.

2. He is likely experiencing a "flashback" which is
    typical of hallucinogen usage.

    Item b, hallucinogens--especially L.S.D. or P.C.P.

3. The repeated inhalation of solvents often leads to an
    organic brain disorder and major organ system
    pathology.

    Items b and c should have been checked.

4. He shows evidence of a central nervous system de-
    pression. The drugs least likely to cause such
    findings are amphetamines, cocaine and hallucinogens.

    Items d, e, and f should have been checked.

        If your answers correspond closely with those above,
please continue reading; if not, please reread the
preceding section until you are confident you know the
material.

SUMMARY

One of this country's major health problems is that of drug and alcohol abuse. Health care professionals should maintain a high level of expertise on the subject of prevention, early diagnosis and treatment of all types of drug problems. The physical and psychological manifestations of several classes of drugs have been presented as an introduction to this widespread and costly problem.

REFERENCES

Goodwin, D., Guze, S., Psychiatric Diagnosis: 2nd Edition, New York: Oxford University Press, 1979.

Greenblatt, D., Shader, R., Drug Abuse and the Emergency Room Physician. Amer. J. Psychiatry, 131:559-562, 1974.

Slaby, A., Lieb, J. and Tancredi, L., Handbook of Psychiatric Emergencies, Flushing: Medical Examination Publishing Co., 1975.

Westermeyer, J., A Primer on Chemical Dependency, Baltimore: Williams and Wilkins Co., 1976.

Chapter 9

Suicide
Charles W. Patterson

Suicide is an important topic for the professional since approximately 75% of the victims will visit a doctor within six months of their death. Awareness of presuicidal symptoms and signs could lead to intervention and prevention.

Since suicide is the tenth leading cause of death in the United States, and is the third leading cause of death for adolescents and adults under thirty, it truly constitutes a major health problem. Suicide is also a problem with which physicians should have personal concern, since the suicide rate for physicians is twice that of the general population.

LEARNING OBJECTIVES

By the time you complete the material in this chapter you should be able to:

1. List five or more demographic characteristics which typify a patient with a high suicide risk.

2. List three or more psychological characteristics of patients which would indicate there is increased risk of suicidal behavior.

3. List five or more findings in the patient's recent history which would suggest a patient with a high suicide risk.

4. List three or more findings in the patient's past history which would suggest a patient with a high suicide risk.

5. List and describe the significance of three or more features of the "suicide plan" about which the physician should specifically inquire when interviewing a potentially suicidal patient.

6. List five or more M.S.E. findings which would suggest a patient with a high suicide risk.

7. Formulate a treatment plan for the patient specifically dealing with:

    a. the need for hospitalization
    b. management of interpersonal relationships
    c. frequency of consultation
    d. the need for ECT

By the conclusion of this chapter and with supervised clinical experience you should be able to:

1. Accurately observe and record a patient's behavior within each of the M.S.E. behavior descriptors.

2. Make a correct differential diagnosis and assess a patient's potential suicide risk given necessary M.S.E. and history information.

3. Indicate the history and M.S.E. findings which enabled you to make a diagnosis.

DEMOGRAPHIC FACTORS

There are a number of factors which affect the degree of suicidal risk: age, sex, race, marital status, job status, the presence of medical illness (real or delusional), prior suicide attempts, and prior psychiatric disorders, to name a few. With respect to age, the suicide rate for both sexes increases until 55-65; thereafter the rate decreases for females but continues to increase for males until 85, after which it decreases. In general, males kill themselves two to four times more frequently than females, but females attempt suicide three to four times more frequently than males. Caucasians are more apt to commit suicide than other races, although recent studies indicate that young urban black men are an exception, having a suicide rate almost twice that of white men. The risk increases for those who were married but are now alone and without a spouse, i.e., divorced, separated, or widowed. The presence of a serious medical illness, especially cancer, or the delusional belief of having a serious illness also increases the risk. Being without a job, either through unemployment or retirement, increases the possibility of suicide. People who have made a prior attempt have a 33-60% chance of trying again and 5-10% will kill themselves. Also, if a patient has a history of a past psychiatric disorder, his risk is higher (e.g., the rate is three and one half times greater for those with a history of psychiatric hospitalization). Further, those persons who lost a parent during childhood (especially via suicide) are at greater risk. Thus, even before

interviewing the patient, if you see from his chart that
he is an elderly white male, divorced, unemployed and
living alone, you have a patient at much higher risk for
suicide.

PSYCHOLOGICAL CHARACTERISTICS INDICATIVE OF INCREASED
RISK

Who is more apt to kill himself? Persons who are
depressed, chronically impulsive or have a Schizophrenic
Disorder are at higher risk.

Remember that all depressed patients are not aware
that their problem is depression. They may present complaints of a depressed mood and thus identification is
easier; some may only complain of feeling "run down" or
"tired," an inability to sleep well, a loss of interest
in sex, or loss of appetite and weight specifically about
their mood. Thus, you may help them identify the problem.
Even if they deny depression, your suspicion should remain
high. The more marked the mood change, i.e., the more
despairing, hopeless and helpless the patient, the greater
the risk. The more agitated the motor component of
depression, the greater the probability that the patient
will implement suicidal thoughts into action. Remember
that a depressed patient with marked psychomotor retardation (slowness of thinking and movement) may become
a greater suicide risk as he starts to improve since,
hypothetically, he now has enough energy to implement his
suicidal plan. There is, then a period of risk lasting
three to six months after a depressive episode.

Evaluation of the suicidal risk in a person with
schizophrenia is more difficult because of the communication problems and unpredictability of behavior. The
risk is higher in those who are hallucinating voices which
tell them to kill themselves. Also, a patient in an acute
psychotically-decompensated state accompanied by strong
affectual feelings (anxiety, fear, depression and panic)
is more vulnerable to suicide. Because of the communication problems, a good relationship with your patient with
frequent contact is invaluable in looking for changes in
mood and behavior. Having schizophrenia does not provide
immunity to depression.

The impulsive person, with a low frustration tolerance
and a tendency to overreact to stress, is also a greater
risk. People who abuse alcohol and drugs tend to fall
into this class. Older alcoholics have intense chronic
self-destructive tendencies and high suicide rates.

Now complete Self-Assessment Exercise #1 on the
following page.

Self-Assessment Exercise #1

1. Check below those categories known to be at higher risk for suicide:

   ___a. older > younger age   ___g. vegetarians
   ___b. younger > older age   ___h. chronic debilitating
   ___c. white > black race   illness
   ___d. black > white race   ___i. drug abusers
   ___e. history of prior   ___j. alcoholics
         psychiatric   ___k. young urban black
         hospitalization   men
   ___f. history of prior   ___l. males > females
         suicide attempt   ___m. females > males
                                  ___n. patients with
                                    schizophrenia

2. What percent of the general population who attempt suicide will ultimately succeed?

   a. 5-10%
   b. 20-30%
   c. 40-50%

3. Assume that three patients are under your care for recent suicide attempts. Without making corrections for gender, what number will ultimately attempt suicide again?

3. Assume that three patients are under your care for recent suicide attempts. Without making corrections for gender, what number will ultimately attempt suicide again?

   a. 0 or 1 patients of the three will try again
   b. 1 or 2 patients of the three will try again
   c. 2 or 3 patients of the three will try again

4. Which of the following statements best describe the suicidal risk of schizophrenics:

   a. seldom kill themselves because they are more concerned with their internal world than with external reality problems
   b. seldom kill themselves because they are too demented to conceive of a suicide plan
   c. are at higher risk for suicide because of their unpredictability, difficulty in establishing close relationships and communicating

When you have completed this exercise to the best of your ability, check your answers with those on the following page.

Self-Assessment Exercise #1 - Feedback

1. The situations at a higher risk for suicide are:

    a. older > younger age
    c. white > black race
    e. history of prior psychiatric hospitalization
    f. history of prior suicide attempt
    h. chronic debilitating illness
    i. drug abusers
    k. young, urban black men
    l. males > females
    n. patients with schizophrenia

2. a. 5-10% of individuals who attempt suicide ultimately kill themselves.

3. b. 1 or 2 (33-60%) of the three patients are likely to attempt suicide again.

4. c. Persons with schizophrenia are at higher risk, in part, because of their unpreditability and difficulty in establishing close relationships.

        If your answers correspond closely with those above, continue your reading on the following page; if not, please reread the preceding section until you are confident you know the material.

SIGNIFICANT FINDINGS OF RECENT HISTORY
What clues might the patient or his family give?
First, listen for statements which directly or indirectly
imply thoughts of suicide. Studies have shown that most
suicidal persons have conveyed their desperate struggle
to others prior to the attempt. Any history of increased
risk-taking, unusual recent behavior (e.g., giving away
valued possessions, unaccountable disrutions of close relationships) or recent changes in their life style (e.g.,
increasing social withdrawal, deteriorating work record,
and increasing dependency on alcohol and medicines for
sleep) may be clues to an impending suicide.
Second, explore for the presence of a depressed mood
and the physical concomitants of depression (it may be
useful to review the chapter on Affective Disorders at
this time).
Third, investigate how he views dying (e.g., as
a desired end or something to fear), and whether the
thoughts reflect active or passive wishes (i.e., "I want
to die." versus "I don't care what happens to me.").
A positive image of death and an active wish to die may
indicate strong suicidal tendencies. A relative lack of
concern for the reaction of others (e.g., family, friends,
etc.) to a planned suicide implies increased risk.
Fourth, evaluate the nature of the resources (social,
financial, health, etc.), available to the patient and the
potential for alleviating the stress that caused the depression. The amount and type of personal strength and
resources greatly affect the prognosis. Likewise, the
degree to which the etiology of the depression can be
lessened or removed will determine the rate of recovery.
Suicidal inclinations originating because of a lost job are
easier to revolve successfully than those due to the death
of a loved one.

SIGNIFICANT FINDINGS OF PAST HISTORY
Past performance is often a good indicator of future
behavior. It is important, therefore, to obtain a clear
picture of the degree of success achieved and the methods
used by the patient when coping with previous life experiences. Especially significant through the years is the
patient's capacity to maintain productive work, sustain
meaningful interpersonal relationships (social, family,
marital) and deal with various life crises without developing signs of psychopathology. It is also helpful to note
how accurately the patient was able to assess the causes
and solutions for past problems. If he has not been able
to conceptualize former difficulties or understand their
origins, he may find it harder to believe that life will
improve. The occurrence of suicide among family members
or close friends increases the likelihood of a similar
response by the patient.

FEATURES OF THE SUICIDAL PLAN

If a suicidal potential is suspected, ask the patient! It is a myth that broaching and discussing this subject will implant thoughts of suicide. Exactly what words to use will depend upon the patient and what fits your conversational style. An example might be: "Have you had any thoughts recently about harming or killing yourself?" If the patient answers affirmatively about a suicide plan, inquire when he began having the thoughts, what method(s) was selected, and the means available for use.

Exploring details of the timing of a planned suicide may provide useful information. The more imminent the planned act, the more increased the risk. Also, anniversaries of significant losses, especially through death, are high risk periods.

Generally, the more available and violent, or lethal, the method selected for suicide the greater the risk (e.g., utilizing a gun or jumping from a high place versus taking a few aspiring or wrist cutting with a dull knife). However, it is important to investigate the patient's belief about the lethality of a means for suicide in order to estimate the seriousness of the intent. For example, the type or dose of an ingested drug cannot by itself indicate the patient's intentions. A more accurate indicator is the patient's impression about the lethality of the medication.

In summary, the more specific the planning, consistent with available means, the greater the risk for suicide.

MENTAL STATUS OBSERVATIONS

Some findings of the mental status examination correlate with increased suicidal risk. They are motor agitation and restlessness, attitudes of hopelessness and helplessness, confused or indecisive thinking, a tendency toward poor or impulsive judgments, the presence of delusions or hallucinations, and a despondent mood. Also, note whether the patient seemed relieved by the opportunity to discuss these feelings and was receptive to help, (favorable prognosis) or seemed untouched by your interest and support (a less favorable outlook).

TREATMENT

Management of high suicidal risk patients requires careful attention to several factors. Hospitalize the patient who is not sufficiently in control of suicidal urges because of depression, psychosis, or impulsiveness, particularly when no supportive relationships to others are immediately available. Provide empathy, hope and realistic assurance that the patient will, in time, experience relief from his distress. If the patient is not hospitalized because he possesses sufficient control over suicidal thoughts, arrange for a close relationship with another person. This person should be readily available to the patient, informed of the problem, and able to make contact with the physician if needed. <u>Separate the patient from the means</u> (e.g., remove drugs or gun from home); this may require hospitalization. <u>See the patient frequently</u> in order to monitor for progress or worsening and to provide constant reassurances from an interested, concerned party. If the patient is highly suicidal, <u>electro convulsive therapy (ECT) may be required</u>, since no other modality can alter the crisis as rapidly. More specific therapeutic intervention will depend upon the diagnosis. ECT is a very safe and highly effective treatment by which to quickly bring about a remission of depressive symptoms.

Now complete Self-Assessment Exercise #2 on the following page.

Self-Assessment Exercise #2

1. Alcoholism is usually associated with a lower suicide
   risk because alcohol acts as a tranquilizer, thus
   making problems less stressful.

   True_____   False_____

2. Physicians are at a lower risk for suicide than
   a general population of the same age and sex because
   their practice has given them an appreciation of life,
   they have learned coping techniques while assisting
   patients in dealing with frustrating problems, and
   they have colleagues to whom they can turn when
   troubled.
   True_____   False_____

3. A patient who is admitted for taking ten tablets of
   Vitamin C in an apparent suicide attempt is:

   a. a high future risk
   b. a low future risk
   c. cannot say

4. Which of these are ideal in the management of all
   suicidal patients who appear appropriate for out-
   patient care? (More than one answer may be
   appropriate.)

   a. frequent appointments initially
   b. tranquilizers
   c. antidepressants
   d. a helpful other person, willing to spend time with
      the patient and capable of contacting the thera-
      pist immediately if necessary.

5. Patients who make serious suicide attempts should:

   a. be permitted to do so under certain circumstances
   b. be chastized for intentionally injuring themselves
   c. generally be hospitalized on a psychiatric ward
   d. immediately be given a series of ECT

When you have completed this exercise to the best of your ability, check your answers with those on the following page.

Self-Assessment Exercise #2 - Feedback

1. False. Persons with a low frustration tolerance, who
    tend to overreact to stress, e.g., alcoholics and
    drug abusers, present a high suicidal risk.

2. False. In spite of their greater medical knowledge
    and expertise the suicide rate for physicians is
    twice that of the general population.

3. c. Statistically any patient who attempts suicide
    irrespective of the lethality of their method, has one
    or two chances in three of again attempting suicide in
    the future. However, to evaluate this specific case,
    the patient's belief about the lethality of Vitamin C
    is necessary.

4. a. and d. Frequent appointments with the therapist
    and ready access to a concerned person should be an
    integral part of the regimen for every patient who
    attempts suicide. All suicidal patients do not require
    tranquilizers or antidepressants.

5. c. A serious suicide attempt is a medical emergency
    requiring hospitalization and careful psychiatric
    evaluation.

    If your answers correspond closely with those above,
proceed to Exercise #3 on the following page; if not,
please reread the preceding section until you are confident
you know the material.

Self-Assessment Exercise #3

Instructions:
      Underline all words and phrases in the following case
history which are related to INCREASED suicidal risk. Use
the left-hand margin to make explanatory comments, if
needed. Then answer the questions at the end of the
exercise.

HISTORY OF PRESENT ILLNESS
      The patient is a 65-year-old white
male, divorced, living alone in a hotel,
admitted in a near comatose condition
yesterday because of an overdose of
of approximately thirty tablets of
Valium, 5 mgm, combined with alcoholic
intoxication. The patient was lavaged,
given supportive care, and is alert at
the present time.
      A heavy drinker, he has been unem-
ployed from his janitorial job for the
past three months because of his
drinking. He acknowledges feeling increasingly depressed since being fired,
and for the past two weeks has had
insomnia, anorexia, and a ten pound
weight loss. He indicates he wanted to
die, had been thinking of suicide for
the past week, planned the overdose,
but had to "get drunk" because "I didn't
have the guts" [to kill myself]. He is
unhappy that the attempt failed, states
that "nobody can help me" and sees no
way to help himself. He denies having
any close relationships or caring how
others would feel if he committed suicide ("who is there who cares?"). He
views death as a "relief." His use
of alcohol has increased considerably
in the past month. He denies having
any hobbies or activities, "just
drinking."

PAST PSYCHIATRIC HISTORY
      Hospitalized in 1965 at Pleasantview
Psychiatric Hospital for three months
following a suicide attempt after his
fourth wife left him. Treated with ECT,
he did "pretty good, but only for about
two years" thereafter.

SOCIAL HISTORY
      An only child, his parents are de-
ceased (father died by suicide when
patient was eight years old; mother

Self-Assessment Exercise #3 (continued)

died of "old age" two years ago).
Raised in Boston, he moved to Los
Angeles at age twenty-one and has lived
here since. Completed eighth grade
(without any repeat) but quit because
"of the Depression" to go to work.
Has never held a job longer than two
years, usually quitting or being fired
because of "my temper." Usually worked
as a laborer. Denies any physical
problems other than feeling "tired all
the time," but has been hospitalized
twice for delerium tremens(1972-1973).
Currently living on Social Security
income, he has no other financial resources. He received a bad conduct
discharge from the army after three
months (during WWII) for "disobeying
an order and punching the officer."
He has had no legal problems other
than several arrests in the past two
years for public intoxication. Married
and divorced four times, he has no
children or close friends.

MENTAL STATUS EXAMINATION
    65 y.o. W/M, short, thin, grey-
haired, unkempt, with 2-3 day-old
beard, lying passively in bed and
avoiding eye contact. His speech was
slow and he did not spontaneously offer
information. Passively cooperative.
Little movement of his extremities.
His facial expression was sad and
immobile.
    Thought processes were logical and
coherent, and no delusions or hallucinations were noted. Theme of talk
centered around how hopeless the future
was and his wishes to be dead. There
were no thoughts about wishing to harm
others.
    Mood was one of depression. He was
oriented to person, place, and time, and
recent and remote memory was intact.
He could perform simple calculations
and his general fund of knowledge was
fair. His intelligence was judged
average.

DIAGNOSTIC IMPRESSION
    1. drug overdose (Valium and alcohol)
    2. Dysthymic Disorder (depressive
       neurosis)
    3. Substance Use Disorder, alcohol
       dependence
Now answer the questions on the following page.

QUESTIONS FOR EXERCISE #3

You have interviewed the patient, obtained the above history, and now have to make some decisions about the patient. He wants to leave the hospital.

1. Is he a significant risk for suicide?

2. Would you:

   a. discharge him as he wishes and with your concurrence?
   b. discharge him against medical advice (A.M.A.)?
   c. discharge him if he promises to see a therapist at a nearby mental health center within the next few days?
   d. hold him and call a psychiatric consultation for purposes of getting him psychiatric inpatient care even though he objects?

3. Discuss briefly why you would not have chosen the other alternatives in question #2.

When you have completed this exercise to the best of your ability, check your answers with those on the following page.

<u>Self-Assessment Exercise #3 - Feedback</u>

HISTORY OF PRESENT ILLNESS
The patient is a 65-year-old white male, divorced, living alone in a hotel, admitted in a near comatose condition yesterday because of an overdose of approximately thirty tablets of Valium, 5 mgm, combined with alcoholic intoxication. The patient was lavaged, given supportive care, and is alert at the present time.
A heavy drinker, he has been unemployed from his janitorial job for the past three months because of his drinking. He acknowledges feeling increasingly depressed since being fired, and for the past two weeks has had insomnia, anorexia, and a ten pound weight loss. He indicates he wanted to die, had been thinking of suicide for the past week, planned the overdose, but had to "get drunk" because "I didn't have the guts" [to kill myself[. He is unhappy that the attempt failed, states that "nobody can help me" and sees no way to help himself. He denies having any close relationships or caring how others would feel if he committed suicide ("who is there who cares?"). He views death as a "relief." His use of alcohol has increased considerably in the past month. He denies having any hobbies or activities, "just drinking."

PAST PSYCHIATRIC HISTORY
Hospitalized in 1965 at Pleasantview Psychiatric Hospital for three months following a suicide attempt after his fourth wife left him. Treated with ECT, he did "pretty good, but only for about two years" thereafter.

SOCIAL HISTORY
An only child, his parents are deceased (father died by suicide when patient was eight years old; mother died of "old age" two years ago). Raised in Boston, he moved to Los Angeles at age twenty one and has lived here since. Completed eighth grade (without any repeat) but quit because "of the Depression" to go to work. Has never held a job longer than two years, usually quitting or being fired because of "my temper." Usually worked as a laborer. Denies any physical problems other than feeling "tired all the time," but has been hospitalized twice for "D.T.'s" (1972, 1973).

Self-Assessment Exercise #3 - Feedback (continued)

Currently living on Social Security income, he has no other financial resources. He received a bad conduct discharge from the army after three months (during WWII) for "disobeying an order and punching the officer." He has had no legal problems other than several arrests in the past two years for public intoxication. Married and divorced four times, he has no children or close friends.

MENTAL STATUS EXAMINATION

65 Y.O. W/M, short, thin, grey-haired, unkempt, with 2-3 day-old beard, lying passively in bed and avoiding eye contact. His speech was slow and he did not spontaneously offer information. Passively cooperative. Little movement of his extremities. His facial expression was sad and immobile.

Thought processes were logical and coherent, and no delusions or hallucinations were noted. Theme of talk centered around how hopeless the future was and his wishes to be dead. There were no thoughts about wishing to harm others.

Mood was one of depression. He was oriented to person, place, and time, and recent and remote memory was intact. He could perform simple calculations and his general fund of knowledge was fair. His intelligence was judged average.

DIAGNOSTIC IMPRESSION
1. drug overdose (Valium and alcohol)
2. Dysthymic Disorder (depressive neurosis)
3. Substance Use Disorder (alcohol dependence)

Answers to Questions:

1. Yes. The patient presents a considerable suicidal risk, with respect to demographic characteristics, psychiatric diagnosis and mental status findings.

2. d. Hold the patient in the hospital and request psychiatric consultation.

3. The patient appears to be actively suicidal at the present time, and may act upon his feelings. Nothing about his life has changed because of his attempt. He

Self-Assessment Exercise #3 - Feedback (continued)

still is lonely, with limited social resources. He
feels no remores for his suicidal behavior and his
future remains unaltered. He must be hospitalized
until some therapeutic progress can be made.

If your answers correspond closely with those above,
please go on to Exercise #4 on the following pages. If
not, reread the preceding section until you are confident
you know the material.

Self-Assessment Exercise #4

Instructions:
Underline all words and phrases in the following case history which suggest a DECREASED suicidal risk. Use the left-hand margin to make explanatory comments, if needed. Then answer the questions at the end of the exercise.

HISTORY OF PRESENT ILLNESS

The patient is a 23-year-old married black female, mother of two, clerk-typist, living with husband, admitted the previous night following an overdose of aspirin. She is alert this morning. "It was stupid taking the pills," she said. The patient indicated that she and her husband had been having marital problems recently--he allegedly drank too much and no longer gave the patient and their two children much attention. He had promised to work harder at improving the marriage and was supposed to take the patient to a movie that night. However, he failed to come home until 10:00 p.m. and smelled "like a brewery" when he arrived. She had become increasingly angry while waiting for him, then consumed three martinis to "cool off." When he did arrive, an argument ensued and he told her he "didn't give a damn about her." Upset, angry, and crying, she ran into the bathroom and impulsively, ingested a bottle of aspirin, thinking at the time that "if he doesn't appreciate me when I'm alive, he'll realize his mistake when I'm gone." However, the patient began to have second thoughts about the overdose, and told her husband, who became concerned and brought her to the hospital. Since admission the patient has been thinking about her problems and thinks they should see a marital counselor. The husband has been around the ward since admission, spending much time with his wife, berating himself for causing the argument, and agreeing with the wife that marital counselling is a good idea.

PAST PSYCHIATRIC HISTORY

No prior history of suicide attempts or psychiatric illness.

SOCIAL HISTORY

The oldest of three children, the patient was born and raised in Los Angeles. Her parents and siblings are in good health, living in Los Angeles, and have a lot of

Self-Assessment Exercise #4 (continued)

social interaction with the patient. A high
school graduate and B+ student, she went to
work at age eighteen as a clerk-typist, is
still working for the same company, and is
being considered for a promotion. In good
physical health, she denied drug abuse and
drank "socially" (her husband stated she
rarely drank, mostly at parties). She
began dating at sixteen, married after high
school and has five-year-old twin daughters
who are in good health and doing well.
Husband is 25 years old, an auto mechanic,
who "drinks too much" but appears willing
to attempt changing his behavior.

MENTAL STATUS EXAMINATION
    23 y.o. B/F, alert, cooperative and
pleasant, who related with open and spon-
taneous speech. Her facial expression was
animated and her motor level adjudged normal.
Thought processes were logical, coherent,
and no delusions or hallucinations were
noted. She denied any further intent to
harm herself, tended to berate herself for
such a "stupid thing," and was concerned
about what others would think. She also
thought her husband was sincere in his
willingness to seek marital therapy with
her. Her mood was one of mild shame, but
she was able to laugh at times and was
optimistic.
    Her orientation, memory, fund of knowledge
and ability of abstract were normal. Average
intelligence.

DIAGNOSTIC IMPRESSION
    1. drug overdose (aspirin)
    2. Adjustment Disorder with depressed
        mood
    3. marital problem

Now answer the questions on the following page.

Self-Assessment Exercise #4 (continued)

QUESTIONS FOR EXERCISE #4

You have interviewed the patient and have obtained the above history. The patient wishes to go home.

1.   What is the potential suicide risk?

2.   Does the fact that the overdose drug was "aspirin" per se (rather than another drug, e.g., phenobarbital) mean the future suicide risk is lower?

3.   Select one or more of the following alternatives:

   a.   discharge patient home with your concurrence?
   b.   discharge patient AMA?
   c.   discharge patient home if she and husband agree to get an appointment within the week with a therapist (psychiatrist, marriage counselor, etc.)?
   d.   discharge patient home but arrange, prior to discharge, an appointment within the week with a therapist (psychiatrist, marriage counselor, etc.)?
   e.   hold the patient and call for a psychiatric consultation for purposes of arranging inpatient treatment?

4.   Briefly discuss why you didn't choose the other alternatives in question #3.

5.   Sometimes patients who make a suicide attempt with a nonlethal intent and for obvious manipulative reasons kill themselves. One reason is that they may choose a drug that is more lethal than suspected or suffer the combined consequence of drug overdose while drinking. Another reason, related to the manipulative element and not technique is....

   When you have completed this exercise to the best of your ability, check your answers with those on the following pages.

Self-Assessment Exercise #4 - Feedback

HISTORY OF PRESENT ILLNESS
   The patient is a 23-year-old married
black female, mother of two, clerk-typist,
living with husband, admitted the previous
night following an overdose of aspirin.
She is alert this morning. "It was stupid
taking the pills," she said. The patient
indicated that she and her husband had been
having marital problems recently--he allegedly drank too much and no longer gave the
patient and their two children much attention. He had promised to work harder at
improving the marriage and was supposed to
take the patient to a movie that night.
However, he failed to come home until 10:00
p.m. and smelled "like a brewery" when he
arrived. She had become increasingly angry
while waiting for him, then consumed three
martinis to "cool off." When he did arrive,
an argument ensued and he told her he "didn't
give a damn about her." Upset, angry, and
crying, she ran into the bathroom and, impulsively, ingested a bottle of aspirin,
thinking at the time that "if he doesn't
appreciate me when I'm alive, he'll realize
his mistake when I'm gone." However, the
patient began to have second thoughts about
the overdose, and told her husband, who became concerned and brought her to the hospital. Since admission the patient has
been thinking about her problems and thinks
they should see a marital counselor. The
husband has been around the ward since admission, spending much time with his wife,
berating himself for causing the argument,
and agreeing with the wife that marital
counselling is a good idea.

PAST PSYCHIATRIC HISTORY
   No prior history of suicide attempts or
psychiatric illness.

SOCIAL HISTORY
   The oldest of three children, the patient
was born and raised in Los Angeles. Her
parents and siblings are in good health,
living in Los Angeles, and have a lot of
social interaction with the patient. A high
school graduate and B+ student, she went to
work at age eighteen as a clerk-typist, is
still working for the same company, and is
being considered for a promotion. In good
physical health, she denied drug abuse and

drank "socially" (her husband stated she
rarely drank, mostly at parties). She
began dating at sixteen, married after
high school and has five-year-old twin
daughters who are in good health and doing
well. Husband is 25 years old, an auto
mechanic, who "drinks too much" but appears
willing to attempt changing his behavior.

MENTAL STATUS EXAMINATION
    23 y.o. B/F, alert, cooperative and
pleasant, who related with open and spon-
taneous speech. Her facial expression was
animated and her motor level adjudged normal.
Thought processes were logical, coherent,
and no delusions or hallucinations were
noted. She denied any further intent to
harm herself, tended to berate herself for
such a "stupid thing," and was concerned
about what others would think. She also
thought her husband was sincere in his
willingness to seek marital therapy with her.
Her mood was one of mild shame, but she was
able to laugh at times and was optimistic.
    Her orientation, memory, fund of knowledge
and ability of abstract were normal. Average
intelligence.

DIAGNOSTIC IMPRESSION
    1.   drug overdose (aspirin)
    2.   Adjustment Disorder with
         depressed mood
    3.   marital problem

Answers to Questions:

1.   The patient presents a low suicidal risk.

2.   No. To assess risk one must know the patient's
     belief about the drug or dose.

3.   Either c. or d. acceptable, but d. is preferable.
     Always attempt to make specific plans prior to
     discharge.

4.   a. and b. have no plans for repairing the marital
     problem. e. is unnecessary--patient doesn't require
     inpatient treatment as she poses no immediate suicide
     risk and can be managed as an outpatient.

Self-Assessment Exercise #4 - Feedback (continued)

5. Several possibilities, e.g.:

    a. the person(s) they were attempting to manipulate
       doesn't find them in time
    b. the person(s) they were attempting to manipulate
       ignore the patient, who may then feel obliged
       (or angry enough) to complete the suicidal
       behavior.

If your answers correspond closely with those above,
continue your reading; if not, please reread the preceding section until you are confident you know the
material.

SUMMARY

In summary, the study of suicide is important for the professional because of the high prevalence of suicidal behavior and the opportunity for intervention. A knowledge of demographic variables, diagnostic groups at risk, appropriate inquiry questions, and mental status observations provide the data upon which treatment decisions are based. The type of intervention will be a function of the potential suicidal risk, psychiatric diagnosis, and the individual's psychosocial resources.

REFERENCES

Aalberg, Veikko: Paper presented at the Ninth International Congress on Suicide Prevention and Crisis Intervention, Helsinki, 1976.   Reported in Psychiat. News of the American Psychiatric Association, October 1977.

Fawcett, J., "Suicidal Depression and Physical Illness," JAMA: pp. 1303-1306, Mar. 6, 1972.

Holden, L. Dwight: "Therapist Response to Patient Suicide: Professional and Personal," J. Cont. Ed. Psychiat., pp. 23-32, May 1978.

Modlin, H. C.:   "Cues and Clues to Suicide," The Five Minute Hour, Summit, N. J.: Geigy Pharmaceuticals, September 1975.

Pokorny, A.:   "Suicide in Depression," in W. E. Fann et al. (eds.) Phenomenology and Treatment of Depression, Chapter 12, New York: Spectrum, 1977.

Rose, K. D. and Rosow, R.:   "Physicians Who Kill Themselves," Arch. Gen. Psychiat., 29:800-805, December 1973.

Schneidman, E. S. (ed.):   Suicidology: Contemporary Developments.   New York: Grune and Stratton, 1976.

Schneidman, E. S.:   "An Overview of Suicide," Psychiat. Ann., 6:11, November 1976.

Tsuang, M. D.:   "Suicide in Schizophrenics, Manics, Depressives, and Surgical Controls," Arch. Gen. Psychiat., 35(2):153-155, February 1978.

Winnik, H. Z.:   Paper presented at Eighth International Congress on Suicidal Prevention and Crisis Intervention, Jerusalem, 1975.   Reported in Ment. Health Soc., 3:175-177, 1976.

Note: The author wishes to credit Harry Zall, M.D. for use of some material from his unpublished outline on suicide.

Chapter 10
Organic Mental Disorders
C. Warner Johnson

An Organic Mental Disorder (O.M.D.) is a condition
caused by an impairment of brain tissue functioning from
any of a number of causes. Although this condition is
frequently associated with the elderly or persons intoxicated with drugs or alcohol, the syndrome often occurs in
connection with a variety of physical illnesses and even
may be the first sign that a medical problem exists. It
is often encountered in inpatient settings and between
5 and 10% of persons admitted to medical hospitals demonstrate some degree of an Organic Brain Syndrome. The incidence sharply increases for persons over 60. For these
reasons, it is important that you, as a health care professional, be well versed in the diagnosis of Organic
Mental Disorders.

LEARNING OBJECTIVES
     By the time you complete the material in this chapter
you should be able to:

1. List the mental status examination findings which
    are typical of an Organic Brain Syndrome.

2. Correctly distinguish between the following
    diagnostic terms:

    delirium
    dementia
    organic brain syndrome
    intoxication syndrome
    withdrawal syndrome

3. Distinguish between delirium and dementia on the
    basis of reversibility of symptoms, course and
    typical mental status findings.

4.   List five major types of physical disorders that can give rise to an Organic Brain Syndrome, and give one example of a medical condition for each type.

5.   List five or more factors that may predispose an individual to developing an Organic Brain Syndrome.

By the conclusion of this chapter and supervised clinical experience, you should be able to do the following:

1.   Accurately observe and record a patient's behavior within each of the M.S.E. behavior descriptors.

2.   Determine whether an O.M.D. is present in a patient, given necessary M.S.E. information.

OVERVIEW

As stated previously, an Organic Mental Disorder results from impairment of brain tissue and functioning from a variety of causes. An O.M.D. should never be equated with a "normal" state of functioning. The signs and symptoms of a developing O.M.D. are manifestations of cerebral impairment and a thorough medical evaluation is essential. These symptoms may be the first indicators of a developing medical problem. In some cases, such as a profound decrease in blood sugar (hypoglycemia) or intracranial bleeding, early recognition of the condition and decisive intervention is necessary in order to prevent irreversible brain damage or death.

Most of the intellectual functions which are so highly valued and unique to man, i.e., creative and abstract thinking, the use of symbols, verbal communications, etc., are dependent upon an intact brain functioning, and any disruption of the integrity of the brain brings about profound changes in one's ability to think and adapt successfully to daily life. Phylogenetically, the structure and functioning of the cerebral cortex are late evolutionary developments and integrated intellectual functioning is rarely attained before the mid to late teen years. The brain structures and functions that are last acquired are also those first lost at a time of illness or injury.

GENERAL DIAGNOSTIC CONSIDERATIONS
The brain dysfunction basic to O.M.D.'s may be
temporary or permanent, mild or marked and variously
affects patient behavior, emotions, and intellectual functioning. O.M.D.'s are further classified into subgroups,
that is, Organic Brain Syndromes (O.B.S.) which are named
according to the nature of the brain dysfunction, clinical
course, and predominant symptoms. In this book when we
refer to a specific subgroup of O.M.D. we will use the
term O.B.S. and reserve O.M.D. as a generic term. Generally, organic brain syndromes are characterized by global
impairment of higher intellectual functioning, orientation,
memory, and abstract thinking. However, the predominant
symptoms of some organic syndromes consist primarily of
impaired memory or abnormalities of affect, or perceptual
dysfunction, or personality and behavioral disturbances
in the absence of significant intellectual impairment.
These latter syndromes are less common and we will confine
our discussion to those which you are more likely to encounter (i.e., delirium, dementia, intoxication and
withdrawal).
There is growing evidence that some of the so-called
"functional" psychoses (i.e., Schizophrenic and Major
Affective Disorders) also may be due to a subtle brain
dysfunction and therefore are "organic" in nature. Although brain dysfunction may be involved in both classes
of disorders, it appears that the underlying abnormalities
are significantly different and, for the foreseeable
future, that diagnostic differentiation should be continued.

MENTAL STATUS FINDINGS
A mental status examination (M.S.E.) will help determine the presence of an organic brain syndrome (O.B.S.)
but cannot discriminate diagnostically between different
etiological factors (i.e., whether an injury or drug in-
gestion were causative). However, M.S.E. observations
provide information about the overall status of the central
nervous system, and whether it is generally excited or
depressed. Therefore, if drug use is suspected, it may be
impossible to infer from patient behaviors whether the
substance taken was a central nervous stimulant or depressant.
The findings of an O.B.S. may obscure or accentuate
those of any preexisting psychopathology, including psychosis, mental retardation, Anxiety Disorder, and others.
The general clinical features of an O.B.S. may show
considerable variation in different individuals, and the
symptoms may change greatly from time to time in the same
individual. Typically, symptoms worsen at night and
improve during daylight hours. The onset and course of
symptoms occurring in an O.B.S. may be gradual or rapid
depending upon the etiology. For example, the onset of
symptoms would be gradual if brain impairment is due to
a slow-growing tumor and rapid in the instance of a sudden
head injury or drug usage.

We will now outline the typical M.S.E. findings of an O.B.S.

Appearance

The greater the impairment of brain functioning, the greater the likelihood that self-care and personal grooming will be neglected. An unkempt appearance, disheveled clothing, uncleanness, unshavenness or lack of attention to makeup are common findings. If a medical problem is present there may be signs of physical illness in the form of chills, nausea, vomiting, pallor or weight loss.

Behavior

Patients with an Organic Brain Syndrome commonly show an abnormality of movement such as decreased or excessive activity, tremulousness, discoordination, an unsteady walk, and impulsive, purposeless movements. Facial expression corresponds with the predominant affect being experienced, be it elation, depression, apprehension or irritability. Speech is often atypical in quality and quantity, and may be indistinct, slurred, or range from loud talkativeness to a soft slow monotone.

Feeling (Mood/Affect)

Patients may demonstrate a variety of feelings. For example, if drugs were taken which depress the central nervous system (i.e., barbiturates, alcohol, or heroin) then the patients are likely to experience lethargy, melancholy or irritability. Conversely, central nervous system stimulants typically cause feelings of euphoria, grandiosity or irritability and belligerence. Generally, the affect shown is consistent with the thought content being expressed but is often labile and can change rapidly.

Perception

Perceptual disturbances in the form of illusions and auditory or visual hallucinations are common, especially in individuals with a delirium, a dementia, or who have taken a hallucinogenic drug. Hallucinations experienced as pure sounds, vivid colors, geometric patterns, animals or insects are commonly associated with an Organic Brain Syndrome caused by chemical intoxicants.

Thinking

Alterations of thinking can be found in almost all persons with an Organic Brain Syndrome, although the degree and type of impairment varies widely. Early signs of impairment occur as fluctuating levels of consciousness, decreased ability to concentrate, and distractibility.
If the central nervous system functioning is depressed from any cause, your patients may become lethargic or stuporous. Delirious patients or those intoxicated with stimulating drugs often seem hyperalert and become easily startled by

minor stimuli. In persons with a significant degree of
Organic Brain Syndrome, orientation, recent memory, concentration, and general intellectual functioning are
impaired. Disorientation successively affects awareness
of time, place and person. The sequence is reversed as
patients improve. Reasoning and judgment are also compromised. Delusions can occur and frequently are paranoid
in nature. An associational disturbance of some degree
is present in many cases of Organic Brain Syndromes.

Integration of Findings
    In most instances, a careful evaluation of findings
from five areas of the M.S.E. will determine whether or
not a patient is experiencing an O.B.S. First, the patient
with an O.B.S. is likely to show some degree of disorientation to time, place, or person. A second finding is that
of memory impairment. Recent memory is more commonly
impaired than remote memory. A third finding is that of
a generalized impairment of intellectual functioning. The
level of consciousness, attention span, the ability to do
abstract thinking and calculations, etc., are all compromised. As the ability to think abstractly decreases, the
patient becomes more literal or "concrete" in his interpretation of the environment. Fourthly, the patient shows
indications of impairment of judgment. It is difficult
to make complex decisions with disordered memory and
intellectual functioning. Finally, individuals with an
organic brain syndrome demonstrate a disturbance of affect.
Their emotions may be highly variable, and strong affective responses may be elicited by modest stimuli. Indifference or apathy to important events may also be observed.

Now complete Self-Assessment Exercise #1 on the
following page.

Self-Assessment Exercise #1

1. List five mental status examination findings which
    generally typify an O.B.S.

2. A young woman struck her head in an automobile acci-
    dent and lost consciousness for several minutes. While
    receiving medical attention she became mentally "con-
    fused." What specific areas of her mental functioning
    should be evaluated further to determine if she has
    an O.B.S.?

        Indicate whether the following statements are true
(T) or false (F).

_____3. The presence of vivid, visual hallucinations in
          a patient are highly suggestive of a diagnosis
          of O.B.S.

_____4. O.B.S. rarely occurs in patients with serious
          medical illness.

_____5. In persons with an O.B.S., recent memory is more
          likely to be impaired than remote memory.

        When you have completed this exercise to the best of
your ability, check your answers with those on the
following page.

Self-Assessment Exercise #1 - Feedback

1. The typical mental status examination findings of
    an O.B.S. are:

    disorientation
    impairment of recent memory
    disordered intellectual functioning
    impaired judgment
    affectual disturbance

2. The patient's mental functioning should be evaluated
    in the areas of:

    orientation
    recent memory
    general intellectual functioning

 T 3. The presence of vivid, visual hallucinations
        in a patient are highly suggestive of a diagnosis
        of O.B.S.

 F 4. O.B.S. rarely occurs in patients with serious
        medical illness.

 T 5. In persons with an O.B.S., recent memory is more
        likely to be impaired than remote memory.

     If your answers correspond closely with those above,
please continue your reading on the following page; if not,
please reread the material in the section preceding until
you are confident you know the material.

PHYSICAL DISORDERS AND THE O.B.S.
     Four major classes of general physical disorders may
give rise to an Organic Brain Syndrome. Endocrine disorders are often accompanied by signs and symptoms of an
Organic Brain Syndrome. Glandular dysfunction of the
pituitary, adrenals, thyroid (both hypo- and hyper-thyroid
states) and pancreas may result in impaired intellectual
functioning. Metabolic and nutritional disorders are
common sources of an O.B.S. Severe vitamin deficiency, an
imbalance of certain chemical substances in the blood and
liver or kidney failure are examples. Systemic infections
of various types including severe pneumonia, thyroid fever,
malaria and rheumatic fever can cause brain dysfunction.
Intoxication by drugs or poisons is the most common type
of medical disorder causing an O.B.S. Prescribed drugs,
"street drugs," hormones (especially steroids), and
various gases (anesthetic agents) may give rise to symptoms
of an O.B.S.
     Intracranial disorders also should be considered.
Cerebral arteriosclerosis, cerebro-vascular disorders
(such as a thrombosis or embolism), epilepsy, central
nervous system degeneration, brain tumors and infections
should be included in the differential diagnosis of an O.B.S.

PREDISPOSING FACTORS
     Certain characteristics of the patient and his en-
vironment make the development of an O.B.S. more likely.
A patient who is especially fearful, depressed or otherwise emotionally disturbed about his condition or hospitalization is more susceptible to an organic brain dysfunction. Prolonged physical inactivity, immobilization
of the extremities and sensory deprivation or overload
may increase the potential for an O.B.S. Other predisposing
factors are sleep deprivation, pre-existing brain damage,
alcohol and/or drug addiction, and being over fifty years
of age.

COMMON ORGANIC BRAIN SYNDROMES
     We will now describe four commonly encountered Organic
Brain Syndromes; namely delirium, dementia, intoxication
and withdrawal.

Delirium
     A delirium is a profound mental disorder arising from
generalized brain dysfunction such as might result from
a high fever, head injury, severe infection, drug withdrawal or similar toxic condition. Typically, the syndrome
develops within a relatively short period of time--hours
to a few days. Early in the course of a delirium, patients
have difficulty maintaining their concentration and attention, and may show fluctuating levels of alertness. They
are easily distracted by unimportant stimuli. Increasing
restlessness, irritability, apprehension, and insomnia
with frightening nightmares follow. Patients often lose
the ability to discriminate between things which are similar, but nonidentical, and may confuse strangers with

relatives or friends. Reality testing is markedly impaired and delusions with vivid hallucinations develop.
Patients typically are disoriented to time, place and
person, and retain little capacity for abstract thinking
or recent memory. Thinking patterns are fragmented and
patients often become totally incoherent. In most cases,
the intensity and duration of a delirium parallels the
course of the underlying medical problem; and as the illness subsides, so does the Organic Brain Syndrome. A delirium implies the presence of an underlying medical
disorder which always warrants prompt evaluation and treatment. In summary, a delirium is characterized by a rapid
onset and fluctuating symptoms. Foremost among the mental
status findings are a disturbance of attention which im-
pairs goal-directed thinking and behavior, disordered
memory and orientation, either decreased or increased
psychomotor activity, hallucinations, delusions, and lethargy or insomnia. The presence of brain dysfunction usually
can be demonstrated by means of history or laboratory
findings.

Dementia
     The diagnosis of dementia is applied to persons who
show gradual and marked deterioration of former levels of
intellectual functioning. Typically, the course of a dementia is gradual and may take months or many years to
develop. The most significant findings include evidence
of severe impairment in the area of thinking, in particular,
abstract thinking ability, problem-solving skills, judgment, orientation, and recent memory. Intellectual deterioration and disordered behavior reach severe proportions
and eventually such patients are unable to manage even
routine decisions of daily living. Persons with dementia
occasionally experience hallucinations, and impaired
reality testing with delusions are common. Judgment is
impaired and these persons are likely to overact emotionally to minor incidents. Dementias result from severe
dysfunction of brain cells as might be caused by tumors,
infections, and blood vessel or degenerative diseases.
Demented persons are predisposed to the development of
a secondary delirium which can be precipitated by medical
illness or various medications. Little can be done to
restore intellectual functioning lost in the course of
a dementia, and treatment consists primarily of providing
custodial and supportive care. A dementia, then is
characterized by deterioration of previously acquired
intellectual abilities including the capacity for memory,
abstract thinking, orientation, impulse control, and
problem-solving abilities. These individuals usually
undergo a personality change. It is often possible to
detect abnormal brain functioning by the laboratory and
other findings.

Intoxication
     This organic brain syndrome is defined as maladaptive
behavior arising from drugs (chemicals) taken to alter

central nervous system functioning. Basic to this diagnosis is the requirement that behavior is present which interferes with regular occupational or social functioning as exemplified by impaired judgment, impulsivity, fighting or other disorderly conduct. As defined here, this diagnostic term does not apply to common intoxication by alcohol or other "recreational" drugs unless intoxication is accompanied by maladaptive behavior. During non-pathologic intoxication, sleepiness or talkativeness, discoordination, an unsteady walk, slurred speech, and slowed thinking can be observed--but not maladaptive behavior. Intoxication can result from a number of drugs or chemicals and patient behavior typically coincides with the general effect which the chemical has on the central nervous system. Central nervous system depressants such as barbiturates, heroin, and psychotropic drugs usually cause slowed thinking and movement, slurred speech, discoordination, and feelings of depression. Respiration and blood pressure are likewise reduced. The opposite is true for drugs which stimulate the central nervous system. Cocaine, amphetamines, and methylphenidate may result in hyperactive behavior, pressured speech, restlessness, and elevated blood pressure and pulse rate. Usually, this type of Organic Brain Syndrome lasts for a few hours but may be extended in duration to several days. Associated medical complications may arise according to the amount and type of drug taken. For example, in the instance of central nervous system depressants, respiratory distress or intoxication by taking a history or examining the patient's blood or urine. Intoxication, then, is an Organic Brain Syndrome which develops soon after taking a drug. The particular behavioral and psychological response depends upon the nature of the drug taken. In addition to the usual finding of intoxication, evidence of maladaptive behavior during the waking state of the patient must be present.

Withdrawal

This Organic Brain Syndrome results from reducing or stopping the intake of a drug upon which a patient has become physically dependent. Such drugs are generally used because of their intoxicating effect upon the central nervous system, and were taken sufficiently often to produce tolerance and physical dependency. The symptoms of withdrawal result as the body readjusts to a decreased level of the drug. Substances which can cause a withdrawal response include tobacco, alcohol, opiates, and various sedatives. Most withdrawal symptoms have in common symptoms of insomnia, distractibility, restlessness, anxiety, irritability, nausea, vomiting, tremulousness and others described earlier in this chapter. Usually a withdrawal response is limited to a few days. If marked physical dependency upon alcohol or sedatives has occurred, withdrawal can result in a delirium and produce serious medical complications. The clinical picture is highly varied with respect to physical and mental status findings, and depends upon the drug taken, the degree of physical dependency, and the speed with which the medication has been decreased.

Now complete Self-Assessment Exercise #2 beginning on the next page.

Self-Assessment Exercise #2

1. A patient was admitted to the hospital for evaluation
    of a poorly controlled diabetic condition. The pa-
    tient was described by the admitting physician as
    being "mentally confused, disoriented and hyperactive."
    Assume that the patient had an O.B.S. Without knowing
    more about the case, what four types of general physical
    disorders, singly or in combination, may be causing
    the patient's mental symptoms? Give one example of
    a representative medical condition for each disorder.

    General Physical Disorder   Medical Condition

        a.
        b.
        c.
        d.

2. A 62-year-old man was brought for evaluation by his
    daughter. The patient was unable to give a relevant
    history. His daughter related that he had become
    increasingly forgetful and confused over the past
    three months. List three or more intracranial con-
    ditions that might be responsible for his symptoms.

        a.
        b.
        c.
        d.
        e.
        f.

3. Many patients who are treated in a C.C.U. (coronary
    care unit) develop symptoms of an O.B.S. List five
    or more environmental factors or patient characteris-
    tics which may predispose them to developing an O.B.S.
    Do not include factors listed in #1 and #2 above.

        a.
        b.
        c.
        d.
        e.

Self-Assessment Exercise #2 (continued)

4. Characterize each of the following syndromes by "yes"
    or "no" answers.

	INTOXICATION (secondary to alcohol)	DELIRIUM	DEMENTIA
potentially reversible			
rapid onset (minutes to hours)			
typically associated with current medical problems			
disorientation usually present			
vivid visual hallu- cinations often present			
markedly impaired intellectual functioning			

   When you have completed this exercise to the best of
your ability, check your answers with those on the
following page.

Self-Assessment Exercise #2 - Feedback

1. The patient's O.B.S. may be due to:

General Physical Disorder	Medical Condition
a. endocrine disorders	hypo- or hyperthyroid-ism, etc.
b. metabolic and nutritional	vitamin deficiency, blood chemical im-balance, liver or kidney failure
c. systemic infections	pneumonia, rheumatic fever, etc.
d. intoxication (drug or poison)	drugs, overdose, anesthetic agents

2. Intracranial conditions which may give rise to an O.B.S. are:

a. cerebral arteriosclerosis
b. cerebro-vascular disorders
c. epilepsy
d. central nervous system degeneration
e. tumors
f. infections

3. Factors which may predispose an individual to developing an O.B.S. are:

a. excessive anxiety
b. prolonged physical inactivity
c. immobilization of the extremities
d. sensory deprivation or overload
e. sleep deprivation
f. preexisting brain damage
g. alcohol and/or drug addiction
h. being over fifty years of age

Self-Assessment Exercise #2 - Feedback (continued)

4. The following syndromes can be characterized as follows:

	INTOXICATION (secondary to alcohol)	DELIRIUM	DEMENTIA
potentially reversible	yes	yes	no
rapid onset (minutes to hours)	yes	yes	no
typically associated with current medical problems	no	yes	no
disorientation usually present	no	yes	yes
vivid visual hallucinations often present	no	yes	no
markedly impaired intellectual functioning	no	yes	yes

If your answers correspond closely with those above, continue reading; if not, please reread the preceding section until you are confident you know the material.

SUMMARY

An O.B.S. is a commonly encountered condition in patients with medical illness. A carefully done mental status examination is an effective diagnostic instrument to determine whether or not the syndrome is present. If the patient manifests symptoms of disorientation, impairment of recent memory, disordered intellectual functioning, impaired judgment and an affectual disturbance, an O.B.S. is likely present.

REFERENCES

Engel, G. and Romano, J.: "Delirium: A Syndrome of Cerebral Insufficiency," J. Chronic Diseases, 9:260-277, 1959.

Freedman, A., Kaplan, H., and Sadock, B.: Comprehensive Textbook of Psychiatry, III, Baltimore: Williams and Wilkins, 1980.

Lipowski, Z.: "Delirium, Clouding of Consciousness and Confusion," J. Ner. and Mental Diseases, 145:227-255, 1967.

Morse, R. and Litin, E.: The anatomy of a delirium, American Journal of Psychiatry, 128:111, 1971.

Wells, C.: Dementia Reconsidered, Arch. General Psychiatry, 26:385, 1972.

Chapter 11

Schizophrenic Disorders
C. Warner Johnson
John R. Snibbe

Schizophrenic Disorders are severe psychopathologic conditions which are characterized by abnormalities of thinking, feeling and behavior. Approximately one percent of the general population develop symptoms of schizophrenia during their lifetime, and more persons require psychiatric hospitalization for this condition than any other form of psychopathology. Schizophrenia typically begins during late adolescence and the early adult years of life and often seriously compromises an individual's capacity for personal relationships, work and social adjustment. The high prevalence and disabling symptoms associated with schizophrenia constitute a major health problem. Early diagnosis and therapeutic intervention are important in order to reduce the incidence of chronic and incapacitating symptoms.

LEARNING OBJECTIVES
By the time you complete the material in this chapter you should be able to:

1. Briefly describe a present day hypothesis about the etiology of Schizophrenic Disorders

2. Describe the mental status examination findings typically associated with Schizophrenic Disorders.

3. Distinguish between Schizophrenic and Schizophreniform Disorders in terms of typical personality type, age and mode of onset, incidence of family psychological symptoms, course and prognosis.

4. Briefly characterize the following subtypes of Schizophrenic Disorders:
   a. paranoid
   b. catatonic
   c. undifferentiated
   d. residual

By the conclusion of this chapter and supervised clinical experience you should be able to:

1. Accurately observe and record a patient's behavior within each of the MSE behavior descriptors.

2. Determine whether a Schizophrenic Disorder is present in a patient, given necessary MSE information.

3. Indicate the history and MSE findings which enabled you to make a diagnosis.

THE ETIOLOGY OF SCHIZOPHRENIC DISORDERS

Present research suggests that the diagnosis "Schizophrenic Disorder" does not represent a single disease or illness, but rather encompasses a group of psychopathologic conditions which have findings in common, but may arise from a different origin and follow a varied course.

Several hypotheses of causation have been advanced. The careful study of close family members with Schizophrenic Disorders have provided evidence that a genetically transmitted predisposition exists for the condition. It is believed by some researchers that the biochemical functioning of the brain may be altered by inherited factors in a way which later leads to the development of schizophrenia.

In contrast to this theory some researchers believe that the basis for Schizophrenic Disorders lies with experiential factors, i.e., maladaptive and traumatic life experiences. Early derangements of the mother/child relationship have been implicated as have chronic, often subtle distortions of family relations and communications. The incidence of severe psychopathology within the family unit has been emphasized by others. Persistent and severe emotional stress, such as occurs during wartime or with other catastrophic life events may precipitate schizophrenia. In some instances Schizophrenic Disorders may result from the use of chemical substances (e.g., hallucinogens like PCP or LSD).

It appears then, that these disorders can be multi-determined and may result from one or a combination of biological, social and psychological factors.

MENTAL STATUS EXAMINATION FINDINGS

No single finding of history or mental status examination (MSE) is characteristic of all persons with Schizophrenic Disorders, and the diagnosis is made by identifying a combination of signs and symptoms and excluding other conditions which may have similar findings. To establish the diagnosis of a Schizophrenic Disorder, hallucinations, delusions and/or a disturbance of thinking should be detected at some time during the course of the condition. It is important to exclude the presence of an Affective Disorder (a manic or depressive syndrome) prior to or during the onset of symptoms and insure that the history and findings are not indicative of an Organic Brain Syndrome. Symptoms persist for at least six months or longer and usually are associated with some deterioration of normal levels of functioning. MSE findings vary considerably from individual to individual and from time to time within the same patient. There are frequently "islands" of personality and intellectual intactness which exists simultaneously with symptoms of severe psychopathology. With this potential for symptom variation in mind, the most characteristic findings of Schizophrenic Disorders will now be presented. Diagnostic subtypes of Schizophrenic Disorders (e.g., paranoid, catatonic, etc.) are classified according to the predominating symptoms and will be described later.

Appearance

Personal appearance is usually affected in proportion
to the severity of the Schizophrenic Disorder. If the
condition is mild, then there may be few or no abnormal
findings. However, if psychological symptoms become
severe, then it is common to find evidence of personal
neglect and highly eccentric or bizarre patterns of dress.

Behavior

Behavior patterns including facial expression, speech
and bodily movements are often atypical, unpredictable
and disorganized. Especially in Schizophrenic Disorders
of an abrupt onset, patients may experience intense anxiety
which is expressed by an apprehensive facial expression,
generalized muscle tension, restlessness and rapid, disjointed speech. However, some patients show a bland, unresponsive facial expression, slowed body movements and
speak with a dull, monotonous voice. Most patients with
a Schizophrenic Disorder are distrustful of interpersonal
relationships and may respond to your, their potential
helper, with anxiety, suspiciousness or defensive hostility.
Because they readily misinterpret your motives, these
patients frequently are negativistic and uncooperative.

Mood and Affect

During the earliest stages of a Schizophrenic Disorder,
patients may complain of feeling persistent depression or
apathy without an identifiable cause. Later, as the onset
of psychosis becomes imminent, they may experience episodes
of intense anxiety and unpredictable fluctuations of mood.
Overt affect is often incongruous with thought content
For example, patients may demonstrate inappropriate smiling
while relating ideas which in normal persons would evoke
feelings of sadness, apprehension or anger. It is difficult to anticipate just how such patients will respond
emotionally, and sudden outbursts of anxiety or anger may
occur for little apparent reason. In many patients, their
overall emotional response seems "flat," "inappropriately
bland," or "blunted." It is often difficult to empathize
with persons experiencing a Schizophrenic Disorder and
you may experience transient feelings of uneasiness when
you talk with them.

Perception

Perceptual disturbances in the form of illusions and
hallucinations are relatively common in persons with
Schizophrenic Disorders. Auditory hallucinations are more
common than visual ones and typically are harassing or
persecutory in nature. Hallucinations involving touch,
smell or taste are less frequently encountered.

Thinking

In Schizophrenic Disorders, both the thought content
and sequential relatedness of ideas are abnormal. Except
in instances when your patient's mental disorganization
is severe, alertness, orientation, memory and calculation

ability are minimally affected. However, concentration, psychological insight and judgment for day-to-day living activities generally are decreased. Abstract thinking frequently shows impairment as evidenced by literal or highly personalized interpretations of common proverbs. Thought content almost invariably will reveal some abnormality in the form of delusional beliefs, impaired reality testing, highly eccentric or bizarre ideation and occasionally homicidal or suicidal ideas. Delusions highly characteristic of this disorder include patient beliefs that his actions and thinking are being controlled by others; that the thoughts of others are being inserted into his mind; or that his thoughts are being broadcast and made known to others. Obsessive thinking and feelings of depersonalization (and derealization) are common. An associational disturbance is almost always present and may be mild or so severe that meaningful communication is difficult. It may be the most noticeable evidence of psychopathology. An example of an associational disturbance follows:

> "I came out to see my husband...he had to see his daughter. There was this time he came to Philadelphia with gifts for her, but that's never been enough. I went to Seattle first, don't know why...guess because I was afraid of his girlfriend. Maybe I should have let him in. He had people sent to our home to rape my little daughter. I knew she's been raped when she came out of the bathroom hopping on one foot. He had me put here so he wouldn't have to pay child support."

Now complete Self-Assessment Exercise #1 beginning on the following page.

Self-Assessment Exercise #1

1. Briefly describe a present day hypothesis about the etiology of Schizophrenic Disorders.

2. Indicate whether the following statements about Schizophrenic Disorders are true (T) or false (F).

_____a. Schizophrenic Disorders are often the result of an interaction of multiple factors.

_____b. reality testing and judgment for routine activities is frequently impaired

_____c. some degree of an associational disturbance is typically present

_____d. thought content is generally unusual or strange

_____e. some Schizophrenic Disorders may result from an inherited biochemical defect

_____f. some Schizophrenic Disorders can be precipitated by a traumatic life event

_____g. auditory hallucinations are more common than visual ones

_____h. most patients with schizophrenia show impairment of orientation and recent memory

_____i. all Schizophrenic Disorders share a common etiology

Self-Assessment Exercise #1 (continued)

3.   In the spaces provided, briefly characterize the
     MSE findings of an individual with a Schizophrenic
     Disorder:

_____

APPEARANCE

_____

BEHAVIOR

_____

AFFECT/MOOD

_____

PERCEPTION

_____

THINKING

_____

When you have completed this exercise to the best
of your ability, check your answers with those on the
following page.

Self-Assessment Exercise #1 - Feedback

1. The etiology of Schizophrenic Disorders is felt to
    involve a genetic predisposition and the presence
    of various external experiential stresses. These
    stresses can include chronic distortions of family
    and communications, derangements of the early mother-
    child relationship, social and cultural factors and
    acute short-lived traumatic experiences.

2.

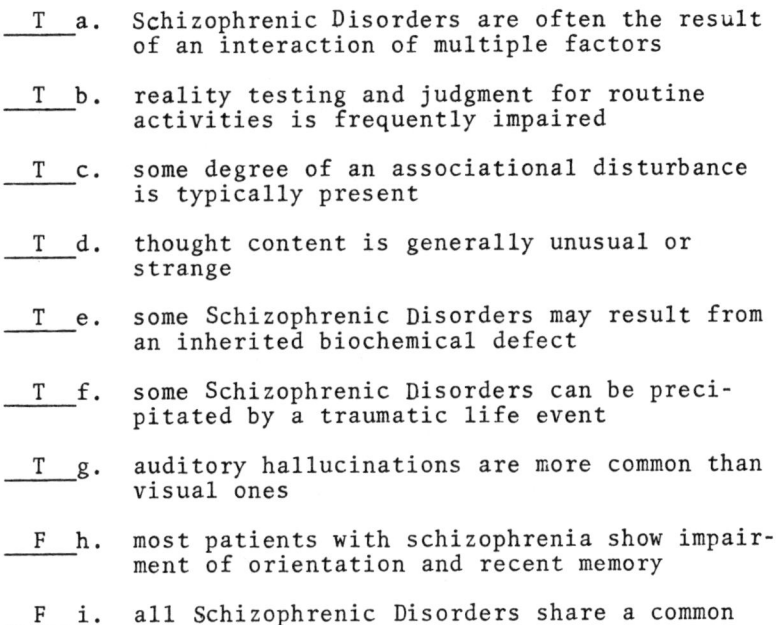

    ___T___ a. Schizophrenic Disorders are often the result
                of an interaction of multiple factors

    ___T___ b. reality testing and judgment for routine
                activities is frequently impaired

    ___T___ c. some degree of an associational disturbance
                is typically present

    ___T___ d. thought content is generally unusual or
                strange

    ___T___ e. some Schizophrenic Disorders may result from
                an inherited biochemical defect

    ___T___ f. some Schizophrenic Disorders can be preci-
                pitated by a traumatic life event

    ___T___ g. auditory hallucinations are more common than
                visual ones

    ___F___ h. most patients with schizophrenia show impair-
                ment of orientation and recent memory

    ___F___ i. all Schizophrenic Disorders share a common
                etiology

3.   Mental Status Findings of a Schizophrenic Disorder

APPEARANCE	Variable according to severity, but typically disheveled, eccentric or bizarre.
BEHAVIOR	Generally atypical or strange. Body movements--erratic, tense or slowed. Facial expression--apprehensive or atypically bland. Speech--rapid and intense or dull, slow, monotone. Therapist-patient relationship--emotional distance; distrust; negativistic; uncooperative.
AFFECT/MOOD	Variable. May range from intense anxiety or hostility to persistent blandness or "blunting." Often inappropriate to thought content.
PERCEPTION	Illusions and/or hallucinations often present. Auditory more frequent than visual hallucinations. Hallucinations are usually critical or persecutory.
THINKING	Alertness, orientation, memory usually intact. Reality testing, judgment typically impaired. Delusions, phobias, depersonalization often present. Ideas are eccentric or bizarre. Associational disturbance almost always present

If your answers correspond closely with those above, please continue reading on the next page. If not, please reread the preceding material.

SCHIZOPHRENIC AND SCHIZOPHRENIFORM DISORDERS
     Many clinicians believe that it is useful to dis-
tinguish between Schizophrenic and Schizophreniform Disorders. Although, in many cases, the MSE findings of the
two conditions are quite similar, the ultimate course
and prognosis may be quite different.
     Schizophrenic Disorders have often been called, "true
schizophrenia," "nonreactive schizophrenia," or "process
schizophrenia." This condition is typified by long-
standing problems with personal relationships, shyness and
marginal school and work performance. There often is
a greater incidence of schizophrenic symptoms among close
family members than in the general population. In this
condition, symptoms usually begin insidiously, taking
months or years to develop, and are difficult to correlate
with any actual life problems. Affective tone generally
is dulled or blunted, and when the patient is initially
evaluated, psychological and behavioral disorganization
is not dramatic. Response to medication and other therapeutic intervention is slow, recovery incomplete, and
relapses which necessitate repeated hospitalization are
common. For this diagnosis to be assigned, symptoms must
be continuously present for six months or longer during
the patient's life time and some residual psychopathology
evident at the time of examination.
     The term "Schizophreniform Disorder" is synonymous in
the psychiatric literature with "reactive schizophrenia" or
"non process schizophrenia." In this condition, the life
adjustment pattern prior to the onset of symptoms is
characterized by relatively stable interpersonal relationships and satisfactory performance at work and school.
There is no significant increased incidence of this disorder in close family members. The symptoms usually develop abruptly, last one week but less than six months, and
the acute phase of this disorder, patients are likely to
show intense affect in the form of anxiety, depression or
hostility. Symptoms of psychosis are typically quite
dramatic with prominent delusions, hallucinations and
mental disorganization. Patient response to medication
and active therapeutic intervention often is good.
     Schizophrenic Disorders do not always end in unre-
mitting debility. Approximately one third of those persons
who suffer an acute episode which then resolves have no
further relapses. Another one third have recurrences of
symptoms which need intensive therapeutic intervention,
but enjoy intervals of productive and well-adjusted living.
The remaining one third of the cases follow an inexorable
downhill course. For these individuals there occurs
a pronounced personality disintegration and progressively
impaired capacity to function effectively in daily life.

SUB-TYPES OF SCHIZOPHRENIC DISORDERS
Diagnostic subtypes of Schizophrenic Disorders are classified according to the prominent findings and symptoms which patients present.

Paranoid
The paranoid type of Schizophrenic Disorder is diagnosed when delusions and/or hallucinations are present which have a prominent theme of persecution, grandiosity and/or jealousy. Major disorganization of patient behavior is rare, but many individuals with this disorder demonstrate hostility, suspiciousness, anxiety and delusions of reference.

Catatonic
Catatonic Schizophrenic Disorders are noted by the presence of extremes of movement ranging from stupor and muscular rigidity to continuous hyperactivity. Patients frequently are verbally unresponsive, negativistic and demonstrate unusual posturing, facial grimaces and other stereotyped behavior. Persons with catatonia sometimes refuse to eat or drink for extended periods of time. They may become exhausted or seriously injure themselves or others.

Undifferentiated
Undifferentiated Schizophrenic Disorders refer to those conditions in which delusions and/or hallucinations are present but lack a control ideational theme (e.g., suspiciousness or grandiosity) or behavioral pattern (e.g., posturing) characteristic of the paranoid or catatonic types described above. Patients with undifferentiated schizophrenia may demonstrate a variety of delusions, hallucinations and disorganized behavior as well as having a disturbance of associations.

Residual
This diagnosis is assigned to persons who have experienced a Schizophrenic Disorder in the past but no longer show prominent delusions, hallucinations or disorganized behavior. Delusions and hallucinations, if present, are of mild intensity. Social withdrawal, inappropriate or blunted affect, atypical behavior and/or the presence of an associational disturbance comprise the most noteworthy findings.

Now complete Self-Assessment Exercise #2 beginning on the following page.

Self-Assessment Exercise #2

1. Compare Schizophreniform and Schizophrenic Disorders
    by indicating whether the findings are "Present"
    or "Absent."

	Schizophreni- form Disorders	Schizophrenic Disorders
a. rapid onset		
b. precipitating life stress often present		
c. good life ad- justment prior to onset		
d. presence of intense anxiety/ affect		
e. presence of emo- tional "blunting"		
f. increased familial incidence of Schi- zophrenic Disorders		
g. good long-term prognosis		
h. symptoms present over six months		

2. For each of the findings below, indicate with which
    of the subtypes of Schizophrenic Disorders it is
    most likely to be associated:

    P=Paranoid   C=Catatonic   U=Undifferentiated
     R=Residual

    _____ a. A teenage patient who moves slowly, stiffly and
              refuses to speak.
    _____ b. A middle aged woman describes intense feelings
              that she is being followed by the Mafia wherever
              she goes and that strangers on the street stare
              at and talk about her.
    _____ c. Six months after being discharged from the hospi-
              tal for psychiatric treatment, the young man kept
              to himself. He maintained some strange ideas
              about special powers he had and spoke in a some-
              what disorganized fashion, but managed his own
              affairs on a day-to-day basis.

Self-Assessment Exercise #2 (continued)

_____ d.   The patient gives a rambling disjointed history
           about being an undercover agent for the F.B.I.;
           she describes auditory hallucinations consisting
           of "voices" arguing inside her head; she is
           very preoccupied with "the meaning of life"
           and is unable to care for herself.

        When you have completed this exercise to the best
of your ability, check your answers with those on the
following page.

Self-Assessment Exercise #2 - Feedback

1.

		Schizophreni-form Disorders	Schizophrenic Disorders
a.	rapid onset	Present	Absent
b.	precipitating life stress often present	Present	Absent
c.	good life adjust-ment prior to onset	Present	Absent
d.	presence of intense anxiety/affect	Present	Absent
e.	presence of emo-tional "blunting"	Absent	Present
f.	increased familial incidence of schizo-phrenic disorders	Absent	Present
g.	good long-term prognosis	Present	Absent
h.	symptoms present over six months	Absent	Present

2.

<u>C</u> a. A teenage patient who moves slowly, stiffly and refuses to speak.

<u>P</u> b. A middle aged woman describes intense feelings that she is being followed by the Mafia wherever she goes and that strangers on the street stare at and talk about her.

<u>R</u> c. Six months after being discharged from the hospital for psychiatric treatment, the young man kept to himself. He maintained some strange ideas about special powers he had and spoke in a somewhat dis-organized fashion, but managed his own affairs on a day-to-day basis.

<u>U</u> d. The patient gives a rambling, disjointed history about being an undercover agent for the F.B.I.: she describes auditory hallucinations consisting of "voices" arguing inside her head; she is very pre-occupied with "the meaning of life" and is unable to care for herself.

If your answers correspond closely with those above, please continue reading on the next page. If not, please reread the preceding material.

SUMMARY

Schizophrenic Disorders are severe mental conditions lasting six months or longer and often characterized by the presence of delusions, hallucinations, a thought disorder and bizarre behavior. These disorders often are severely debilitating and constitute a major health problem for affected patients and society in general. Early recognition and therapeutic intervention may favorably affect the outcome of those conditions.

ACKNOWLEDGMENTS

The authors wish to credit Laurance S. Reid, M. D. for the material on schizophrenia published in the first edition of this book upon which much of the present chapter is based.

REFERENCES

Bellak, L. (ed): The Disorders of the Schizophrenic Syndrome. New York: Basic Books, 1979.

Mendel, W.: Supportive Care. Los Angeles: Mara Books, 1975.

Rakoff, V. M., Stancer, H. C., Kedivard, H. D. (editors): Psychiatric Diagnosis. New York: Brunner/Mazel, 1977.

Spitzer, R. L., Anderson, N. D., Endicott, J.: Schizophrenia and Other Psychotic Disorders in DSM III. Schizophrenia Bulletin 4(4):489-509, 1978.

Stephens, J. H.: Long Term Prognosis and Follow up in Schizophrenia. Schizophrenia Bulletin 4:25-47, 1978.

Strauss, J. S., Carpenter, W. T., Jr.: Characteristic Symptoms and Outcome in Schizophrenia. Archives of General Psychiatry, 30:429-434, 1974.

Chapter 12

Affective Disorders
C. Warner Johnson

Affective Disorders comprise a group of psychopathologic conditions in which prominent alterations of mood and activity occur, ranging from depression and underactivity to mania and hyperactivity. Affective Disorders may occur in varying intensities and combinations of symptoms and can be associated with such factors as physical illness, the use of medications, psychological stress and heredity. These disorders are relatively common, and in their most disabling form affect approximately one percent of the population. In this chapter we will discuss Affective Disorders in terms of their typical findings, etiology, causes and significant subtypes.

LEARNING OBJECTIVES
By the time you complete the material in this chapter you should be able to:

1. Describe the physical and mental status examination findings typical of a depressive syndrome.

2. Describe the physical and mental status examination findings typical of a manic syndrome.

3. Correctly define and apply to case histories the following terms:

        Bipolar Disorder
        Major Depression
        Major Affective Disorder
        Cyclothymic Disorder
        Dysthymic Disorder (Depressive Neurosis)
        Unipolar Disorder

4. Briefly describe the three differentiating etiological factors that should be considered in persons manifesting an Affective Disorder.

By the conclusion of this chapter and with supervised clinical experience you should be able to:

1. Accurately observe and record a patient's behavior
   within each of the M.S.E. behavior descriptors.

2. Determine whether an Affective Disorder is present
   in a patient, given necessary M.S.E. information.

3. Indicate the history and M.S.E. findings which enabled you to make a diagnosis.

MENTAL STATUS FINDINGS OF AFFECTIVE DISORDERS
    There is considerable variability in the way individuals
manifest an affective disorder. However, if you become thoroughly familiar with the classic findings of depression and
mania, you will be able to recognize their presence in most
instances. We shall present separately the depressive and
manic syndromes.

Mental Status Examination (M.S.E.) Findings in Depressive
Syndromes.
    Appearance. The appearance of depressed persons gen-
erally corresponds with the severity of their disorder. For
example, if the depression is mild, they may show little abnormality of their appearance. However, in instances where
the disorder is more severe, the patients likely will appear
disheveled. Such patients often give the impression of being
fatigued or perhaps physically ill.

    Behavior. The facial expression associated with depres-
sion usually appears bland and unresponsive or lined by a
furrowed brow and down-turned mouth. Smiling rarely occurs.
Patients usually are slumped and show slowed and infrequent
movement and gestures. Exceptions to this are instances of
agitated depression during which patients may be markedly
tense, restless and fidgety. Speech generally is decreased
in amplitude and volume in most depressive conditions.

    Feeling. Most depressed persons will describe feeling
a combination of sadness, depression, a sense of futility
and an inability to feel pleasure. Their feelings typically
are appropriate to the expressed thought content.

    Perception. Illusions and hallucinations are relatively
rare phenomena. When hallucinations occur, their content
usually reflects those of guilt, personal loss or nihilism.

    Thinking. In all but the most severe depressions, in-
tellectual functioning ability remains intact. Therefore,
alertness, the ability to perform calculations or think abstractly, and orientation are mostly unaffected. The capacity for mental concentration may be impaired because of
self-preoccupation with sadness. Ideas of helplessness,
worry, hopelessness, self-recriminations and apathy are common findings. Suicidal ideation is regularly present and
should be explored fully. When psychosis is present, delusions which reflect exaggerated bodily concerns, sinfulness,
suspiciousness or guilt are frequent. An associational dis-

turbance does not occur but thinking can be greatly slowed.

M.S.E. Findings in Manic Syndromes

Mania, like the syndrome of depression, can be manifested by a combination of symptoms of varying intensities, but a triad of findings which are common to most persons with mania include an elated mood, hyperactivity and rapid, continuous speech.

Appearance. The patient's general appearance usually is in keeping with their emotional state and ranges from appropriate personal grooming to the wearing of outlandish clothing and being unkempt.

Behavior. Persons experiencing some degree of mania typically show an increase in the speed and amount of behavior and activity. They tend to be continuously active, pacing or fidgeting and punctuating their speech with expansive gesturing. Their facial expression and speech is typically quite animated. Speech is rapid and continuous. Because of their high levels of energy and talkativeness, manic persons may tend to dominate the interview.

Feeling. Characteristically, patients with mania demonstrate an elated, euphoric affect. This mood can rapidly change to one of irritability and antagonism if they become frustrated. Thought content and the affect being shown are congruent.

Perception. If psychosis is present, patients may describe auditory and visual hallucinations which usually have a theme to match their predominant affect, i.e., these phenomenon often reflect grandiosity.

Thinking. The intellectual functioning of persons with manic symptoms is generally intact. These patients are overly alert, and usually can be distracted by environmental stimuli. Although memory, orientation, the ability to calculate and think abstractly are intact, affected patients may have difficulty in completing intellectual tasks because of their distractibility. Insight and judgment are impaired, and these patients often act impulsively in accordance with their immediate feelings without considering long-range consequences. Many patients experience somewhat grandiose ideas about themselves and their capabilities. These expansive ideas may reach delusional proportions in which case they reflect themes of great personal power, wealth, importance, etc. An associational disturbance is usually present and patients characteristically jump rapidly from topic to topic as they speak.

Physical Symptoms Associated With Depressive and Manic Syndromes

There are many physical findings which are regularly associated with depressive and manic syndromes. In some cases, these findings may be the first indication that an Affective Disorder is present and helps to establish the correct diagnosis.

In a depressive syndrome, a disturbance of appetite, sleep and energy is typically present. Characteristically patients will describe a loss of appetite, weight, sleep and energy, but in some cases excessive eating and sleeping may occur. Depressed persons often complain of persistent bodily weakness, muscle pains and easy fatigability. Constipation, indigestion and disinterest in sexual activities are typical.

Manic patients often possess such an abundance of energy and interest in an array of projects that they neglect adequate rest and food. In some instances, they are unable to sleep because of their restless energy. Speech and physical activity is generally accelerated and continuous and most patients are tense, restless and talk uninterruptedly.

Now complete Self-Assessment Exercise #1 on the following page.

Self-Assessment Exercise #1

1. For each of the findings listed, indicate whether they are <u>most</u> characteristic of:

    M = a manic syndrome
    D = a depressive syndrome
    B = both a manic and depressive syndrome

    _____   a. impaired appetite and sleep

    _____   b. a sense of increased energy and capability

    _____   c. slowed speech and general activity

    _____   d. suicidal ideation

    _____   e. delusions and hallucinations

    _____   f. intact intellectual functioning, i.e., orientation, memory, etc.

    _____   g. feelings of self-recriminations and guilt

    _____   h. distractibility

    _____   i. feelings of helplessness and hopelessness

    _____   j. an associational disturbance

2. Briefly describe the M.S.E. findings typical to the manic and depressive syndromes in terms of:

	DEPRESSIVE SYNDROME	MANIC SYNDROME
rate of speech		
amount of physical activity		
predominant affect		
theme of thought content		
presence of an associational disturbance		

When you have completed this exercise to the best of your ability, check your answers with those on the following page.

Self-Assessment Exercise #1 - Feedback

1.   M = a manic syndrome
        D = a depressive syndrome
        B = both a manic and depressive syndrome

___B___   a. impaired appetite and sleep

___M___   b. a sense of increased energy and capability

___D___   c. slowed speech and general activity

___D___   d. suicidal ideation

___B___   e. delusions and hallucinations

___B___   f. intact intellectual functioning, i.e. orienta-
               tion, memory, etc.

___D___   g. feelings of self-recrimination and guilt

___B___   h. distractibility

___D___   i. feelings of helplessness and hopelessness

___M___   j. an associational disturbance

2.

	DEPRESSIVE SYNDROME	MANIC SYNDROME
rate of speech	decreased	increased
amount of physical activity	decreased	increased
predominant affect	depression, sadness	elation, euphoria, irritability
theme of thought content	hopelessness, loss, helplessness	optimism, grandiosity, expansiveness
presence of an associational disturbance	absent	present

        If your answers correspond closely with those above,
please continue reading; if not, please reread the preceding
section until you are confident you know the material.

ETIOLOGICAL FACTORS
        Although individuals may experience similar symptoms
suggestive of an Affective Disorder, the causes and courses
of their respective conditions can be very different. For
example, symptoms of elation and hyperactivity may result
from a person taking a central nervous system stimulant such
as amphetamine. These symptoms usually will disappear after
the drug is discontinued. Another individual initially may
demonstrate comparable hyperactivity which is secondary to
an inherited disorder and can episodically recur throughout
their life. In these examples the initial symptoms of an
affective disturbance are similar, but the prognosis and
treatment may vary considerably.

        One or a combination of physical, psychological and
hereditary factors may be involved in causing significant
changes in affect and behavior. It is important that you
investigate these factors in each patient with a prominent
affective disturbance. Examples of psychological factors
which can produce a depressive disorder (or more rarely mania)
are significant personal losses, i.e., health, finances, or
relationships. Physical factors commonly implicated in bringing about affective changes are various medical illnesses and
prescribed medications or "street drugs." Thyroid disorders,
viral infections, prescribed medications (i.e., sedatives
hormones, and psychotropic drugs) as well as illicitly used
drugs (i.e., PCP, cocaine, LSD and amphetamines) can cause
mild or profound alterations of movement and behavior. Depressive and manic syndromes due to physical factors are
classified as Organic Affective Syndromes. Hereditary factors may be involved in some cases which may predispose an
individual to developing particular types of Affective Disorders, i.e., a Bipolar Disorder (to be described later).
Ask persons with Major Affective Disorders if they have close
family members (parents, siblings, etc.) who have been troubled by depressive or manic behavior, psychiatric problems
or alcoholism. Many persons overuse alcohol when attempting
to reduce symptoms of depression.

DIAGNOSTIC CLASSIFICATION OF AFFECTIVE DISORDERS
        In this chapter we will adopt the terminology of Affec-
tive Disorders presented in the Diagnostic and Statistical
Manual of Mental Disorders, Third Edition (DSM - III). To
assist your learning we suggest that you read Table 1 which
compares DSM - III diagnoses with those used in the past.
It is important to note that depression or manic syndromes
secondary to illness or drugs are defined as Organic Affective Syndromes. Similarly, common grief reactions or affective disturbances associated with schizophrenia should not
be classified as Affective Disorders.

        Major Affective Disorders are psychopathologic conditions
in which episodes of manic and/or depressive syndromes occur
that are separated by intervals of normal functioning. The
intervals between attacks can last from weeks to years. The
manic or depressive symptoms are usually severe and cause
considerable impairment of daily functioning. Delusions and/
or hallucinations may occur.

TABLE 1

NEWLY RECOMMENDED DSM-III DIAGNOSES
COMPARED WITH THOSE USED FORMERLY (DSM-II)

DSM-III (Recommended Terminology)	DSM-II
MAJOR AFFECTIVE DISORDERS	
Bipolar Disorder	Manic-Depressive Illness
mixed	Manic-Depressive Illness, circular type
manic	Manic-Depressive Illness, manic type
depressed	Manic-Depressive Illness, depressive type
Major Depression	Involutional Melancholia
single episode	Psychotic Depressive Reaction (reactive depressive psychosis)
recurrent	Manic-Depressive Illness, depressive type
OTHER SPECIFIC AFFECTIVE DISORDERS	
Cyclothymic Disorder	Cyclothymic Personality
Dysthymic Disorder (or depressive neurosis)	Depressive Neurosis

The Major Affective Disorders include two diagnostic
subtypes. Bipolar Disorders[1] and Major Depression[2]. A Bipolar Disorder implies that discreet episodes of mania and
depression will both occur during the course of the condition. A typical Bipolar Disorder will begin before the age
of 30 and runs a course of alternating episodes of mania and
depressive symptoms. Patients who experience a single manic
attack as well as those who already have had cycles of mania
and depressive symptoms, are assigned this diagnosis. By
definition, a Bipolar Disorder is a recurrent condition and
inherited genetic factors are often implicated in this type
of psychopathology.

A Major Depression consists of a moderately severe depressive syndrome which lasts at least one week. The depressive symptoms can be manifested as a single episode or
recur and be present in varying degrees of severity. Delusions and/or hallucinations may be present. Significant
life stress or loss can precipitate a single episode of Major
Depression whereas recurrent episodes of depression may be
caused by inherited factors.

Cyclothymic Disorders and Dysthymic Disorders (depressive neurosis) are milder conditions in which alternating
periods of mood may occur. In comparison with Major Affective Disorders, these conditions are of milder severity and
do not interfere so much with daily functioning. The Cyclothymic Disorder is a condition in which persons have alternating episodes of mild depression and manic syndromes. The
diagnosis of a Dysthymic Disorder (depressive neurosis) is
assigned to persons with depressive symptoms which are of excessive duration or intensity in relationship to causes of
events. In many cases, no specific etiological factors can
be identified.

Now complete Self-Assessment Exercise #2 on the following page.

----

[1]Terms indicating "polarity" are widely used for class-
ifying affective disorders. The term "unipolar" signifies a condition charactered by a single affect,
i.e. depression. Whereas a bipolar disorder refers
to a condition which includes episodes of both mania
and depression.

[2]Major Depressive Disorders encompass a variety of
conditions which were formally diagnosed separately
as Psychotic Depressive Reaction, Involutional Melan-
cholia, and Manic Depressive Illness, Depressive
Type.

Self-Assessment Exercise #2

1. Indicate whether the following statements are true (T) or false (F):

_____ a. A Major Depression may occur or be limited to a single episode.

_____ b. The depressive symptoms of a Dysthymic Disorder are more prolonged than those of a Major Depression.

_____ c. Delusions and/or hallucinations may be found in Cyclothymic and Dysthymic Disorders.

_____ d. A manic syndrome caused by drugs is classified as an Organic Affective Syndrome.

_____ e. A Major Depression is by definition a Bipolar Disorder.

_____ f. The depressive syndrome following the death of a loved one is appropriately classified as a Major Affective Disorder.

_____ g. Major Affective Disorders are episodic in nature and attacks are separated by periods of relatively normal functioning.

2. For each case vignette below, indicate the most appropriate diagnosis from the following:

   a. Bipolar Disorder
   b. Major Depression
   c. Organic Affective Syndrome
   d. Cyclothymic Disorder
   e. Dysthymic Disorder (or depressive neurosis)

A. The young woman described intense feelings of depression and hopelessness. She showed evidence of slowed movement, speech and expressed suicidal ideation. The onset of her symptoms coincided with being placed on birth control pills.

_____

B. A middle-aged business man developed symptoms of a progressively severe depression over a several-month period. He was in good health, not taking any medications and never had previous psychological problems. His depression reached severe proportions and he was not able to function at his job.

_____

C.   Over an 8-year period, a 35-year-old woman had experienced three episodes of hyperactive behavior and an elated affect, which lasted several weeks or more. She intermittedly had depressive attacks which were characterized by marked loss of energy, insomnia, and weight loss. She was not able to manage her daily affairs during episodes of affective disturbances.

_____

D.   A 26-year-old man sought treatment for persistent depressive feelings of at least four years duration. The symptoms were persistent but mild in nature and did not severely impair his daily activities. He was unable to identify specific causes for his feeling of depression.

_____

3.   List three possible factors which singly or in combination may be causative of Affective Disorders.

When you have completed this exercise to the best of your ability, check your answers with those on the following page.

Self-Assessment Exercise #3 - Feedback

1. The following statements are true or false as indicated:

___T___   a. A Major Depression may recur or be limited to
               a single episode.

___T___   b. The depressive symptoms of a Dysthymic Disorder
               are more prolonged than those of a Major De-
               pression.

___F___   c. Delusions and/or hallucinations may be found
               in Cyclothymic and Dysthymic Disorders.

___T___   d. A manic syndrome caused by drugs is classified
               as an Organic Affective Syndrome.

___F___   e. A Major Depression is by definition a Bipolar
               Disorder.

___F___   f. The depressive syndrome following the death of
               a loved one is appropriately classified as a
               Major Affective Disorder

___T___   g. Major Affective Disorders are episodic in na-
               ture and attacks are separated by periods of
               relatively normal functioning.

2. The most appropriate diagnosis for each case vignette
    is as follows:

    A.   (c)   Organic Affective Syndrome

    B.   (b)   Major Depression

    C.   (a)   Bipolar Disorder

    D.   (e)   Dysthymic Disorder (or depressive neurosis)

3. The possible factors which singly or in combination
    may be causative of Affective Disorders are:

            physical factors
            psychological factors
            hereditary factors

    If your answers correspond closely with those above,
please continue reading; if not, please reread the preceding
section until you are confident you know the material.

SUMMARY
Affective Disorders comprise a group of mood disturbances which have in common symptoms of mania and/or depression. These conditions may be caused by a variety of factors. Accurate diagnostic classification is important for treatment purposes and should be based upon a consideration of M.S.E. findings, and symptom course of each patient.

REFERENCES

Diagnostic and Statistical Manual of Mental Disorders, Third Edition, Washington, D.C., American Psychiatric Association, 1979.

Goodwin, D. and Guze, S.: Psychiatric Diagnosis, Second Edition, Oxford University Press, 1979.

Price, J.S.: Chronic Depressive Illness, Brit. Med. J., 1:1200-1201, 1978.

Van Valkenburg, C., et al: Depressive spectrum disease versus pure depressive disease. J. Nerv. Ment. Disease, 165:341-347, 1977.

Windcur, G.: Types of depressive illness. Brit. J. of Psychiatry, 120:265-266, 1972.

Woodruff, R., Murphy, G. and Herjanic, M.: The natural history of affective disorders. J. Psychiat. Res., 5:255-263, 1967.

Diagnostic and Statistical Manual of Mental Disorders, 3rd Edition, Washington, D.C., American Psychiatric Association, 1979.

Chapter 13

Anxiety Disorders
John R. Snibbe

This chapter deals with a group of emotional disorders which are characterized either by painfully intense
feelings of anxiety or behaviors (phobias, compulsions,
etc.) which attempt to control it.

Symptoms of anxiety are among the most commonly
described emotional complaints in our society. Many of
the patients seen by therapists in office or hospital
practices will demonstrate some signs of anxiety. In fact,
many medical problems are aggravated or even caused by the
presence of severe anxiety. It is helpful, therefore, to
be able to recognize these common problems.

Symptoms of anxiety can be associated with a variety
of psychiatric disorders. However, for this diagnostic
classification, major personality disorganization is rare
and loss of contact with reality unusual. Most individuals
with anxiety disorders can maintain employment and continue
to function in their usual roles and activities.

It is important for the therapist to become familiar
with different manifestations of anxiety since they are
presented by patients independent of, or in conjunction
with, all types of physical and psychological problems.

LEARNING OBJECTIVES
By the time you complete the material in this chapter
you should be able to:

1. Correctly define the term <u>anxiety</u>.

2. Describe for each of the five major categories of
   the mental status examination the findings typical
   of an individual manifesting a:

   a. schizophrenic disorder
   b. organic mental disorder
   c. anxiety disorder

4. Briefly describe the distinguishing characteristics for each of the following:

   a. Generalized Anxiety Disorder
   b. Panic Disorder
   c. Phobic Disorder (phobic neurosis)
   d. Obsessive-Compulsive Disorder (obsessive
      compulsive neurosis).

By the conclusion of this chapter and the supervised
clinical experience you should be able to:

1. Accurately observe and record a patient's behavior
   within each of the M.S.E. behavior descriptors.

2. Determine whether an anxiety disorder is present
   in a patient, given necessary M.S.E. information.

3. Indicate the history and M.S.E. findings which
   enabled you to make a diagnosis.

MENTAL STATUS FINDINGS

Anxiety is the feeling of dread or apprehension that
is typical of a response to a marked physical or psychological threat. Feelings of anxiety are usually accompanied by physical symptoms such as restlessness, muscle
tension, sweating, tremors and irritability.

Under each category of the Mental Status Examination
listed below are the typical findings that one might expect in a patient with an anxiety disorder.

Appearance

Many patients with Anxiety Disorders appear normal
and show little outward sign of their internal suffering.
However, this is not always the case with persons with
severe anxiety. Sometimes the "wear and tear" of emotional
discomfort will show as a tired look, circles under the
eyes, tenseness and similar signs of stress or pressure.
These patients may tremble or appear pale and frightened.
They may also perspire freely.

Behavior

Very often anxious patients show some disturbance of
their behavior. They often act and speak as if tense and
anxious. They may appear restless, jumpy and overreact
to personally significant events that other people would
ignore. Their behavior is not bizarre, but frequently one
can sense that something is "not right" with them. The
therapist patient relationship in many ways. At times the
act of consulting a professional may be a "cry for help"
expressing an emotional problem rather than actual physical
pathology. The physical concomitants of anxiety such as
stomach upset, headache, fatigue and rapid heartbeat may
prompt a patient to seek medical attention. If the
physician is not alert to this possibility, he may misinterpret the patient's motives and erroneously feel the
patient to be malingering, demanding, or uncooperative.

Feeling (Affect and Mood)

Some manifestations and derivatives of anxiety are
always present in these patients. For example, they often
report that they "feel badly." They complain of feeling
anxious, "nervous," apprehensive or "I'm not myself."
They may feel unrealistically guilty about things that
they have done. Their affect, however, is generally appropriate and corresponds to their thought content.

Perception

Sensory perception is usually unaffected by the presence of anxiety. An individual with an anxiety disorder
may experience an illusion (a misinterpretation of a real
stimulus) but not hallucinations (a sensory perception in
the absence of a real or external stimulus).

Thinking
        Anxious patients do not often show a marked thinking
disorder. They may be overly preoccupied with themselves
and their problems, but generally their intellectual
functions, (the ability to use abstract thought and make
mathematical calculations) are within normal limits.
Memory and orientation are intact. Because of their
anxiety, decision-making may be difficult or faulty and
hence **judgment** may be impaired. Meaningful insight is
typically decreased.

        The thought content of anxious persons is often
"abnormal." They do not experience delusions or paranoid
ideas; however, they may have inappropriate fears of
harmless things or situations (phobias). At times, they
may feel compelled to perform repetitive acts (compulsions)
or experience recurrent unwanted thoughts (obsessions).
They may express a feeling of impending catastrophe or
personal disaster. Despite the unusual content of their
thinking, their use of logic is not impaired greatly, and
associational disturbances are not found. In the presence
of anxiety, thought flow may be increased.

        Now complete Self-Assessment Exercise #1 on the
following page.

Self-Assessment Exercise #1

1.   Define the term Anxiety.

2.   Indicate below the mental status findings associated
     with Anxiety.

     a.   Appearance

     b.   Behavior

     c.   Feeling (Affect and Mood)

     d.   Perception

     e.   Thinking

     When you have completed this exercise to the best of
your ability, check your answers with those on the
following page.

Self-Assessment Exercise #1 - Feedback

1. Anxiety is a common emotional symptom characterized
    by feelings of mild to severe apprehension and/or
    may be manifested by maladaptive behaviors; such as
    phobia, and compulsions. Daily functioning remains
    intact and no psychotic symptoms are present.

2. The mental status findings associated with anxiety
    are:

    a. Appearance: Tiredness, tensions, signs of "wear
        excessive perspiration.

    b. Behavior: Restlessness, overreacting and jumpy.

    c. Feeling (affect and mood): Sense of "not being
        oneself," withdrawal, an overriding sense of
        fear and apprehension.

    d. Perception: Illusions possible. No hallucina-
        tions.

    e. Thinking: Preoccupation with self, inappropriate
        fears, recurrent unwanted thoughts, increased
        thought flow, worry, fear that something bad will
        happen (impending catastrophe). No true associa-
        tional disturbance; no impairment of orientation,
        memory or intellectual functioning. No delusions.

     If your answers correspond closely with those above,
please continue your reading on the following page; if
not, please reread the preceding section until you are
confident you know the material.

ANXIETY DISORDERS DISTINGUISHED FROM OTHER EMOTIONAL DISORDERS

The intensity and kind of symptoms present in an Anxiety Disorder differs greatly from those of a Schizophrenic Disorder. In the former, persons are troubled and unhappy, but they manage to function and their thinking patterns and feelings are not grossly impaired. In contrast, individuals with schizophrenia are generally markedly disordered in terms of their daily living activities, feelings and thinking. The person with a Schizophrenic Disorder may also show significantly more social and vocational instability. Typically they have a history of past emotional problems including impaired reality testing (the ability to distinguish personal feelings and wishes from the real world). Persons with Schizophrenic Disorders tend to blame others, or "powers" for their problems and may also be delusional. Patients with schizophrenia may also show an associational disturbance and severe perceptual disturbances such as hallucinations.

The mental status findings of persons with an Anxiety Disorder differ significantly from patients with an Organic Mental Disorder. Individuals with an Organic Mental Disorder usually show impaired recent and remote memory, disorientation and mental confusion. Their intellectual functions are also impaired. Perceptual abnormalities such as illusions and/or hallucinations may occur. Persons with an Anxiety Disorder do not have such symptoms.

Now complete Self-Assessment Exercise #2 on the following pages.

Self-Assessment Exercise #2

1. Compare and contrast the mental status findings for
    Anxiety Disorders, Schizophrenic Disorders, and
    Organic Mental Disorders.

	ANXIETY DISORDERS
BEHAVIOR	
FEELING (AFFECT AND MOOD)	
PERCEPTION	
THINKING	

SCHIZOPHRENIC DISORDERS	ORGANIC MENTAL DISORDER

Self-Assessment Exercise #2 (continued)

2. R. W., a 48-year-old male was brought by ambulance
to a hospital emergency room for consultation. He
was observed to be breathing deeply and rapidly and
to be quite apprehensive, restless and was perspiring.
Mr. W. complained that he felt "dizzy" and just
"couldn't get enough air." He described a sensation
of numbness in both of his hands and about his face,
and was panicked by the thought that a "stroke" was
imminent. A cardiac and a cursory physical examination were performed and were within normal limits.
The physician's firm verbal reassurance and injection
of a mild sedative brought about a remission of
symptoms. After Mr. W. became calm, he related a coherent history that the episode was the third of its
kind during the past six weeks. His breathing,
however, was normal in between the episodes. Each
incident of rapid breathing began as a vague sense
of uneasiness and soon escalated to a feeling of
impending disaster or sudden death. The symptoms,
each time, followed a violent argument with his
teen-age son.

   a. Assuming that actual physical pathology was ruled
   out, which diagnosis would be appropriate for
   Mr. W.? Check one.

   Organic Mental Disorder
   Schizophrenic Disorder
   Anxiety Disorder

   b. List M.S.E. and other findings from the above
   history that substantiate your judgment.

When you have completed this exercise to the best of your ability, check your answers with those on the following pages.

Self-Assessment Exercise #2 - Feedback

	ANXIETY DISORDER
BEHAVIOR	variable
FEELING (AFFECT AND MOOD)	predominant mood is anxiety; feelings are appropriate to thought content
PERCEPTION	no abnormalities
THINKING	no major intellectual impairment (i.e., memory orientation), phobias and/or obsessions may be present. No delusions

SCHIZOPHRENIC DISORDERS	ORGANIC MENTAL DISORDER
often atypical, unusual	variable, may be restless
inappropriate to thought content and/or excessive	variable
illusions and/or hallucinations (auditory)	variable; may be hallucinations (usually visual)
intellectual functioning and orientation intact; disordered insight, delusions frequently present, reality testing impaired; associational disturbance common	impaired; level of consciousness, orientation, recent memory, intellectual functioning

Self-Assessment Exercise #2 - Feedback (continued)

2. a. The appropriate diagnosis for Mr. W. would be an
        anxiety disorder.

    b. No indication of O.M.D. or schizophrenia on M.S.E.
        finding (recent memory intact, history is co-
        herent, no perceptive abnormalities noted).
        Patient appears to be anxious and describes
        similar feelings.

        Somatic signs and symptoms are consistent with
        feelings of intense anxiety.

      If your answers correspond closely with those above,
please continue your reading on the following page; if
not, please reread the preceding section until you are
confident you know the material.

TYPES OF ANXIETY DISORDERS
The following syndromes represent four commonly encountered sub-types of Anxiety Disorders. It should be
kept in mind that, while most disorders contain a mixture
of symptoms, the specific diagnosis is determined by the
most pervasive and predominant symptoms.

Generalized Anxiety Disorders
This disorder is characterized by chronic anxiety
ranging from mild discomfort to periods of severe apprehension that last at least six (6) months. The patient
constantly feels nervous and frightened, often for no
obvious reason. There may be physiological manifestations
such as sweating palms, dizziness, hot and cold spells,
dry mouth and upset stomach. Motor tension may also be
chronically present, manifested as tenseness, muscular
aches or an inability to relax. These patients also con-
tinually worry, ruminate and anticipate disastrous events.
Finally anxious expectation may result in sleep problems,
impatience, irritability and hyper-vigilance. The following is an example of a Generalized Anxiety Disorder:

> A 23-year-old woman has consulted her physician be-
> cause of "sleep problems." She reports she is too
> "nervous" to sleep and has felt tense and irritable
> for over a year. She occasionally gets a dry mouth
> and upset stomach and "can't seem to sit still." She
> also occasionally feels that something terrible will
> happen but is not clear exactly what. She reports no
> unusual events in her life and is at a loss to explain
> her experiences. During the interview she appeared
> tense, restless, apprehensive and distractible.

Panic Disorder
This disorder is characterized by periodic episodes of
severe and crippling anxiety or nervousness. These episodes are often so intense that they are frequently referred
to as "Panic Attacks." These attacks do not coincide with
any event, episode, or particular stimuli which the patient
can identify. These periods are episodic, recurrent, and
patients with this disorder appear and act normally at all
other times. These attacks can be characterized by the
intense experience of at least four of the following symptoms: palpatations, chest pain, choking, hot or cold
flashes, feeling faint, sweating, fear of dying, dizziness,
trembling, and a sense of unreality. Occasionally patients
with this disorder become so fearful of an impending attack that they are reluctant to leave home or other "safe
environment." The following is an example of a Panic
Disorder:

Mr. M. was driving with his wife to catch the
morning commuter train. He said "I don't feel well."
He pulled the car over and grabbed his chest. He
became pale, sweaty, and gasped for breath. He said
"I'm dying, I'm dying." When rushed to an emergency
room he was found to be in normal health and physical
condition. Gradually over a two-hour period he re-
covered his composure and was feeling fine. He
experssed concern that this might happen again.

Now complete Self-Assessment Exercise #3 beginning
on the next page.

Self-Assessment Exercise #3

1. For each of the descriptions below indicate in the
    space provided whether it is a:

    a. Generalized Anxiety Disorder
    b. Panic Disorder
    c. Both a and b.

    _____(1) Physical symptoms may be present such as sweating,
    rapid heartbeat, and a sense of dread.

    _____(2) Causes of anxiety are unclear to the patient.

    _____(3) Symptoms of anxiety are present for 6 months or
    longer.

    _____(4) Symptoms are severe, intense, brief and not
    caused by an external event which the patient
    can identify.

2. A 26-year-old man comes to a mental health clinic in
    severe distress. He is "jittery," restless, fidgeting
    and can't sit still in the waiting room. When asked
    to enter your office he shakes hands and his palms
    are wet. He complains of upset stomach and diarrhea.
    He says recently he has begun to worry about every
    little thing. He says he can't sleep and is always
    looking around expecting something bad to happen.
    He can't explain why this is happening but felt that
    way almost a year. Recently he was divorced but was
    not visibly upset at that time.

    a. Based upon the history, which diagnosis would be
        generally applied to this man? Check one.

        _____Generalized Anxiety Disorder

        _____Panic Disorder

    b. Substantiate your diagnosis.

    When you have completed this exercise to the best of
your ability, check your answers with those on the
following page.

Self-Assessment Exercise #3 - Feedback

1. For each of the following descriptions below indicate
    in the space provided whether it is a:

    a. Generalized Anxiety Disorder
    b. Panic Disorder
    c. Both a and B.

    __c__ (1) Physical symptoms may be present such as sweating,
               rapid hearbeat, and a sense of dread.

    __c__ (2) Causes of anxiety are unclear to the patient.

    __a__ (3) Symptoms of anxiety are present for 6 months
               or longer.

    __b__ (4) Symptoms are severe, intense, brief and not
               caused by an external event which the patient
               can identify.

2.a. The diagnosis generally applied to the man in this
     case would be Generalized Anxiety Disorder.

  b. Severe motor tension, hyperactivity, apprehension,
     vigilance. No apparent reason for his fears.
     Symptoms over 6 months duration.

        If your answers correspond closely with those above,
please continue your reading on the following page; if not,
please reread the preceding section until you are confident you know the material.

TYPES OF ANXIETY DISORDERS (Continued)

Phobic Disorder
    The most prominent symptom of a Phobic Disorder
(phobic neurosis) is an intense and exaggerated fear of
a situation or object that in reality is relatively harmless. Common phobias include those of animals, fear of
closed-in places such as elevators, fear of heights, being
in crowds or of leaving home, etc. The phobic individual
realizes that his fear is inappropriate and excessive but
his fear remains unabated by reasoning or logic. Exposure
to a particular situation may cause feelings of panic and
physical manifestation associated with fear. Reassurance,
logic, persuasion and punishment have little effect on
the phobic person. In come instances, this type of disorder can be incapacitating.

        Following a change of job responsibility, a young ex-
        ecutive experienced an intensification of some boyhood
        fears. He noted his becoming very uneasy and rest-
        less when finding himself in enclosed places such
        as elevators, airplanes, buses, etc. The feelings
        became more persistent and soon he was unable to
        travel at all in an elevator without developing pal-
        pitations and great apprehension. His office was on
        the 10th floor. He felt perplexed and embarrassed
        about his symptoms but could not overcome them.

Obsessive Compulsive Disorder (Obsessive Compulsive
Neurosis)
        This disorder is characterized by a persistent in-
trusion of unwanted thoughts (obsessions) and/or actions
(compulsions)into an individual's life or awareness. In
the instance of obsessive thinking, the person is preoccupied with recurring ideas or feelings which cannot be
diminished by conscious intent. Likewise, compulsive
rituals cannot be "willed" or reassured away. The person
will experience great anxiety if not allowed to complete the
action. Obsessive thinking and compulsive behavior are
frequently combined. They may be present in a mild form
or be so severe as to incapacitate the patient. Mild and
transient obsessional thinking, compulsive behavior and
phobias may occur in "normal" persons from time-to-time.
Two examples of this disorder follow:

        A young mother was somewhat ambivalent about assuming
        the responsibilities of parenthood. She began to
        experience repetitive ideas that she would somehow
        harm her baby. She became very preoccupied with these
        thoughts and could not exclude them from her mind.
        Reassurance that she was a good mother did not relieve
        her symptoms.

The second example follows:

A prominent musician was greatly concerned with disease and cleanliness. He avoided touching or shaking hands whenever possible. When he had to shake hands, he felt it imperative to immediately wash them. If this was not possible, he experienced great tension and restlessness.

Now complete Self-Assessment Exercise #4 on the following page.

Self-Assessment Exercise #4

1.   Correctly match the symptoms in Column B with the
     disorder sub-type in Column A.

<u>COLUMN A</u>   <u>COLUMN B</u>

_____Phobic Disorder   a.   constant and unwanted
                                          thoughts about sexual
_____Obsessive Compulsive   activity
       Disorder
                                     b.   vague but intense fears of
_____Generalized Anxiety   impending personal disaster
       Disorder
                                     c.   sudden onset of intense
_____Panic Disorder   fear, choking sensation,
                                          palpitations, chest pain,
                                          but no physical pathology
                                          found

                                     d.   excessive fear of riding
                                          in cars and driving in
                                          traffic

        When you have completed this exercise to the best of
your ability, check your answers on the following page.

Self-Assessment Exercise #4 - Feedback

1.

COLUMN A	COLUMN B

___d___ Phobic Disorder

___a___ Obsessive Compulsive Disorder

___b___ Generalized Anxiety Disorder

___c___ Panic Disorder

a. constant and unwanted thoughts about sexual activity

b. vague but intense fears of impending personal disaster

c. sudden onset of intense fear, choking sensation, palpitations, chest pain, but no physical pathology found

d. excessive fear of riding in cars and driving in traffic

SUMMARY

Anxiety Disorders are commonly encountered in professional practice. Although they may take different forms, feelings of anxiety, expressed directly or indirectly, are characteristic. The severity of the condition may vary considerably. However, delusions and hallucinations are not present. Intellectual functions, orientation and memory are generally intact. The thought content may be unusual but not bizarre. No associational disturbance is present. Anxiety Disorders can be distinguished readily from functional psychosis and organic brain syndrome in most cases.

REFERENCES

Diagnostic and Statistical Manual of Mental Disorders (Third Edition): Washington: American Psychiatric Association, 1980.

Goodwin, D., Guze, S.: Psychiatric Diagnosis, 2nd Ed., New York: Oxford University Press, 1979.

Marks, I., Lader, M.: Anxiety States (anxiety neurosis): A Review, J. Nerv. Ment. Dis., 156:3-18, 1973.

Nemiah, J. C., Anxiety Neurosis in: Freedman, A. M. Kaplan, H. L., Sadock, B. J. (Editors): Comprehensive Textbook of Psychiatry III, Baltimore: Williams and Wilkins Co., 1980.

Woodruff, R. A., Guze, S. B., Clayton, P. J.: Anxiety Neurosis Among Psychiatric Outpatients, Compr. Psychiat., 13:165-170, 1972.

Chapter 14
Somatoform Disorders
Warren Procci

Scientific research, as well as clinical experience, has clearly demonstrated that an individual's emotional life can manifest itself through somatic symptoms. Few of us need look further than our own personal experience to confirm this. A patient in psychotherapy with me was recently going through a very painful separation from his wife. He had chronic abdominal pain which he described vividly as "a feeling that I've been kicked in the stomach." Many of us have witnessed in elderly relatives the "heartache" they experienced after the loss of a long-time loved one. Beginning hunters frequently find their trigger hand paralyzed when they are confronted with their first buck. Who amongst us has not at one time or another literally "frozen with anger" or fright? Inevitably, these "bodily" changes are a reflection of powerful emotions. Patients, however, frequently identify such symptoms as being exclusively of a physical origin. As a result of this, physicians performing primary medical care, see and treat many individuals suffering from Somatoform Disorders. These disorders are characterized by symptoms that strongly suggest an organic, physical illness although the patient's primary care physician finds none despite careful and thorough evaluation (hence somatoform). Rather, they are the result of emotional influences. These individuals may be referred by their general physicians to mental health professionals.

LEARNING OBJECTIVES
By the time you complete the material in this chapter you should be able to:

1. Correctly define the term Somatoform Disorder

2. List the different types of Somatoform Disorders
    and characterize them with respect to:

    a. Sex Ratio
    b. Type of Onset
    c. Course of Illness
    d. Typical Organ System(s) Involved
    e. Possible Complications

3. Distinguish Somatoform Disorders from:

    a. Factitious Disorders
    b. Malingering
    c. Depressive Disorders
    d. Schizophrenic Disorders

By the conclusion of this chapter and supervised
clinical experience you should be ablt to:

1. Accurately observe and record a patient's be-
    havior within each of the MSE behavior descriptors.

2. Determine whether a Somatoform Disorder is present
    in a patient, given the necessary history and
    MSE information.

3. Indicate the history and MSE findings which en-
    abled you to make the diagnosis.

GENERAL CHARACTERISTICS

As mentioned above, the Somatoform Disorders simulate organic, physical illness so that the patient may complain of loss or alteration of function in one or in a number of organ systems. Headache, fatigue, abdominal pain, a distressing feeling of a rapid and pounding heart (palpitations), trouble walking, back pain, menstrual difficulties and sexual problems are just a few of the myriad of symptoms which may occur.

Careful and thorough diagnostic appraisal by the patient's primary care physician invariably fails to demonstrate pathology of the presumably affected organ or organ systems. Frequently, this will fail to assuage these patients as there is often a very demanding and insistent quality to them and their complaints. They are often convinced about the physical origin of their difficulties and may take up a great deal of the primary care physician's limited time. If their complaint is pain, they may constantly ask for medications to relieve this.

For instance, a middle aged woman with long-term abdominal pain has visited her physician at least once a month for many years. He has performed repeated X-ray studies of the stomach and intestines and has even performed direct visual examination of the stomach (gastroscopy). He has never found a trace of organic pathology. Rather than reassuring her, this lack of corroborating evidence has been greeted with great indignation. This commonly occurs with the Somatoform Disorders. As a result, some primary care physicians will often vigorously treat these disorders as though actual organ pathology were present. In the case mentioned above, the patient was evaluated with an excessive number of diagnostic procedures and was treated with a large number of medications without any benefit. Indeed, there is the possibility of the misuse of medication and even unnecessary surgical intervention in some cases.

Dissatisfaction with the primary care physician's "failure" to adequately diagnose and cure their ills may prompt many of these patients to "comparison shop" from doctor to doctor. A shared feeling of ill will is an all too frequent result and by the time referral to a mental health professional occurs, the patient and the primary care physician may be at loggerheads.

Etiology

In the Somatoform Disorders, psychological factors play a primary etiologic role. The physical symptoms actually represent a substitute form of expression for the underlying emotional needs which have no other outlet. For example, a number of bodily complaints may serve the purpose of obtaining a measure of attention, comfort and concern in an individual who is depressed but who, for a variety of reasons, cannot acknowledge the underlying depression. Indeed he may not even be consciously aware of the depression.

Etiology (Continued)

Emotions other than depression may also be involved and, in fact, more than one emotion may be operative in a given case of a Somatoform Disorder. For example, physical symptoms may allow someone to gratify strong dependency needs which cannot be openly acknowledged. Guilt over powerful angry feelings may result in any number of bodily complaints. A temporary paralysis of the right arm was seen in a young man who became enraged with his irritable and irritating invalid father. He felt it was "wrong" to be furious at his father, especially since he was ill. The anger could not find direct expression so it was expressed indirectly.

The level of stress experienced by a person is a contributing factor in the expression of the Somatoform Disorders. Someone under a great deal of pressure for a lengthy period of time is more susceptible to any kind of illness and the Somatoform Disorders are no exception.

It is crucial to emphasize that those who suffer from these disorders are in no way consciously aware of the underlying emotional state. To them, the illness is perceived as a very real organic, physical ailment. They are not able to exert any volitional control over these symptoms. This very often frustrates those who must live with them. It is common for relatives to think that these symptoms can be simply removed by an act of will. If expressed, this attitude generally serves only to antagonize the patient who may well feel that his family sees him as "faking" illness. I can vividly recall a 59-year-old judge who suffered very severe headaches. No physical basis for this was ever found despite extensive medical studies. His severe depression was obvious to his family, friends and physician, but not to himself. His wife repeatedly told him that his headaches were the result of depression. He perceived this as meaning that she didn't believe his headaches were "real" and this drove a wedge into their relationship which further deepened his depression.

Typical Mental Status Examination Findings

Appearance. In general, these individuals are neatly and appropriately dressed with no out-of-the-ordinary quality to their appearance. There is a very distinct subgroup of women with this condition who dress in a sexually provocative fashion (e.g. they wear copious amounts of makeup, tightly fitting or revealing clothing,etc.).

Behavior. There is usually nothing unusual in the posture, facial expressions, body movements and speech of these people. The relationship with the health care professional is usually characterized by a superficial cooperation which may quickly turn into an adversarial relationship if the patient feels his or her needs are not being taken seriously. They are very sensitive to any innuendo concerning the genuineness of their somatic symptoms.

Behavior (continued)

The subgroup of female patient referred to above will likely demonstrate sexually seductive posture and body movements at least sometime during an evaluation. They also may have a breathy, theatrical type of speech, and a dramatic style to their facial expressions. An overly submissive relationship to the mental health worker may be present.

Feeling. Feelings are generally appropriate in both quality and quantity. There is no characteristic predominant mood although depression, sadness and anxiety are frequently seen.

Occasionally one will see a peculiar absence of any feeling towards the physical symptoms while at the same time there is a perfectly appropriate range of feelings regarding all other matters. This is seen more frequently in females, especially the subgroup described above. This blasé attitude is referred to as "la belle indifference."

Perception. Hallucinations or illusions are not a part of the Somatoform Disorders.

Thinking. Typically, there are no alterations in intellectual functioning, orientation, judgment, memory or the stream of thought. There is usually a dramatic lack of insight into the underlying emotional state which is at the core of this condition. The thought content may be completely dominated by a description of the somatic complaints and concern about the adequacy of their physical evaluation.

We can see that these disorders can occur in patients with no overt evidence of psychopathology. It is possible for these conditions to occur in combination with any other psychiatric disorder. Depressive Disorders are not infrequently found to coexist with Somatoform Disorders. The subgroup of women referred to above fit very classicly the criteria for histrionic personality disorder, as well as do a number of other patients with Somatoform Disorders.

Now complete Self Assessment Exercise #1 beginning on the following page.

Self-Assessment Exercise #1

1. Define, in your own words, the term Somatoform
    Disorder.

2. Discuss the etiology of a Somatoform Disorder.

3. Describe the typical MSE findings of a patient with
    a Somatoform Disorder.

    Appearance:

    Behavior:

    Feeling:

    Perception:

    Thinking:

When you have completed this exercise to the best of
your ability, check your answers with those on the
following page.

Self-Assessment Exercise #1 - Feedback

1. Somatoform Disorders are conditions which are charac-
    terized by symptoms which strongly suggest an organic,
    physical illness although a careful and thorough
    medical evaluation reveals no evidence of physical
    disorder (hence somatoform). These disorders are
    rather the result of emotional influences.

2. Psychological factors play a primary etiologic role
    in the somatoform disorders. The physical symptoms
    represent a substitute form for the expression of
    strong underlying emotional needs which can find no
    other outlet. These underlying emotions are usually
    not consciously accessible to the individual suffering
    from a Somatoform Disorder.

3. Typical MSE findings of an individual with a Somatoform
    Disorder are:

    Appearance: Unremarkable with the exception of a sub-
    group of females who dress in a sexually provocative
    manner.

    Behavior: Generally appropriate. Very sensitive to
    remarks seeming to question the genuineness of their
    symptoms. The subgroup of female patients referred to
    may exhibit sexually seductive posture and body move-
    ments, as well as a submissive relationship to the
    interviewer.

    Feeling: Generally appropriate. Group of females
    referred to above sometimes have an indifference toward
    their symptoms ("la belle indifference").

    Perception: No illusions and/or hallucinations.

    Thinking: Usually dominated by concern with physical
    symptoms, but there is a lack of insight into the
    underlying emotional state.

        If your answers correspond closely with those above,
please continue your reading on the following page;
if not, please reread the material in the preceding section until you are confident you know it.

TYPES OF SOMATOFORM DISORDERS
There are several different types of Somatoform Disorders. Although there is an overall similarity, each type has its unique aspects and the health care professional should be familiar with them.

Somatization Disorder
This is a chronic disorder which is much more common in women than men. A very characteristic feature is its onset early in life. It usually begins during the teenage years. These individuals exhibit many physical complaints involving many parts of the body. They are described in a vague, yet dramatic fashion. There are no symptoms which are specific for this condition but this multiple body part involvement is a characteristic feature. These patients go to their doctor over and over again for these complaints and invariably, despite very careful and thorough study, no physical illness is found. The patient's persistence will frequently lead the treating physician to reexamine them repeatedly. They may be subjected to many diagnostic tests that are expensive and perhaps even risky. On occasion, these patients are unnecessarily brought to surgery. It is not uncommon to see multiple scars on the abdomens of these individuals.

Although this condition is psychologically induced the patient is often not aware of this and, in most cases, if this is suggested he or she will very quickly reject it. The chronicity and intensity of the illness attest to the profound emotional disturbance. Pain is a common accompaniment of these disorders, and since the psychological difficulty is great the pain is often intense. As a result, these patients are a high risk group for the development of addiction to pain relieving medications as well as to tranquilizers.

The condition does wax and wane but it is chronic. The patient is never really free from the condition for any lengthy period of time and, in a sense, somatic symptoms become part of their lives. Certainly if they are under a great deal of stress their symptoms are likely to flare up.

A 48 year-old woman recently seen in consultation described pain in her lower abdominal and genital regions. She stated very dramatically that it had been present for several years. On further inquiry, she described a thirty-year history of numerous pains. She had had several major surgeries in the past including removal of her gall bladder, appendix and part of her stomach. As best as could be ascertained from reviewing her old medical records, no evidence of physical illness was ever found in these organs. Her current problem had led to a hysterectomy several months ago. Upon much more careful questioning, she described a great feeling of loss since she and her husband had separated several years ago. She also stated that she was afraid her late teenage children would soon be "grown up" and would inevitably depart from home. However, she adamantly stated that in no way could these concerns be related to her abdominal pain.

Conversion Disorder (or Hysterical Neurosis, Conversion Type)

This is a condition which is acute in onset and short in duration. Usually only one organ system is affected with only one presenting complaint. Both men and women are affected. Conversion symptoms are most frequently limited either to the parts of the body which are under voluntary control or to the organs which serve the function of perception. However, the autonomic and endocrine systems may be affected too. The most common conversion symptoms are neurological such as paralysis of any extremity or part thereof, blindness, loss of sensation (anesthesia) or a strange, funny sensation (paresthesia).

These symptoms will often not conform to any known anatomical or physiological pathway. For example, a patient will complain of a loss of feeling in their hand which in no way coincides with the manner in which nerves supply the hand with its capacity to feel. Also, these individuals may exhibit the bland reaction to the symptom described above ("la belle indifference").

Conversion symptoms generally occur when an individual is suddenly confronted with a very stressful psychological predicament. Usually, come very strong feeling is stimulated which the patient finds very disturbing. As a result, the feeling is not expressed, but is "converted" into a physical symptom. Often the individual will receive a great deal of attention from people surrounding him or her. This has the unfortunate effect of reinforcing the patient for being sick and this may be especially difficult in cases involving those who don't receive much attention from their loved ones when they are well. This reinforcement for ill role behavior is referred to as secondary gain and it may well prove to be the key factor in maintaining the symptom. However, these disorders usually resolve spontaneously within a short period of time, especially if the precipitating stressful condition is relieved.

A 47 year-old man was being evaluated by the neurology service for paralysis of his right arm. Diagnostic appraisal uncovered no evidence of organic illness. Psychiatric consultation was obtained. During the initial interview the patient stated that he and his wife had a long history of marital difficulty. Two weeks ago, she informed him that she had had a recent affair and wanted a divorce. He became enraged and feared he would lose control of his temper. However, he felt very upset with his anger because he had been brought up very strictly. Anger was not tolerated especially if it were directed towards a woman. The following morning he awoke and found his arm paralyzed. Since then, his wife has been taking care of him and has stated that she will postpone initiating the divorce proceedings until there is some understanding of his illness and an established treatment program.

Psychogenic Pain Disorder
       This is a disorder which is characterized by the
complaint of pain. As in the Conversion Disorders, they
are acute in their onset and they have a short duration.
Both men and women are affected. There is no evidence of
organic physical illness to explain the pain. The pain
will usually not conform to what would be expected based
on known anatomy, physiology and pathology. For example,
the patient may complain of pain in the chest which is
completely different from what typically occurs based on
the nerve supply to this area.
       While there is little or no evidence which supports
the presence of organic, medical illness, there is evidence
for the etiological role of psychological factors. The
patient usually refuses to consider that his emotions have
anything to do with the pain. Careful questioning will
usually reveal evidence of a major recent alteration of
importance in the patient's personal or vocational life.
However, he or she will not attach any importance to the
concurrent occurrence of this change and the pain. Although these patients express a great deal of discomfort
as a result of the pain and seek relief, they are usually
much less worried about what causes the pain.
       Because these patients can be very insistent with
their complaints and their desire to obtain relief, the
primary care physician may prescribe various pain relieving
medications. This is usually fruitless, however, as these
individuals fail to respond to these medications. Unlike
Somatization Disorders, there is little risk of the development of addiction to pain relieving medications since
the disorder is acute, does not last for any lengthy period
of time, and the pain relieving medications are ineffective
anyway.
       This disorder will usually subside spontaneously
especially if the precipitating psychological events are
altered. Less frequently, the condition becomes chronic
and the patient may adopt pain as part of a "way of life."
Strong secondary gain for the pain may contribute to this
chronicity.
       A 34 year-old junior executive was evaluated for
abdominal pain. His primary care physician was unable to
find any organic cause for the pain despite a detailed
evaluation. The young man stated that the pain began three
weeks ago. He said the pain felt "like a knife sticking
right through my stomach." He described an increasing
amount of pressure and stress at work for the past two
years. He and an older man were both being considered for
a soon to be vacated position. Five weeks ago, the company
president announced that the position would be given to
the older man. The patient stated that he was very bitter
about this since he had worked much harder. He felt that
the other man was given the job because he was a close
social friend of the president.

Hypochondriasis (or Hypochondriacal Neurosis)
       This is an unusual, but dramatic disorder in which the
individual is preoccupied with the functions of his or her

body to the extent that some dreadful illness is feared
to be present. Both males and females are affected. The
individual complains insistently of a physical complaint
but there is no demonstrable organic finding despite the
most careful workup. Hypochondriasis can be differentiated
from Somatization Disorder since there is not an early onset
to this condition. The onset is usually insidious but
occurs in adult life. Furthermore, the hypochondriac does
not have the multiplicity of symptoms which the sufferer
from Somatization Disorder does. It is more likely in
hypochondriasis for the patient to have only a few complaints centered around one organ or organ system. The
hypochondriac characteristically has a very dreadful fear
that he or she has some catastrophic illness while the
somatization disorder patient generally does not believe
this.

These patients are typically left unsatisfied by the
reassurance and support of their primary care physicians.
They greet with resentment and frustration the results of
laboratory tests which fail to confirm the presence of
very serious organic illness. These patients may be subject to unnecessary medical studies and perhaps even
unnecessary surgery. They will repeatedly go from doctor
to doctor often bringing meticulous records of their
symptoms. Their disorder seems to be the exclusive focus
of their life. The health care professional will often
note that the hypochondriac leads a life which is severely
restricted with regard to friends, vocational and avoca-
tional interests.

Hypochondriacs often become the bane of their primary
care physicians who often will initiate referral to a mental
health professional. In general, the hypochondriac is
very reluctant to accept the idea that psychological problems are a significant contributor to the illness so they
may present themselves to the mental health professional
with a very skeptical attitude about the possible role
psychological factors might play in their disorder.

The tenacity with which these patients believe that
very catastrophic illness is present, despite unequivocally
negative medical investigations, has led some psychiatrists
to view these individuals as being close to delusional.
Because of their persistence, they may well be placed on
analgesic or tranquilizing medications and abuse of these
agents may occur.

A 59 year-old lawyer was admitted to a general medical
ward with a complaint of headache. He carried with him
a detailed notebook describing the time of onset, duration,
location and quality of each headache suffered over the
past six months. He pulled out a chart which graphically
demonstrated an increase in their frequency. He stated
that he must have a brain tumor. Three previous workups
were unable to unearth any evidence of an organic medical
illness. In addition, he was convinced his mental faculties
were drastically deteriorating as a result of this "tumor."

He was not reassured by results of IQ testing which demonstrated a full scale IQ of 139 and no evidence of any
impairment. Upon very careful questioning, he stated he
had been pressured by his wife for several years to retire
at age 60. She had always insisted that this was "long
enough" to work. He and his wife had been argumentative
with each other for several months and she had recently
moved out of their master bedroom to the guest room.

    Now complete Self-Assessment Exercise #2 beginning
on the following page.

Self-Assessment Exercise #2

Part I

Characterize the different types of Somatoform Disorders by completing the chart below.

	Somatization Disorder	Conversion Disorder	Psychogenic Pain Disorder	Hypochondriasis
Sex Ratio				
Type of Onset				
Organ System(s) Affected				
Course of Illness				
Possible Complications				

Self-Assessment Exercise #2 (continued)

Part II

Please answer the questions following each of the
case histories below.

Patient #1

A 20 year-old college coed sought medical consultation because of an impairment of her ability to speak.
Initially, she responded to questions by writing answers
rather than speaking when urged to do so, however, she
could communicate but in a whispered voice. She described
a feeling of a "scratchy sore throat" and a "lump in the
back of my throat." She complained of difficulty swallow-
ing solid foods. Physical examination revealed only
a minimal degree of redness and no sign of enlarged lymph
nodes. Upon further questioning, the patient stated she
had been staying away from her classes. She was doing
very poorly in a public speaking class, primarily because
she felt very self-conscious in front of a group of people.
She had to give a major presentation to the public speaking
class on the very next day but now felt unable because of
her speaking difficulty.

What type of Somatoform Disorder is this patient
experiencing?

What information enabled you to make the diagnosis?

Self-Assessment Exercise #2 (continued)

Patient #2

A 36 year-old woman sought assistance from her general practitioner. This was her seventh visit in a six-month period of time. She stated that she had "terrible excrutiating" discomfort in the lower abdomen. She also stated that she had "intense stabbing" pains in the genital area. Furthermore, she had difficulty with her breathing.

This woman had a long medical history with frequent medical diagnostic procedures which had generally proven inconclusive. She had exploratory abdominal surgery on two occasions. The first, when she was sixteen years old, however, no distinct abnormalities were found.

The patient was dressed neatly in a short skirt and low cut sweater. She wore a great deal of makeup. Several times she pleaded with the physician to examine her, "find out what's wrong and make me well."

What type of Somatoform Disorder is this patient experiencing?

What information enabled you to make the diagnosis?

Self-Assessment Exercise #2 (continued)

Patient #3

   A 52 year-old man sought medical consultation for
recurrent chest pain of several years duration. He stated
that the pain was constant and excrutiating. He described,
at length, the various shifts in intensity of the pain
which had occurred during the past few years. He stated
that he had tried numerous medications to relieve the pain
and produced a list with drug names, dosages, and dates
of use. He insisted that a serious, life threatening
heart disease was present and the doctor must find it.
The patient informed the physician that this problem caused
him so much trouble that he saw very little of his friends
and family and had cut his work as a professional photog-
rapher by more than half. A thorough physical examination
and cardiac workup revealed no abnormalities. When informed of this, the patient responded that the tests were
probably not properly performed or interpreted.

   What type of Somatoform Disorder is this patient
experiencing?

   What information enabled you to make the diagnosis?

Self-Assessment Exercise #2 (continued)

Patient #4

A 43 year-old male accountant saw his general physician due to headache pain. He stated the pain had begun suddenly the day before. He pointed to his forehead and stated he felt as though his head had "a tight noose around it." Upon further questioning, he reluctantly stated that earlier that week, one of his major clients received notification of an income tax audit. To his dismay, the accountant discovered a large error in one of the tax returns which would be subject to scrutiny.

What type of Somatoform Disorder is this patient experiencing?

What information enabled you to make the diagnosis?

When you have completed this exercise to the best of your ability, check your answers with those on the following page.

Self-Assessment Exercise #2 - Feedback

Part I

	Somati-zation Disorder	Conver-sion Disorder	Psycho-genic Pain Disorder	Hypochon-driasis
Sex Ratio	More common in females	Both males and females	Both males and females	Both males and females
Type of Onset	Early in life (teenage years)	Acute, follow-ing recent psy-chological stress	Acute, fol-lowing recent psy-chological stress	Insidious, during adult life
Organ System(s) Affected	Multiple	Usually single in an organ system under vol-untary control, or an or-gan of percep-tion	Patient complains of pain, any organ system may be affected	Usually only a few symp-toms. Any organ sys-tem(s) may be affected. Symptom(s) described in meticu-lous detail
Course of Illness	Chronic	Usually resolves quickly after re-moval of stressful circum-stances	Usually resolves quickly after re-moval of stressful circum-stances	Chronic
Possible Compli-cations	Unneces-sary medical and sur-gical pro-cedures. Misuse of medi-cations.	Rare	Rare	Unnecessary medical and surgical procedures. Misuse of medications. Constric-tion of life interests and symptoms become sole focus of their lives.

Self-Assessment Exercise #2 - Feedback (continued)

Part II

Patient #1 - Conversion Disorder

>   Acute onset, following very stressful event
>   (class presentation), single organ which is
>   under voluntary control is involved (larynx).

Patient #2 - Somatization Disorder

>   Patient is female and this disorder is more
>   common in females. Condition began very early
>   in life (note exploratory surgery at age 16).
>   Numerous organ systems are affected. She has
>   had a chronic illness with a long medical
>   history including many diagnostic procedures
>   but with little or no organic pathology ever
>   established.

Patient #3 - Hypochondriasis

>   Condition is of several years duration and
>   began in adult life. Patient describes only
>   on symptom but with meticulous detail and
>   insistence in the belief that there is some-
>   thing dreadfully wrong with him. He has been
>   treated with many medications for his symptoms
>   but has gained no relief. His symptoms have
>   become the central focus of his life and his
>   vocational and avocational interests have
>   greatly constricted.

Patient #4 - Psychogenic Pain Disorder

>   The patient's complaint is one exclusively
>   involving pain. There is a recent acute
>   psychological stress (a possible serious
>   business mistake which could have grave con-
>   sequences) preceding the onset of the pain.

If your answers correspond closely with those above, please continue your reading on the following page; if not, please reread the preceding section until you are confident you know the material.

DISTINGUISHING FEATURES

For diagnostic and treatment purposes, both medically and psychologically, it is important to be able to distinguish the Somatoform Disorders from both the Factitious Disorders and Malingering. These latter two groups are conditions in which there is the voluntary production by the patient of somatic symptoms. In the Somatoform Disorders, there is no such volitional production of symptoms. With the malingerer, one can usually detect an obvious direct reward to the patient for being ill. Not uncommonly, the malingerer is seeking to obtain some financial benefit, such as money from an insurance company or disability income as compensation for an "injury." In the Factitious Disorders, the patient's goals are not so obviously recognized unless the health care professional has a careful knowledge of the patient's background. For unknown reasons, patients with Factitious Illness derive a great deal of reward from being seen as physically ill. In the Somatoform Disorders there is no direct reward to the patient for his physical symptoms. However, if the patient receives an increased amount of attention and concern as a result of symptoms, this may well become powerfully rewarding and help maintain the symptoms. This, of course, is the secondary gain discussed earlier.

It is also crucially important to distinguish the Somatoform Disorders from the Depressive Disorders and Schizophrenic Disorders. Depressive Disorders may present a variety of physical symptoms. Headaches, muscular aches and pains, chest pain and a feeling of profound fatigue are very common presenting symptoms of depression. More dramatic somatic symptoms, such as the belief that there is something catastrophically wrong with the body are less common but occur frequently enough so that most primary care physicians see at least several in their careers. Such an individual may have the conviction that there is an inoperable tumor growth in his or her brain. This conviction may well persist despite weighty evidence to the contrary. This is referred to as a somatic delusion and is usually indicative of very serious depression. With the Depressive Disorders, careful history taking will reveal the constellation of other symptoms more typically associated with depression such as hopelessness, insomnia, appetite loss, depressed mood and generalized loss of interest in previously pleasurable activities (anhedonia).

Somatoform Disorders may, at times, be confused with Schizophrenic Disorders. It is not at all unusual for schizophrenics to become very concerned and preoccupied with the inner workings of their bodies. They may complain of various bodily aches, pains and malfunctions. In severe cases, they can develop somatic delusions similar to the more common symptoms of schizophrenia, such as bizarre behavior, delusions, hallucinations and disordered thinking is apparent and helps the mental health professional make the appropriate distinction.

It is also crucially important to distinguish the Somatoform Disorders from true organic physical illness.

The consequences for failure to identify a physical illness can be profound. This can be an exquisitely difficult task particularly since some organic illnesses can be present with vague complaints. However, there are some factors which can help guide the mental health professional through this hazardous exercise. For instance, the Somatoform Disorders often consist of symptoms which just do not conform to what is known about anatomy and physiology. A Conversion Disorder is frequently accompanied by unusual casualness of attitude about even serious symptoms ("la belle indifference"). In Conversion Disorder and Psychogenic Pain Disorder, the mental health worker may find that there is an obvious and apparent symbolic meaning for the symptom. For example, conversion blindness may occur immediately after viewing a disturbing event. An individual's past history has some relevance in determining whether or not organic physical illness is present. While there is always a first time, it is typical that most individuals with Conversion Disorder or Psychogenic Pain Disorder have a previous history of other conversion symptoms or pain. The Somatization Disorder patient will usually have a very long history of repetitive somatic complaints without any apparent cause.

In general, the Somatoform Disorders should be treated with a psychological approach. Organic physical illnesses are, of course, treated by the appropriate medical intervention. Schizophrenic and Depressive Disorders require the appropriate combination of specific psychopharmacologic and modest psychotherapeutic interventions. Individuals suffering from Malingering or Factitious Illness are very difficult to treat either medically of psychologically. In fact, psychological approaches are rarely, if ever, helpful in regard to these patients.

Now complete Self-Assessment Exercise #3 beginning on the following page.

Self-Assessment Exercise #3

Please read the following case histories and answer the questions that follow.

Case #1

A 32 year-old male has been referred to a mental health professional for evaluation by his primary care physician. The patient states that since sustaining a "whiplash neck" injury in an automobile accident six years ago, he has been unable to perform heavy work. He had been a heavy construction worker but was reassigned to a desk job. For several years, he has tried unsuccessfully for disability income. He states that his persistent neck pain makes it "impossible to do anything." He angrily states that no doctor has been able to help him.

What diagnosis should be suspected?

Why?

Self-Assessment Exercise #3 (continued)

Case #2

A 47 year-old female sought medical attention for profound fatigue during the past four months. Upon further questioning, she described a number of other complaints including a headache, difficulty breathing, serious loss of sleep, appetite loss with 12 pounds weight loss and a generalized lack of interest in the world around her. She stated that six months ago she was fine and she had never experienced any similar problems in the past. Midway through the interview, she became very upset and began to cry. Five months ago, she found out her husband was having an affair with a woman twenty years his junior. They were actively considering a divorce. She wondered if her problems might be "nerves."

What diagnosis should be suspected?

Why?

Self-Assessment Exercise #3 (continued)

Case #3

A 29 year-old man sought medical assistance for bowel difficulty. He stated he was convinced that he had "cancer eating away at my insides." He denied any symptoms of abdominal changes which might be consistent with a cancer of the gastrointestinal tract. He described this in an emotionless voice. When the physician asked him why he thought he had cancer, he stated that his next door neighbor and he had a recent altercation. As a result of this, he suspected his neighbor had interfered with his food and placed cancer causing agents in it.

What diagnosis should be suspected?

Why?

When you have completed this exercise to the best of your ability, check your answers with those on the following page.

Self-Assessment Exercise #3 - Feedback

Case #1 - Malingering should be suspected. This patient
         has an obvious potential financial gain to
         obtain from being ill. Patients with Somatoform
         Disorders seldom exhibit this.

Case #2 - Depression should be suspected. The combination
         of fatigue, sleep loss, appetite loss, weight
         loss and lack of interest along with a number
         of physical complaints such as a headache and
         difficulty breathing, strongly suggest depression.
         Somatoform Disorder patients will seldom be
         found to cry openly and show major feelings of
         unhappiness. Indeed, Somatoform Disorder
         patients rarely associate feelings with symptoms
         as this woman did.

Case #3 - A Schizophrenic Disorder should be suspected.
         While fear of dreadful illness may be seen in
         Somatoform Disorders, the lack of emotional
         expressiveness ("flat affect") and the probable
         paranoid delusions are not consistent with
         Somatoform Disorders but clearly fit with
         a Schizophrenic Disorder.

     If your answers correspond closely with those above,
please continue your reading on the following page; if
not, please reread the preceding section until you are
confident you know the material.

SUMMARY
       The Somatoform Disorders are a group of conditions
which are frequently observed in the primary care
physician's office. They are, of course, the product of
emotional factors. It is axiomatic that the therapist
closely attend to the emotional aspects of these disorders
while he plans for medical treatment. Referral to a mental health professional is frequently appropriate.

REFERENCES

Canter, A., Imboden, J. F., Cluff, L. E.: "The Frequency
of Physical Illness as a Function of Prior Psychological
Vulnerability and Contemporary Stress," Psychosom. Med.,
28:344, 1966.

Cassell, E.: The Healer's Art, Philadelphia: J. B.
Lippincott, 1976.

Engel, G. L.: "A Psychological Setting of Somatic Disease:
The 'Giving-Up' Complex," Proceeding of the Royal Society
of Medicine, 60:533, 1967.

Frazer, A., Winokur, A. (Eds.), Biological Basis of
Psychiatric Disorders, New York: Spectrum, 1977.

Friedman, M., Roseman, R. H.: Type A Behavior Pattern:
Its Association with Coronary Heart Disease. Annals
Clinical Research, 3:300-312, 1971

Hinkle, L. E., et. al.: "An Investigation Between Life
Experiences, Personality Characteristics and General
Susceptibility to Illness," Psychosom. Med., 20(4):278,
1958.

Lipowski, A. J.: "Psychosomatic Medicine in the 80's:
An Overview" American Journal of Psychiatry, 134:233-244, 1
1977.

Paykel, E. S.: "Life Stress and Psychiatric Disorder," in
Dohrenwend, B. S. and Dohrenwend, B. P. (eds.), Stressful
Life Events: Their Nature and Effects, New York: Wiley,
1974, pp. 135-149.

Rahe, R. H., et. al.: "Social Stress and Illness Onset,"
J. Psychosom. Research, 8:35, 1964.

Rahe, R. H.: "Life Change Measurement as a Predictor of
Illness," Proceedings of the Royal Society of Medicine,
61:1124, 1968.

Rahe, R. H., Folstad, I., Bergon, T. et. al.: A Model for
Life Change Illness Research. Archives of General Psychiatry, 31:172-177, 1974.

Weiner, H.: Psychobiology and Human Disease, New York: Elsevier North-Holland, 1977.

Weiss, J. M.: Influence of Psychological Variables on Stress-Induced Pathology. Psychological Emotions and Psychosomatic Illness. Amsterdam: CIBA Foundation Symposium 8, Excerpta Medica, 1972.

Wittkower, E. D., and Warnes, H.: Psychosomatic Medicine, Its Clinical Application, New York: Harper and Row, 1977.

Chapter 15

Personality Disorders
John R. Snibbe

Personality disorders are deeply ingrained and pervasive maladaptive behavior patterns of sufficient severity to cause impairment in interpersonal relationships and functioning. These maladaptive behaviors usually become prominent in adolescence and continue throughout life. Personality disorders are less disabling than a psychosis and rarely incapacitate the affected individual. However, their presence is usually out of the patient's awareness and constitute a recurrent source of work and relationship problems. They are frequently encountered. It is, therefore, important that health care professionals recognize and deal with personality disorders effectively.

LEARNING OBJECTIVES

By the time you complete the material in this chapter you should be able to:

1. Correctly define personality disorder.

2. List the key findings from a patient's history and M.S.E. which are characteristic of a patient with a personality disorder.

3. Briefly describe the distinguishing characteristics of each of the following personality disorders:

paranoid	histrionic
antisocial	schizoid
compulsive	dependent
narcissistic	borderline
	passive-aggressive

By the conclusion of this chapter and supervised clinical experience you should be able to:

1. Accurately observe and record a patient's
    behavior within each of the M.S.E. behavior
    descriptors.

2. Determine whether a personality disorder is
    present in a patient, given necessary M.S.E. and
    history information.

3. Indicate the history and M.S.E. findings which
    enabled you to make a diagnosis.

OVERVIEW

Personality Disorders represent a pervasive style of adapting to life that is nonfunctional and persists unchanged over time. In order to diagnose this disorder these maladaptive behaviors should be present for a minimum of one year. Frequently, individuals with a Personality Disorder are experienced by others as problematic even though the patients themselves are oblivious to their maladaptive behavior pattern. These persons often are puzzled regarding the origins of repeated difficulties in coping with daily living. A word of caution must be added. Personality Disorders merge imperceptibly with the "normal," itself a vague and inexact term. While reading the description of personality types in this chapter, you will probably feel that you recognize yourself at least once. Keep this in mind when you are dealing with your patients. A danger lies with overdiagnosis and pejorative labeling. Unless a Personality Disorder is severe and warrants treatment, it is usually sufficient only to note its presence and make allowances for it in planning patient care.

Personality Disorders are characterized by lifelong maladaptive behavior patterns. The behaviors are firmly ingrained and so much a part of the life style that the afflicted individuals usually are oblivious of their presence. These behavioral patterns are most probably the result of learning and/or experiential factors. It must be pointed out that these patterns of behavior can sometimes facilitate vocational success--e.g., the compulsive exactness of an accountant or the hardworking and precise attitude of the typical physician--but if they are exaggerated or overused, difficulties do appear. Then the individual will typically report his troubles as "I'm doing things I always do but things just are going bad for me...and I don't know why!"

MENTAL STATUS FINDINGS

Appearance

No findings of appearance are diagnostic. Most individuals with a Personality Disorder are appropriately dressed and well groomed. Some persons may be excessively fastidious (Compulsive Personality Disorder), others may be provocative and revealing in their attire (histrionic personality disorder); few may be unkempt, unclean and without usual regard for appearance (Borderline Personality Disorder).

Behavior

Posture is generally appropriate. In some cases it may be distinguished by an unusual rigidity (compulsive) or a sexually enticing quality (histrionic). Facial expression can reveal anxiety, depression, anger, or suspicion, however, it is not bizarre or inappropriate. Body movements and speech are generally not unusual.

Behavior (continued)
The quality of the therapist-patient relationship is
one of the most valuable areas for establishing a diagnosis
of Personality Disorders. The individual may be suspicious
and nontrusting (paranoid), or he may attempt to manipu-
late and "use" the interviewer (antisocial). The inter-
change may be dominated by thinly disguised, procrastinating resistance (passive-aggressive) and some individuals
will relate with marked helplessness and without stamina
or willpower (dependent).

Feeling (Affect and Mood)
Feeling may be manifest as anxious, vigilant, anger,
elation, depression or a feeling of emotional coldness.
Affect is not characterized by the inappropriate, the
bizarre, or the unusual, and has no "schizophrenic feel"
to it.

Perception
Illusions and hallucinations are not present. Perception is normal.

Thinking
Intellectual functioning, orientation and memory are
generally intact. Judgment is not literally impaired,
though individuals may repeatedly involve themselves in
similar, somewhat self-defeating situations. Insight is
often limited; usually individuals with Personality Disorders see nothing maladaptive about their "life style."
Obsessions and compulsions may occur, but they are not as
incapacitating as those associated with the Anxiety Disorders. There is no depersonalization. There may be
paranoid tendencies, but delusions and ideas of reference
do not occur. The stream of thought is normally logical
and well structured.

History
A carefully taken life history is often helpful in
making the diagnosis of a Personality Disorder. Because
the M.S.E. findings are not usually diagnostic, the major
indication of a Personality Disorder is the presence of
a lifelong pattern of maladjustment, unhappiness, suspicion, difficulty with the law or interpersonal relations,
or a striking lack of accomplishments. Generally, subjective feelings of discomfort--especially anxiety and
depression--are not as prominent in the Personality Disorders as with Anxiety Disorders and Affective Disorders.
Remember, the diagnosis of Personality Disorder should not
be based on a single episode or behavior or affect that is
problematic. This disorder reflects long-term chronic
behavior patterns that resists change.

Now complete Self-Assessment Exercise #1 on the
following page.

Self-Assessment Exercise #1

1. Define personality disorder.

2. List the key findings from an individual's history
    and M.S.E. which are characteristic of a patient with
    a personality disorder.

    Appearance:

    Behavior:

    Feeling:

    Perception:

    Thinking:

    History:

    When you have completed this exercise to the best of
    your ability, check your answers with those on the
    following page.

Self-Assessment Exercise #1 - Feedback

1. A Personality Disorder is a common mental disorder,
   generally of long-standing and characterized by maladaptive behavior patterns. A Personality Disorder
   is less disabling than a psychosis or Anxiety Disorder.
   Usually little subjective anxiety or d.pression is
   experienced. These disorders commonly begin during
   childhood or adolescence and continue during adult
   life.

2. Appearance: generally unremarkable, though some
                  patients may be too fastidious,
                  provocative or unkempt

   Behavior: generally appropriate, though posture
                  may be overly rigid or sexually enticing

   Feeling: not unusual; generally no prominent
                  anxiety or depression

   Perception: no abnormalities

   Thinking: seeming lapses of judgment; limited
                  personal insight; otherwise unremarkable

   History: a long history of maladjustment; an
                  unchanging lifelong pattern of dis-
                  content, maladaptive and/or self-defeating
                  behavior

   If your answers correspond closely with those above,
please continue reading; if not, please reread the preceding section until you are confident you know the
material.

TYPES OF PERSONALITY DISORDERS

Paranoid
This disorder is characterized by pervasive suspiciousness and distrust of others. These individuals may be hypervigilant, guarded, very defensive, concerned with "hidden motives," and pathologically jealous. They also tend to be quick to take offense, exaggerate problems and seem tense or irritable. As far as feelings are concerned, persons with Paranoid Personality Disorders are cold, aloof, serious, unemotional, and lack "soft" and tender qualities.

Antisocial
Individuals with this disorder are characterized by an inability to sustain regular work and personal relationships and to accept usual social norms. These persons are often socially aggressive, impulsive and have recurrent problems with authority and law enforcement figures. Drug or alcohol abuse is common. Antisocial behavior becomes permanent after age 18. Prior to age 15 these persons are often involved in truancy, stealing, drug and alcohol abuse, vandalism, and sexual promiscuity.

Compulsive
This disorder is characterized by emotional inflexibility and an excessive need to be in control of most life matters. These individuals have difficulty expressing emotions and tend to be overly serious, perfectionistic and "workaholics." They often are stubborn, indecisive and easily become worried. Pleasure and interpersonal relationships are felt not as important as productivity and work. They are prone to ruminate about even minor decisions.

Histrionic
Persons with histrionic personalities are overdramatic, and often react in an intense way to seemingly insignificant events. Their emotions are exaggerated. They seek constant attention, crave excitement and often have tantrums. Others may see these persons as shallow, self-preoccupied, vain, helpless and socially manipulative.

Schizoid
The main quality of schizoid personalities is the inability to form close interpersonal relationships. They tend to be socially isolated, cold, aloof and lack emotional warmth. They seem somehow indifferent to the praise or criticism of others and prefer solitary pursuits.

Dependent
Individuals having dependent personalities are characterized by their willingness to allow others to assume major responsibility for their lives. These individuals do not rely on their own decision-making capacity and delegate that authority to their spouse, lover, parent or other

persons. These individuals lack a positive sense of
self-worth and tend to subordinate their own needs to
those of others upon whom they depend.

Narcissistic

Persons with narcissistic personalities exaggerate
their sense of self-worth to such a degree that they do
not function well in interpersonal relationships. They
have an inflated sense of their own importance, continu-
ally fantasize about success, and brag to others about
themselves. Their affect varies according to their perceived self-worth and ranges widely. They lack empathy
and can be interpersonally very exploitive.

Borderline

Persons with borderline personalities are unpredictable
in behavior and affect. They often show impulsivity in
terms of spending, sex habits, substance abuse, overeating
or even physically self-damaging acts. Their interpersonal
relations are marked by intense and unstable feelings that
vacillate between love and hate. These persons may
demonstrate explosive tempers and can become very upset
and moody for no apparent reason. Their vocational and
personal lives lack stability and are marked indicating
lack of self-concept and identity. Borderline individuals
chronically feel empty or bored and occasionally make
suicidal gestures, get into fights, or have accidents.

Passive-Aggressive

Individuals with passive-aggressive personalities
resist the requests of others in indirect ways. Instead
of saying "No" or "I can't manage that" they procrastinate,
dawdle or simply "forget" the request. Because of this
stubborn resistance they are socially and vocationally
ineffective and inefficient. Even when it is possible to
do the job or fill the request easily, these people simply
cannot follow through without some "message" of dis-
pleasure via indirect means.

Now complete Self-Assessment Exercise #2 on the
following page.

Self-Assessment Exercise #2

1. Briefly describe the distinguishing characteristics
    for each of the following types of personality
    disorders:

    a. Paranoid

    b. Antisocial

    c. Compulsive

    d. Histrionic

    e. Schizoid

    f. Dependent

    g. Narcissistic

    h. Borderline

    i. Passive-Aggressive

Self-Assessment Exercise #2 (continued)

2. On the line provided indicate the type of Personality
   Disorder which each of the following vignettes suggests.
   Remember that a Personality Disorder is a maladjustment of "life style." Diagnosis is not based upon an
   isolated episode. Diagnosis requires evidence of
   a recurring, established maladaptive pattern.

   a. Arthur is 38 years old and lives with his mother.
      He rarely dates and seems devoted to her. She
      frequently buys his clothes, makes major pur-
      chases for him and organizes their social life.
      Arthur rarely talks about himself and seems only
      to care about how his mother might feel about
      things. He often describes himself as "helpless
      without her."

      _____

   b. Bob is a truck driver who makes long runs across
      country. He prefers to work alone and a succes-
      sion of occasional co-drivers describe him as "a
      cold fish." No matter what people say to him
      about his work or attitude he seems not to care
      much. He lives alone in a rundown hotel, eats out
      mostly and has no real friends. He does not appear
      to act in an odd way, but seems aloof and lacking
      in warm feelings.

      _____

   c. Nancy works as a secretary for a major corporation.
      She is active in union activities. Whenever
      fellow employees talk to her she invariably tells
      them how the company is "out to get them" and her.
      She even feels the union will "betray us the first
      chance they get." She always locks her desk and
      worries about "crime today." Her co-workers re-
      port she is quick to take offense, seems cold and
      distraught, never laughs and can't seem to relax.

      _____

   d. Sue is 39-years old and has been married four times.
      She dresses in a flamboyant, sexy way and seems
      always to be "on the make." When she is upset she
      seems to feel the whole world will end and when
      she's happy it is "total joy." She always wants
      to "liven things up" and needs constant stimula-
      tion. Her ex-husbands describe her as vain, de-
      manding, self-indulgent and shallow.

      _____

Self-Assessment Exercise #2 (continued)

e. Dave is 19 and already has had at least 10 arrests.
    At age 12 he was a serious problem in school and
    was expelled. He would rarely attend classes and
    when he did, would disrupt the program. He was
    aggressive and impulsive. He would come to school
    drunk and on one occasion assaulted a teacher.
    Since turning 18 he has not worked consistently
    and has been involved in two robberies. His
    aggressiveness has increased and he is always in
    trouble.

    _____

f. Grace is 23 and just does not seem to know who she
    is. She feels "lost" most of the time and can't
    seem to "find herself." She has a history of
    slashing her wrists when things go wrong. She is
    also chronically overweight and has abused drugs.
    Lately she reports she hates to be alone and has
    severe mood swings. She feels empty and bored with
    little hope for the future. She has been in
    several vocational retraining programs but never
    was able to complete a course.

    _____

g. Bob is a computer scientist for a large electronics
    firm. His friends describe him as "fastidious,
    proper, serious and logical." However, since
    going to work for this firm his supervisors have
    found that Bob does not seem to be able to com-
    plete an assignment. He "gets lost in the details"
    and spends hours solving minor problems while the
    major project goes unfinished. He works many hours
    and seems devoted but is inefficient. Despite
    feedback from his supervisors he stubbornly re-
    fuses to change his behavior.

    _____

h. Clara works as a personnel officer in a state
    agency. A serious backlog in hiring has developed
    in recent years because of Clara's refusal to
    process various forms. Somehow they always get
    "lost" or are "incomplete" and need more work.
    Occasionally she says she "forgets" things. Her
    supervisors have asked her to speed up her work
    and she has been unable to change. Now all forms
    have been routed through another personnel officer
    while Clara stubbornly refuses to change her be-
    havior. Her previous supervisor admits that she
    was the same in her past assignments and this has
    held up her promotions and now threatens her job.

    _____

Self-Assessment Exercise #2 (continued)

    i. Ron is an insurance salesman who is always in financial trouble. His grandiose schemes have lost much money, but he maintains an exaggerated view of his financial prowess. He goes to bars and buys drinks for all and entertains the patrons with jokes and stories. He dreams of the day he will be a millionaire. His financial dealings have ruined several partners whom he blames for his failures. He seems to "care less" for his ex-partners and people in general.

When you have completed this exercise to the best of your ability, check your answers with those on the following page.

Self-Assessment Exercise #2 - Feedback

1. The distinguishing characteristics of the following personality disorders are:

    a. Paranoid -- suspicious, distrustful, hyper-vigilant, defensive, cold, aloof and quick to offend.

    b. Anti-social -- unable to sustain work, delinquent, aggressive, hostile, school problems, lies, reckless, alcohol abuse.

    c. Compulsive -- rigid, "workaholic," stubborn, indecisive, worried, ruminative, concerned about trivial details.

    d. Histrionic -- craves excitement, overdramatic, over-reacts to small things, tantrums, shallow, vain and self-indulgent.

    e. Schizoid -- isolated, cold, aloof, few friends and indifferent to praise or criticism.

    f. Dependent -- willing to allow others to take re-sponsibility for their lives, poor sense of self-worth, and indecisive.

    g. Narcissistic -- exaggerated sense of self-worth, "uses" others, brags, dislikes any criticism, and fantasizes about success and fame.

    h. Borderline -- recurrent problem with sex, money, eating, self-abuse, temper tantrums, labile affect, poor self-concept.

    i. Passive-Aggressive -- resists demands from others, procrastinates, "forgets," and poor job performance.

2. The type of personality disorder that best fits these cases are:

    a. Dependent -- Arthur cannot take charge of his own life; his mother's needs take precedence over his own; he is "helpless" without her.

    b. Schizoid -- Bob is a "loner," is "cold," not odd in any way, aloof and lacking warm feelings.

    c. Paranoid -- Nancy is suspicious, distrustful, cold, distant, vigilant, no sense of humor, and tense.

    d. Histrionic -- Sue is overdramatic, seductive, craves excitement, is vain, demanding and self-indulgent.

Self-Assessment Exercise #2 - Feedback (continued)

e. Anti-social -- Dave has a history of delinquency and truancy, aggressive problems, alcohol abuse assaultive, graduated to major crimes, and poor work history.

f. Borderline -- Grace displays a sense of being "lost," self-abuse, drug abuse, eating problems, moody, unable to train for a job, and feels empty and bored.

g. Compulsive -- Bob is rigid, over-attends to details, is indecisive, fastidious, overworks without positive result, and stubborn.

h. Passive-Aggressive -- Clara stands in the way of things in a passive way by "forgetting" or procrastinating, refuses to change and may face loss of her job.

i. Narcissistic -- financial instability, exaggerated self-worth, "cares less" for people, "uses" others for his own gain, and likes attention.

If your answers correspond closely with those above, please continue reading; if not please reread the preceding section until you are confident you know the material.

SUMMARY
    A Personality Disorder is a condition characterized
by long-standing maladaptive behavior. It is a commonly
encountered disorder in professional practice, one that
often directly affects the therapist-patient relationship
and thereby patient care. Awareness of these disorders
should facilitate the effective and efficient delivery of
health care.

ACKNOWLEDGMENTS

    The authors wish to credit Laurance S. Reid, M. D.
for the material on Personality Disorders published in
the first edition of this book upon which much of the
present chapter is based.

REFERENCES

Kolb, L.: Modern Clinical Psychiatry, Chapter 26. Philadelphia: W. B. Saunders, 1973.

Lewis, J. M. et al.: No Single Thread: Psychological
Health in Family Systems, New York: Brunner/Mazel, 1977.

Lion, J. R. (ed.): Personality Disorders, Baltimore:
Williams and Wilkins, 1975.

Rollin, H. R.: "Personality Disorders," Brit. Med. J.,
1:655-667, 1975.

Steiner, C.: Scripts People Live, New York: Grove Press,
1975.

Thomas, A., and Chess, S.: Temperament and Development,
New York: Brunner/Mazel, 1977.

Vaillant, G. E.: Sociopathy as a human process: A view-
point, Archives of General Psychiatry, 32:178-183, 1975.

Vaillant, G. E.: Adaptation to Life, Boston: Little,
Brown, 1977.